Company's Coming®

Weekend Cooking

40 menus
for casual entertaining

Photo Legend front and back cover:

1. Pasta Pronto, page 108
2. Tangy Mixed Salad, page 107
3. Hot Garlic Bread Sticks, page 107
4. Balsamic Vegetables, page 108
5. Italian Colours, page 108

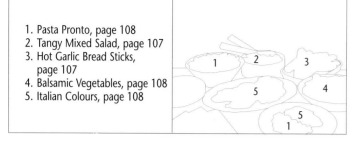

Second Printing August 2003

National Library of Canada Cataloguing in Publication

Paré, Jean
    Company's coming weekend cooking : 40 menus for casual entertaining / Jean Paré

(Special occasion series)
Includes index.
ISBN 1-896891-58-6

    1. Cookery. 2. Entertaining. 3. Menus. I. Title. II. Title: Weekend Cooking. III. Series.

TX731.P36 2003   642'.4   C2002-905501-6

Published by
COMPANY'S COMING PUBLISHING LIMITED
2311 – 96 Street
Edmonton, Alberta, Canada T6N 1G3
Tel: 780.450.6223 Fax: 780.450.1857
www.companyscoming.com

Company's Coming is a registered trademark owned by Company's Coming Publishing Limited

Colour separations by
Friesens, Altona, Manitoba, Canada

Printed in China

Pictured at left:

Top: Grilled Lemon And Lime, page 61
Centre Left: Coconut Rice Salad, page 61
Bottom: Mango-Stuffed Chicken, page 62

Weekend Cooking was created thanks to the dedicated efforts of the people and organizations listed below.

COMPANY'S COMING PUBLISHING LIMITED

Author	Jean Paré
President	Grant Lovig
Production Manager	Derrick Sorochan
Senior Designer	Zoë Henry
Publishing Coordinator	Shelly Willsey

The Recipe Factory

Research & Development Manager	Nora Prokop
Editor	Laurel Hoffmann
Editorial Assistant	Rendi Dennis
Associate Editors	Stephanie Amodio
	Josie Wong
Copywriter	Debbie Dixon
Proofreaders	Audrey Dahl
	Connie Townsend
Food Editors	Lynda Elsenheimer
	Lovoni Walker
Test Kitchen Supervisor	Jessica Assaly
Test Kitchen Staff	James Bullock
	Gloria Clare
	Sandra Clydesdale
Photo Editor	Patricia Meili-Bullock
Principal Photographers	Stephe Tate Photo
	John McDougall
Cover Photographer	Bluefish Studios
Prep Kitchen Coordinator	Audrey Smetaniuk
Prep Kitchen Assistant	Linda Dobos
Prop Stylists	Paula Bertamini
	Snezana Ferenac
Registered Dietitian	Margaret Ng

Our special thanks to the following businesses for providing extensive props for photography:

Anchor Hocking Canada	Montana's Cookhouse Saloon
Browne & Co. Ltd.	Pfaltzgraff Canada
Canadian Tire	Pier 1 Imports
Canhome Global	PROP abilities corp.
Casa Bugatti	Pyrex® Serveware
C C On Whyte Inc.	Sears Canada
Cherison Enterprises Inc.	Stokes
Choy Hope Trading Ltd.	The Bay
Dansk Gifts	Wal-Mart Canada Inc.
Island Pottery Inc.	Winners Stores
La Cache	Wiltshire®
Linens 'N Things	Zellers
Mikasa Home Store	

Table of Contents

#	Menu Chart	page	serves	brunch & lunch	dinner	after-dinner	inter-national	outdoor	indoor	make-ahead
1	Company's Coming	8	6	●					🏠	
2	Dim Sum	12	6	●			🌐		🏠	🕐
3	Family Brunch	18	6	●					🏠	
4	Mediterranean Lunch	22	6	●			🌐		🏠	
5	Patio Party	26	8	●	✕			🍃		🕐
6	Afternoon Grill	31	4	●				🍃		
7	Aussie Barbie	34	6	●			🌐	🍃		
8	Beach Party	38	10	●	✕			🍃		🕐
9	Boating Fare	42	6	●	✕			🍃	🏠	🕐
10	Pool Party	46	8	●	✕			🍃		
11	Seafood Barbecue	51	8	●	✕			🍃	🏠	🕐
12	Tailgate Party	56	8	●				🍃	🏠	🕐
13	Tropical Barbecue	60	6	●	✕			🍃		🕐
14	Après-Toboggan Party	65	4		✕				🏠	🕐
15	Cabin Cooking	69	6		✕				🏠	🕐
16	Campfire Cookout	72	4		✕			🍃		
17	Make-Ahead Family Supper	76	6		✕				🏠	🕐
18	Picnic In The Park	80	6	●				🍃		🕐
19	Rainy Day Supper	84	6		✕				🏠	🕐
20	Simple Supper	88	4	●	✕				🏠	
21	Sunday Roast	92	6		✕				🏠	
22	Unexpected Guests!	97	6	●	✕				🏠	
23	Weekend Baking Bee	101	n/a						🏠	🕐
24	A Taste Of Italy	106	6		✕		🌐		🏠	
25	African Safari	110	6	●	✕		🌐		🏠	🕐
26	Asian Night	113	6		✕		🌐		🏠	
27	Casual Dinner Party	118	8		✕				🏠	
28	Curry Night	123	8		✕		🌐		🏠	🕐
29	Mexican Fiesta	128	6	●	✕		🌐	🍃	🏠	
30	Romantic Dinner	133	2		✕				🏠	
31	Vegetarian Dinner Party	137	6	●	✕				🏠	
32	Winter Dinner Party	141	6		✕				🏠	
33	An Evening Of Appetizers	145	10			▮			🏠	🕐
34	Dessert And Coffee	151	8			▮			🏠	🕐
35	Feeding Frenzy!	155	25			▮			🏠	🕐
36	Fondue Fun	160	8		✕	▮			🏠	
37	Games 'N' Cards Night	164	6		✕	▮			🏠	🕐
38	Hot 'N' Spicy Night	168	4		✕	▮			🏠	
39	Pizza And Video Night	173	6		✕				🏠	🕐
40	Platters Of The World	177	8			▮	🌐		🏠	

At last it's the weekend—time to kick off your shoes and settle in for a few days of rest and relaxation. Are house guests expected? Is it barbecue weather? Is The Big Game on television tonight?

The weekend is yours to enjoy, and it's a perfect opportunity to celebrate the end of a busy week with family and friends. Welcome them into your home with some casual entertaining ideas from *Weekend Cooking*.

Before assembling this collection of recipes, we thought about how we could help you with your party plans. Our solution was to create "theme packages" of recipes—40 very unique menus suitable for practically any weekend occasion. By doing this, we've hopefully helped you eliminate the time-consuming task of searching through stacks of cookbooks for the perfect combination of recipes. After all, it's your free time and you don't want to waste a minute of it!

Every recipe features easy-to-follow instructions and is beautifully pictured in full colour. This makes it easy to choose a menu, plus it provides a good visual reference for making your grocery list. Brunches, dinners, theme parties, barbecues, quick crowd-pleasing menus and more are included for your weekend fun.

Start weekend entertaining as early as Friday night with Pizza And Video Night or perhaps just Dessert And Coffee. You're winding down from a busy week, so you might want to think about

Top and Bottom: French Toast Cinnamon Buns, page 19, with Raisin Cream Topping, page 19
Centre Left: Fresh Fruit Platter, page 20, with Fluffy Peach Dip, page 20

keeping the evening simple and relaxed. Saturday, on the other hand, is traditionally a good time to put party plans into full swing. Large or small, every get-together is worthy of a fun menu—something you are certain to find in our chapter on Evening Entertaining. These eight distinctive menus are suitable for quiet get-togethers or lively party events.

Casual dinners are great for bringing together good conversation and good food, and you'll find nine very different menus in Table Travels to help you do just that. All you have to do is decide how elaborate you want the evening to be. We'd like to suggest a few special menus that can add a worldly essence to the evening—Asian Night, African Safari, Mexican Fiesta and A Taste Of Italy hold the spotlight, with a featured blend of exotic flavours to seduce the senses.

Of course, perfect barbecue weather can't be ignored when it lands so nicely on your days off, so look for some inspiration in our selection of eight Summer Fare menus. Our Tailgate Party, Beach Party and Seafood Barbecue are just a few examples. There's even a fun Aussie Barbie menu featuring classic dishes from our friends Down Under.

Don't forget the importance of family. The weekend is the perfect opportunity to make the most of precious family time together. Menus can be simple and fun—Campfire Cookout, Weekend Baking Bee, Rainy Day Supper and Picnic In The

Park are among the 10 menu choices in our Family Fun section. Get everyone involved in the plans, including the kids!

Mid-afternoon entertaining is perfect on a Sunday, and appetites can get pretty big if it's been a busy morning. Five menus are featured in our Morning 'Til Noon section, each one adaptable to suit your crowd. If you're lucky enough to have a warm, sunny day for brunch, try our Patio Party menu. And if the weather isn't cooperative, you can create your own warmth and sunshine with featured dishes from our Mediterranean Lunch menu.

Weekend Cooking offers 40 different ways to wrap up your busy week in a happy, relaxed and entertaining manner. So don't let the weekend slip by without planning something fun—host a card game, a toboggan party or a barbecue—and give friends and family something memorable to talk about on Monday morning.

Jean Paré

Each recipe has been analyzed using the most up-to-date version of the Canadian Nutrient File from Health Canada, which is based on the United States Department of Agriculture (USDA) Nutrient Database. If more than one ingredient is listed (such as "hard margarine or butter"), then the first ingredient is used in the analysis. Where an ingredient reads "sprinkle," "optional," or "for garnish," it is not included as part of the nutrition information.

Margaret Ng, B.Sc. (Hon), M.A.
Registered Dietitian

Company's Coming

Whether after a late sleep or early church service, that's the time of day when appetites are at their peak. Appease mid-morning cravings with this relaxed, buffet-style brunch.

serves 6

Citus Starter

✹

Multi-Grain Toast

✹

Prosciutto And Mushroom Omelet

✹

Asparagus And Salmon Crêpes

✹

Raspberry Streusel Muffins

✹

Assorted Melon Plate

✹

Blueberry Little Cakes

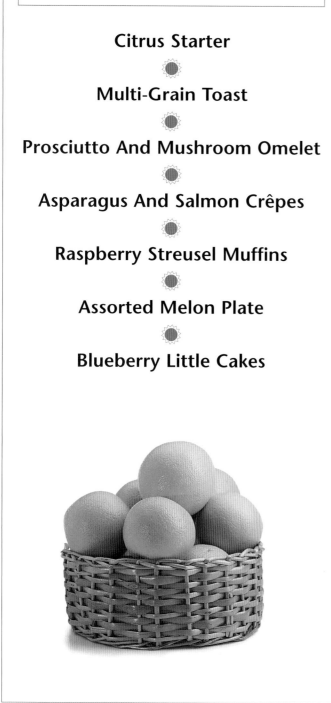

Citrus Starter

Serve freshly squeezed orange juice or pink grapefruit juice for a refreshing start to the day. Choose whatever ratio suits your taste. 1 medium orange = about 1/3 cup (75 mL) juice. 1 medium pink grapefruit = about 2/3 cup (150 mL) juice. When choosing fruit (oranges, grapefruit, lemons) that you will be squeezing for juice, look for smoother skin with smaller, shallower indentations. This indicates a thinner skin so there will be more fruit and juice inside. Pictured on page 9 and on page 11.

Multi-Grain Toast

Thick slices of multi-grain bread, toasted and buttered. Pictured on page 9.

Prosciutto And Mushroom Omelet

A hearty omelet with prosciutto, mushroom and white Cheddar cheese flavours throughout. The prosciutto adds a natural saltiness.

Cooking oil	1 tbsp.	15 mL
Sliced fresh brown (or white) mushrooms	2 cups	500 mL
Sliced prosciutto (or ham), chopped	3 oz.	85 g
Large eggs	6	6
Chopped fresh parsley (or 1 tbsp., 15 mL, flakes)	1/4 cup	60 mL
Salt	1/4 tsp.	1 mL
Pepper	1/4 tsp.	1 mL
Grated sharp white Cheddar cheese	1/2 cup	125 mL

Heat cooking oil in large frying pan on medium. Add mushrooms. Cook for about 5 minutes until golden.

Add prosciutto. Heat and stir for about 5 minutes until prosciutto starts to crisp.

Whisk next 4 ingredients in small bowl until frothy. Add to mushroom mixture. Stir. Cook on medium-low for 3 to 5 minutes until almost set.

Sprinkle with cheese. Cover. Heat for 2 to 3 minutes until cheese is melted. Fold omelet in half. Cuts into 6 wedges.

1 wedge: 224 Calories; 17.7 g Total Fat (7.6 g Mono, 2.3 g Poly, 6.3 g Sat); 238 mg Cholesterol; 2 g Carbohydrate; trace Fibre; 14 g Protein; 452 mg Sodium

Pictured on page 11.

Asparagus And Salmon Crêpes

Light crêpes filled with asparagus and smoked salmon in a creamy sauce.

CRÊPES

All-purpose flour	1 cup	250 mL
Milk	1 cup	250 mL
Large egg	1	1
Salt	1/8 tsp.	0.5 mL
Cooking oil	1 1/2 tsp.	7 mL

FILLING

Cooking oil	1 tbsp.	15 mL
Finely chopped onion	1/2 cup	125 mL
All-purpose flour	2 tbsp.	30 mL
Milk	1 1/2 cups	375 mL
Fresh asparagus, trimmed of tough ends and finely chopped	1 lb.	454 g
Smoked salmon, chopped	4 oz.	113 g
Salt	1/4 tsp.	1 mL
Pepper	1/8 tsp.	0.5 mL

Crêpes: Combine first 4 ingredients in medium bowl until smooth.

Heat 9 inch (22 cm) frying pan on medium-high. Add 1/4 tsp. (1 mL) cooking oil to pan. Add 1/3 cup (75 mL) batter to pan, tilting and swirling pan so batter evenly coats surface. Cook for about 1 minute until lightly browned on bottom. Turn over. Cook for about 1 minute until lightly browned on bottom. Remove to plate. Repeat with remaining cooking oil and batter. Makes 6 crêpes. Keep warm.

Filling: Heat cooking oil in large saucepan on medium. Add onion. Cook for about 5 minutes until onion is soft.

Add flour. Heat and stir for 1 minute to cook flour. Gradually add milk. Heat and stir for 5 minutes.

Add asparagus. Heat and stir for 5 to 7 minutes until asparagus is tender-crisp and mixture is thickened. Remove from heat.

Add salmon, salt and pepper. Stir until well combined. Lay crêpes flat. Place about 1/2 cup (125 mL) mixture down 1 side of each crêpe. Roll up. Makes 6 crêpes.

1 filled crêpe: 221 Calories; 6.6 g Total Fat (3.1 g Mono, 1.5 g Poly, 1.5 g Sat); 45 mg Cholesterol; 28 g Carbohydrate; 2 g Fibre; 12 g Protein; 364 mg Sodium

Pictured below.

Top Centre: Citrus Starter, page 8 Bottom: Asparagus And Salmon Crêpes, above Top Right: Multi-Grain Toast, page 8

Raspberry Streusel Muffins

Golden brown muffins with a soft crumb and sweet crumble topping.

STREUSEL TOPPING		
All-purpose flour	1/3 cup	75 mL
Brown sugar, packed	3 tbsp.	50 mL
Ground cinnamon	1 tsp.	5 mL
Hard margarine (or butter)	3 tbsp.	50 mL
All-purpose flour	2 cups	500 mL
Brown sugar, packed	3/4 cup	175 mL
Baking powder	1 tbsp.	15 mL
Fresh (or frozen, thawed) raspberries	1 1/3 cups	325 mL
Grated apple (your choice)	1/2 cup	125 mL
Large eggs, fork-beaten	3	3
Cooking oil	1/3 cup	75 mL
Buttermilk (or reconstituted from powder)	1/3 cup	75 mL

Streusel Topping: Combine first amounts of flour and brown sugar in small bowl. Add cinnamon. Stir. Cut in margarine until consistency of fine crumbs.

Mix second amounts of flour and brown sugar in large bowl. Add baking powder. Stir.

Add raspberries and apple. Mix well.

Combine eggs, cooking oil and buttermilk in separate small bowl. Add to raspberry mixture. Stir until just moistened. Do not overmix. Grease muffin cups with cooking spray. Fill cups 3/4 full. Sprinkle each with streusel topping. Bake in 375°F (190°C) oven for about 20 minutes until wooden pick inserted in centre of muffin comes out clean. Let stand in pan for 5 minutes before removing to wire rack to cool. Serve warm or cold. Makes 12 muffins.

1 muffin: 276 Calories; 10.9 g Total Fat (6.2 g Mono, 2.5 g Poly, 1.5 g Sat); 54 mg Cholesterol; 41 g Carbohydrate; 2 g Fibre; 5 g Protein; 157 mg Sodium

Pictured on page 11.

Assorted Melon Plate

Arrange watermelon, cantaloupe and honeydew on a plate or tray. Keep the pieces small so that your guests can place a few on their plate with the other brunch food. Pictured on page 11.

Blueberry Little Cakes

The perfect combination: blueberry and lemon. This rich and cakey treat will become an all-time favourite. Flat on top like a cake, but the size of a muffin.

Hard margarine (or butter)	3/4 cup	175 mL
Ground almonds	1 cup	250 mL
Egg whites (large), fork-beaten	6	6
Icing (confectioner's) sugar	1 1/2 cups	375 mL
All-purpose flour	1/2 cup	125 mL
Fresh blueberries	1 cup	250 mL
Finely grated lemon zest	2 tsp.	10 mL

Icing (confectioner's) sugar (optional)

Melt margarine in large saucepan.

Add next 6 ingredients. Stir until just combined. Grease muffin cups with cooking spray. Fill cups 2/3 full. Bake in 375°F (190°C) oven for about 25 minutes until wooden pick inserted in centre of cake comes out clean. Let stand in pan for 10 minutes before removing to wire rack to cool.

Dust with icing sugar. Makes 12 little cakes.

1 little cake: 239 Calories; 15.3 g Total Fat (5.5 g Mono, 1.1 g Poly, 7.9 g Sat); 33 mg Cholesterol; 23 g Carbohydrate; 1 g Fibre; 4 g Protein; 153 mg Sodium

Pictured on page 11.

1. Citrus Starter, page 8
2. Raspberry Streusel Muffins, this page
3. Prosciutto And Mushroom Omelet, page 8
4. Assorted Melon Plate, this page
5. Blueberry Little Cakes, above

Dim Sum

This dim sum menu features exotic, established Chinese recipes, certain to tempt even the fussiest appetite. Impress guests with this delightful tradition that can be made ahead and warmed up just before serving.

serves 6

Shrimp Spring Rolls

Ginger Soy Dipping Sauce

Spicy Dipping Sauce

All About Tea

Sticky Rice Packets

Shrimp-Stuffed Peppers

Barbecue Pork Buns

Rich Egg Custard Tarts

Mango Pudding

Shrimp Spring Rolls

Crispy, savoury spring rolls with a colourful shrimp filling. Serve with Spicy Dipping Sauce, page 13, or Ginger Soy Dipping Sauce, page 13.

FILLING

Raw shrimp, peeled, deveined, blotted dry and finely chopped	8 oz.	225 g
Finely grated carrot	1 tbsp.	15 mL
Finely chopped green onion (or cilantro)	1 tbsp.	15 mL
Low-sodium soy sauce	2 tsp.	10 mL
Cornstarch	2 tsp.	10 mL
Sesame seeds, toasted (see Note)	1 tsp.	5 mL
Finely grated peeled gingerroot	1/2 tsp.	2 mL
Minced garlic (optional)	1/2 tsp.	2 mL
Granulated sugar	1/2 tsp.	2 mL
Water	2 tbsp.	30 mL
All-purpose flour	1 tbsp.	15 mL
Spring roll wrappers (8 1/2 inch, 21 cm, square)	9	9

Peanut (or cooking) oil, for deep-frying

Filling: Combine first 9 ingredients in small bowl.

Stir water into flour in small cup until smooth.

Cut each wrapper in half into 2 rectangles. Keep wrappers covered with damp cloth to prevent drying out. Brush all 4 edges of 1 rectangle with flour paste. Place 2 tsp. (10 mL) filling across centre of 1 short end. Roll up, tucking in sides to enclose filling, into small finger-sized cylinders. Repeat with remaining filling and rectangles.

Deep-fry spring rolls, in 3 batches, in hot (375°F, 190°C) peanut oil for about 3 minutes, turning often, until crisp and golden. Remove to paper towels to drain. Makes 18 spring rolls.

3 spring rolls: 291 Calories; 8.6 g Total Fat (3.5 g Mono, 2.9 g Poly, 1.5 g Sat); 49 mg Cholesterol; 40 g Carbohydrate; trace Fibre; 12 g Protein; 463 mg Sodium

Pictured on page 13.

Note: To toast sesame seeds, place in single layer in ungreased shallow pan. Bake in 350°F (175°C) oven for 5 to 10 minutes, stirring or shaking often, until desired doneness.

Ginger Soy Dipping Sauce

A dark brown, slightly salty sauce with a hint of sweetness and a wonderful ginger taste. Makes a nice dip for Shrimp Spring Rolls, page 12.

Soy sauce	1/2 cup	125 mL
Rice vinegar	2 tbsp.	30 mL
Brown sugar, packed	2 tbsp.	30 mL
Slice of peeled gingerroot, 1/4 inch (6 mm) thick	1	1
Green onion, cut into 3 pieces	1	1
Sesame oil (optional)	1 tsp.	5 mL

Process all 6 ingredients in blender until almost smooth. Pour into small saucepan. Heat and stir on medium until boiling. Reduce heat to medium-low. Simmer, uncovered, for 5 minutes. Cool. Spoon into 2 or 3 tiny dishes. Place at intervals on table. Makes 2/3 cup (150 mL).

1 1/2 tbsp. (25 mL): 35 Calories; trace Total Fat (0 g Mono, 0 g Poly, 0 g Sat); 0 mg Cholesterol; 7 g Carbohydrate; trace Fibre; 2 g Protein; 1453 mg Sodium

Pictured below.

Spicy Dipping Sauce

Combine equal amounts of Worcestershire sauce and chili sauce in small cup. Spoon into 2 or 3 tiny, shallow dishes. Place on table in several spots so they are easily accessible to your guests. Excellent with Shrimp Spring Rolls, page 12.

All About Tea

- Green and oolong teas are most commonly served at dim sum.

- There are 3 methods of processing tea leaves with the results being labelled "green," "oolong" and "black."

- Green tea is high in vitamins and antioxidants because less of the essential oils (responsible for the flavour) have been allowed to oxidize.

- **To make:** Measure 2 tsp. (10 mL) green tea leaves or 1 1/2 tsp. (7 mL) oolong leaves into teapot for each 1 cup (250 mL) water. Add a final 2 tsp. (10 mL) green tea or 1 1/2 tsp. (7 mL) oolong tea. Pour very hot, but not boiling, water over tea leaves. Steep for 1 to 2 minutes before serving.

- Tea bags can also be used.

- Sweetener or milk should not be added to green tea.

Green Tea pictured on page 15.

Ginger Soy Dipping Sauce, above

Shrimp Spring Rolls, page 12

Sticky Rice Packets

This popular dim sum dish can be made the day before, chilled and steamed the next day.

Dried bamboo (or banana or lotus) leaves (available in Chinese grocery stores)	18	18
Boiling water, to cover		
Short grain white rice, rinsed and drained	1 cup	250 mL
Water	1 1/2 cups	375 mL
Cooking oil	1 tbsp.	15 mL
Finely grated peeled gingerroot	2 tsp.	10 mL
Diced fresh brown (or white) mushrooms	1/2 cup	125 mL
Lean ground chicken	8 oz.	225 g
Oyster sauce	1 tbsp.	15 mL
Dry sherry	1 tbsp.	15 mL
Water	1 tbsp.	15 mL
Soy sauce	2 tsp.	10 mL
Cornstarch	2 tsp.	10 mL
Sliced Chinese barbecued (or cooked) pork	2 oz.	57 g

Soak leaves in boiling water in large bowl for 20 minutes. Drain. Trim any hard edges. Set aside.

Stir rice and water in medium saucepan. Bring to a boil. Reduce heat to low. Cover. Simmer for 10 minutes. Remove from heat. Do not lift lid. Let stand for 10 minutes. Turn into separate large bowl. Fluff slightly with fork. Cool. Divide into 3 portions.

Heat cooking oil in wok or large frying pan on medium-high. Add ginger, mushrooms and ground chicken. Stir-fry for about 5 minutes until browned.

Stir next 5 ingredients in small cup. Add to chicken mixture. Stir until boiling and thickened. Cool. Lay 3 leaves vertically, slightly overlapping on long edges, on work surface. Lay 3 leaves horizontally, overlapping on long edges, over top. Spoon 1 portion of rice onto bottom of centre leaf. Spoon about 1/3 cup (75 mL) chicken mixture onto centre of rice, pushing down into middle so rice surrounds it.

Place 2 or 3 slices of pork on top. Fold in sides over filling. Fold to enclose. Use more leaves if necessary to wrap and form secure package. Tie with butcher's string if desired. Repeat twice more with remaining fillings and leaves. Set packets, seam-side down, in large bamboo steamer or on rack over rapidly boiling water in wok or Dutch oven. Cover. Steam for about 15 minutes until packets are fragrant. Add more boiling water to wok or pot as required to keep water boiling rapidly. To serve, cut string and discard. Cut open packets. Makes 3 packets. Serves 6.

1 serving: 229 Calories; 4.6 g Total Fat (2.2 g Mono, 1.1 g Poly, 0.9 g Sat); 34 mg Cholesterol; 32 g Carbohydrate; trace Fibre; 13 g Protein; 413 mg Sodium

Pictured on page 15.

Shrimp-Stuffed Peppers

These attractive, tender-crisp green pepper "boats" hold a delightful shrimp filling. Make them the day before and reheat in the microwave for a quick and easy treat.

Raw shrimp, peeled, deveined, blotted dry and finely chopped	6 oz.	170 g
Cornstarch	1 tbsp.	15 mL
Dry sherry	2 tsp.	10 mL
Green onion, finely sliced	1	1
Garlic powder, sprinkle		
Ground ginger, sprinkle		
Medium green peppers, cut lengthwise into 6 pieces each	2	2
Commercial black bean sauce (see Tip, page 16)	1/2 cup	125 mL

Combine first 6 ingredients in small bowl.

Spoon about 2 tsp. (10 mL) filling onto each green pepper piece, packing down slightly to cover. Set in large bamboo steamer or on rack over rapidly boiling water in wok or Dutch oven. Cover. Steam for 6 to 7 minutes until peppers are tender-crisp and shrimp is pink. Add more boiling water to wok or pot as required to keep water boiling rapidly.

Drizzle with black bean sauce before serving. Makes 12 pieces.

2 pieces: 73 Calories; 2.1 g Total Fat (1 g Mono, 0.7 g Poly, 0.2 g Sat); 32 mg Cholesterol; 8 g Carbohydrate; 1 g Fibre; 6 g Protein; 851 mg Sodium

Pictured on page 15.

1. Green Tea, page 13
2. Barbecue Pork Buns, page 16
3. Shrimp-Stuffed Peppers, above
4. Sticky Rice Packets, this page

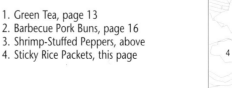

Barbecue Pork Buns

Authentic-looking buns with a sweet, savoury pork filling coated in a deliciously thick sauce. Make the day before, or just re-steam frozen buns for about five minutes when required.

Water	1/3 cup	75 mL
Cornstarch	2 tbsp.	30 mL
Soy sauce	2 tbsp.	30 mL
Oyster sauce	1 tbsp.	15 mL
Granulated sugar	3 tbsp.	50 mL
Pepper, sprinkle		
FILLING		
Sesame (or cooking) oil	1 tsp.	5 mL
Green onion, sliced	1	1
Garlic clove, minced (or 1/4 tsp., 1 mL, powder)	1	1
Finely grated peeled gingerroot	1/2 tsp.	2 mL
Diced Chinese barbecued (or cooked) pork	1 cup	250 mL
DOUGH		
Water	1/2 cup	125 mL
Milk	1/4 cup	60 mL
Granulated sugar	2 tbsp.	30 mL
Salt	1/2 tsp.	2 mL
All-purpose flour	2 1/3 cups	575 mL
Instant yeast	1 1/2 tsp.	7 mL

Stir water into cornstarch in small cup until smooth. Add remaining 4 ingredients. Stir. Set aside.

Filling: Heat sesame oil in large frying pan on medium. Add green onion, garlic and ginger. Stir-fry for about 1 minute, stirring constantly, until soft. Stir cornstarch mixture. Stir into green onion mixture until boiling and thickened.

Add pork. Stir until coated. Turn into medium bowl. Chill for at least 1 1/2 hours until cold. Makes 1 cup (250 mL) filling.

Dough: Heat and stir water, milk, sugar and salt in small saucepan until sugar is dissolved. Cool slightly. You should be able to hold your finger in water mixture and it should be almost hot.

Process flour and yeast in food processor for 2 seconds until just combined. With motor running, gradually add liquid through food chute until dough comes together and forms a ball. Process for 30 seconds. Turn dough out onto floured surface. Knead for 2 minutes, adding more flour if necessary to prevent sticking. Place in large greased bowl, turning once to grease top. Cover with tea towel. Let stand in oven with light on and door closed for about 1 hour until doubled in bulk. Punch dough down and knead gently to remove any air pockets. Roll into cylinder shape. Cut crosswise into 12 portions. Roll or flatten each portion into 4 inch (10 cm) circle. Spoon rounded tablespoon of filling onto centre. Gather edges together over filling, twisting in clockwise direction to form "top knot." Place each bun, smooth side down, on waxed paper cut into squares about 2 1/2 inch (6.4 cm) size. Cover with tea towel. Let stand for about 1 hour until slightly risen. Set buns with waxed paper, about 1 1/2 inches (3.8 cm) apart, in large bamboo steamer or on rack over rapidly boiling water in wok or Dutch oven. Cover. Steam for 15 minutes. This may have to be done in batches. Makes 12 buns.

1 bun: 163 Calories; 2.7 g Total Fat (1.1 g Mono, 0.5 g Poly, 0.9 g Sat); 11 mg Cholesterol; 27 g Carbohydrate; 1 g Fibre; 7 g Protein; 418 mg Sodium

Pictured on page 15.

Tip

When purchasing black bean sauce, please note that there are two very different products available with the same name. The concentrated sauce is thick, somewhat chunky and has fermented black beans as the first ingredient. It should be used in small amounts since it has a strong flavour. The prepared sauce (what we refer to as commercial black bean sauce) is thinner and smoother than the concentrated sauce and has water as the first ingredient. It can be used as is from the bottle without being overpowering.

Rich Egg Custard Tarts

A sweet, smooth, egg-tasting custard in a light, flaky pastry. Enjoy warm or at room temperature.

TART PASTRY

All-purpose flour	1 cup	250 mL
Cold lard, cut into 4 pieces	1/4 cup	60 mL
Cold hard margarine (or butter)	2 tbsp.	30 mL
Egg yolk (large)	1	1
Ice water	1 tbsp.	15 mL

CUSTARD

Granulated sugar	1/4 cup	60 mL
Custard powder	1 1/2 tsp.	7 mL
Water	1/3 cup	75 mL
Half-and-half cream	2 1/2 tbsp.	37 mL
Drop of yellow food colouring (optional)	1	1
Large eggs	2	2

Tart Pastry: Process flour, lard and margarine in food processor with on/off motion until lard and margarine are pea size.

Beat egg yolk and ice water in small cup with fork. Remove food processor cover. Pour water mixture over flour mixture. Secure cover. Process with on/off motion several times until mixture just comes together. Turn out onto lightly floured surface. Shape into ball. Flatten into disc shape. Wrap in plastic wrap. Chill for at least 1 hour. Roll out pastry on lightly floured surface to 1/4 inch (6 mm) thickness. Cut into 3 1/2 inch (9 cm) circles with floured cutter. Line tart or muffin pan with circles.

Custard: Stir sugar and custard powder in small saucepan. Slowly add water until smooth. Heat and stir on medium until just starting to boil and sugar is dissolved. Pour into small bowl. Cool, stirring several times.

Stir in cream and food colouring.

Beat each egg individually in small cup with fork. Stir into custard mixture, 1 at a time. Fill tart shells to within 1/4 inch (6 mm) of top. Bake on bottom rack in 300°F (150°C) oven for about 45 minutes until knife inserted in centre of tart comes out clean and custard is set. Let stand in pan for 10 minutes before removing tarts. Serve warm. Makes 6 to 9 tarts.

1 tart: 274 Calories; 16 g Total Fat (7.6 g Mono, 1.8 g Poly, 5.5 g Sat); 122 mg Cholesterol; 27 g Carbohydrate; 1 g Fibre; 5 g Protein; 79 mg Sodium

Pictured on this page.

Mango Pudding

Tangy pudding with a smooth, velvety texture and a refreshing mango flavour. The perfect finish to your homemade dim sum meal.

Envelope of unflavoured gelatin	1/4 oz.	7 g
Reserved mango syrup, plus water to make	3/4 cup	175 mL
Granulated sugar	1/3 cup	75 mL
Lemon juice	1 tsp.	5 mL
Can of sliced mango, drained and syrup reserved	14 oz.	398 mL
Carton of prepared mango juice	3/4 cup	175 mL
Half-and-half cream	1 cup	250 mL

Sprinkle gelatin over reserved mango syrup in small saucepan. Let stand for 2 minutes. Add sugar and lemon juice. Heat and stir on medium until gelatin and sugar are dissolved.

Purée mango in blender until smooth. Add gelatin mixture and mango juice. Process. Pour into 6 individual 1/2 cup (125 mL) molds or 3 cup (750 mL) mold. Chill for several hours or overnight. Dip molds briefly into hot water before turning out.

Spoon small amount of cream over top of pudding. Serve remaining cream on side to pour over individual servings. Serves 6.

1 serving: 183 Calories; 4.5 g Total Fat (1.3 g Mono, 0.2 g Poly, 2.7 g Sat); 13 mg Cholesterol; 36 g Carbohydrate; 1 g Fibre; 3 g Protein; 25 mg Sodium

Pictured below.

Top: Rich Egg Custard Tarts, this page   Bottom: Mango Pudding, above

Family Brunch

Treat your family to a special brunch
this weekend. Bring everyone to
the table for this tempting feast
and some engaging conversation.

serves 6

Sunrise Beverage

Fried Peameal Canadian Bacon

French Toast Cinnamon Buns

Raisin Cream Topping

Fluffy Peach Dip

Fresh Fruit Platter

Sunrise Beverage

*This refreshing, peachy drink separates into layers for a
beautiful sunrise effect.*

Can of frozen concentrated peach punch	12 oz.	341 mL
Water	2 cups	500 mL
Lemon juice	2 tbsp.	30 mL
Frozen large bananas, cut into 4 pieces each	2	2
Ice cubes (about 24)	4 cups	1 L
Grenadine syrup	1/2 cup	125 mL

Orange slices, for garnish
Maraschino cherries, for garnish

Process first 4 ingredients in blender for about 30 seconds
until smooth. Remove and set aside 1/2 of mixture.

Add 1/2 of ice cubes through hole in lid, 1 at a time,
processing after each addition until smooth. Pour into large
pitcher. Process remaining 1/2 of peach mixture and ice
cubes. Add to mixture in pitcher.

Pour 4 tsp. (20 mL) grenadine into bottom of six 14 oz.
(398 mL) glasses. Add peach mixture until glasses are 3/4 full.
Stir gently in bottom of glass to achieve sunrise appearance.

Garnish with orange slice and cherry skewered on wooden
pick. Serves 6.

1 serving: 244 Calories; 0.7 g Total Fat (0.1 g Mono, 0.2 g Poly, 0.1 g Sat);
0 mg Cholesterol; 62 g Carbohydrate; 1 g Fibre; 1 g Protein; 27 mg Sodium

Pictured on page 19.

Fried Peameal Canadian Bacon

Cut back bacon into 1/8 to 1/4 inch (3 to 6 mm) slices.
Fry in lightly greased non-stick frying pan on medium,
turning once, until lightly browned and crusty. Keep
warm, covered, in oven that has been heated to 200°F
(95°C) and then turned off. Pictured on page 21.

French Toast Cinnamon Buns

A quick and easy breakfast with the delicious taste of French toast and cinnamon.

Large eggs	3	3
Milk	3/4 cup	175 mL
Vanilla	1 tsp.	5 mL
Salt	1/4 tsp.	1 mL
Hard margarine (or butter)	1 tbsp.	15 mL
Day-old cinnamon buns (4 inch, 10 cm, size), cut horizontally into 2 layers	6	6

Beat first 4 ingredients in medium bowl until smooth.

Melt 1/2 of margarine in large non-stick frying pan on medium until sizzling. Reduce heat to medium-low.

Quickly dip cinnamon bun halves, 1 at a time, into egg mixture. Cook, about 6 at a time, for 3 to 4 minutes per side until lightly browned. Keep warm in oven that has been heated to 200°F (95°C) and then turned off. Repeat with remaining margarine, buns and egg mixture. Serves 6.

1 serving: 517 Calories; 24.5 g Total Fat (13.2 g Mono, 3.1 g Poly, 6.4 g Sat); 188 mg Cholesterol; 63 g Carbohydrate; 2 g Fibre; 12 g Protein; 629 mg Sodium

Pictured on page 21.

Raisin Cream Topping

This fluffy, lightly sweetened topping is the perfect complement to hot French Toast Cinnamon Buns, above.

Sultana raisins	1/3 cup	75 mL
Boiling water	1 cup	250 mL
Whipping cream	1 cup	250 mL
Instant vanilla pudding powder	2 tbsp.	30 mL
Ground cinnamon	1/4 tsp.	1 mL

Stir raisins and boiling water in small bowl. Let stand for about 10 minutes until raisins are plump. Drain. Blot raisins dry with paper towels. Cool completely.

Beat whipping cream, pudding powder and cinnamon in medium bowl for about 2 minutes until soft peaks form. Fold in raisins. Makes about 1 2/3 cups (400 mL).

2 tbsp. (30 mL): 79 Calories; 6.1 g Total Fat (1.8 g Mono, 0.2 g Poly, 3.8 g Sat); 22 mg Cholesterol; 6 g Carbohydrate; trace Fibre; 1 g Protein; 48 mg Sodium

Pictured on page 21.

Sunrise Beverage, page 18

Fluffy Peach Dip

The consistency of soft whipped cream with a delicate peach flavour. Goes perfectly with fresh fruit.

Liquid whip topping (such as Nutriwhip)	1 cup	250 mL
Peach-flavoured jelly powder (gelatin)	1 tbsp.	15 mL
Vanilla	1/2 tsp.	2 mL
Peach yogurt	3/4 cup	175 mL

Beat topping, jelly powder and vanilla in medium bowl for about 5 minutes until stiff peaks form.

Beat in yogurt until combined. Makes 3 1/2 cups (875 mL).

2 tbsp. (30 mL): 25 Calories; 1.6 g Total Fat (trace Mono, 0 g Poly, 0.1 g Sat); trace Cholesterol; 2 g Carbohydrate; 0 g Fibre; trace Protein; 4 mg Sodium

Pictured on this page.

Fresh Fruit Platter

Arrange whole grapes, blueberries, strawberries, and slices of honeydew, cantaloupe and kiwifruit on platter around Fluffy Peach Dip, above. Pictured on page 20/21.

1. Fluffy Peach Dip, above
2. French Toast Cinnamon Buns, page 19
3. Raisin Cream Topping, page 19
4. Fried Peameal Canadian Bacon, page 18
5. Fresh Fruit Platter, above

Mediterranean Lunch

The flavours in this casual luncheon menu will bring rays of sunshine and thoughts of warm ocean breezes into your home, no matter what the weather is outside.

serves 6

Warm Chicken Salad

❋

Tuna And Lemon Pasta

❋

Antipasto Platter

❋

Tomato Salad

❋

Lemon Syrup Cake

Warm Chicken Salad

A colourful, hearty salad with a zesty lemon kick balanced by the sweetness of honey and a hint of garlic.

Olive (or cooking) oil	1 tsp.	5 mL
Garlic clove, minced (or 1/4 tsp., 1 mL, powder)	1	1
Chopped fresh rosemary (or 1/2 tsp., 2 mL, dried, crushed)	2 tsp.	10 mL
Finely grated lemon zest	1 tsp.	5 mL
Pepper	1/2 tsp.	2 mL
Boneless, skinless chicken breast halves (about 2)	1/2 lb.	225 g
Bag of arugula (or other baby greens), about 6 cups (1.5 L), stems removed	4 1/2 oz.	128 g
Can of chickpeas (garbanzo beans), rinsed and drained	19 oz.	540 mL
Prosciutto (or ham) slices, cooked crisp and crumbled	8	8
Thinly sliced English cucumber (with peel)	3/4 cup	175 mL
LEMON GARLIC DRESSING		
Olive (or cooking) oil	1/3 cup	75 mL
Lemon juice	1/4 cup	60 mL
Liquid honey	2 tbsp.	30 mL
Garlic clove, minced (or 1/4 tsp., 1 mL, powder)	1	1
Hot pepper sauce	1/2 tsp.	2 mL
Salt	1/4 tsp.	1 mL
Pepper	1/4 tsp.	1 mL

Combine first 5 ingredients in medium bowl. Add chicken. Turn until coated. Cover. Chill for 30 minutes. Preheat gas barbecue to medium. Cook chicken on greased grill for about 5 minutes per side until no longer pink inside. Cut into 1/4 inch (6 mm) thick strips.

Put next 4 ingredients into large bowl. Add chicken. Toss gently.

Lemon Garlic Dressing: Combine all 7 ingredients in jar with tight-fitting lid. Shake well. Makes 3/4 cup (175 mL) dressing. Drizzle over chicken mixture. Toss gently. Makes 8 cups (2 L). Serves 6.

1 serving: 354 Calories; 23.4 g Total Fat (14.2 g Mono, 2.7 g Poly, 5 g Sat); 36 mg Cholesterol; 19 g Carbohydrate; 2 g Fibre; 18 g Protein; 476 mg Sodium

Pictured on page 23.

Tuna And Lemon Pasta

A creamy, colourful dish that will have your guests asking for more!

Medium red peppers, quartered	2	2
Olive (or cooking) oil	1 tbsp.	15 mL
Green onions, chopped	8	8
Garlic cloves, minced (or 1/2 tsp., 2 mL, powder)	2	2
Dry white (or alcohol-free) wine	1/2 cup	125 mL
Whipping cream (or whole milk)	1 1/2 cups	375 mL
Frozen baby peas	1 cup	250 mL
Chopped fresh mint leaves (or 1 1/2 tsp., 7 mL, dried)	2 tbsp.	30 mL
Chopped fresh dill (or 1 1/2 tsp., 7 mL, dill weed)	2 tbsp.	30 mL
Finely grated lemon zest	1 tsp.	5 mL
Cans of flaked white tuna, packed in water (6 1/2 oz., 184 g, each), drained	2	2
Salt	1/2 tsp.	2 mL
Pepper	1/8 tsp.	0.5 mL
Large shell pasta (about 8 oz., 225 g)	3 cups	750 mL
Boiling water	9 cups	2.25 L
Salt	1 tsp.	5 mL

Top Left: Tomato Salad, page 24 Top Right: Antipasto Platter, below
Bottom: Warm Chicken Salad, page 22

Arrange red pepper, skin-side up, on ungreased baking sheet. Broil 5 inches (12.5 cm) from heat for about 10 minutes, rearranging as necessary, until skins are blistered and blackened. Remove to small bowl. Cover with plastic wrap. Let sweat for 10 to 15 minutes until cool enough to handle. Remove and discard skins. Cut into 1/4 inch (6 mm) strips. Set aside.

Heat olive oil in large frying pan on medium-high. Add green onion and garlic. Cook for about 3 minutes until green onion is soft.

Add wine. Stir. Bring to a boil. Reduce heat to medium. Boil gently, uncovered, for about 3 minutes until almost all liquid is evaporated.

Add red pepper strips and next 8 ingredients. Heat and stir for about 5 minutes until hot. Keep warm.

Cook pasta in boiling water and second amount of salt in large uncovered pot or Dutch oven for 8 to 10 minutes, stirring occasionally, until tender but firm. Drain well. Return pasta to pot. Add tuna mixture. Mix well. Makes about 7 cups (1.75 L). Serves 6.

1 serving: 383 Calories; 24 g Total Fat (7.9 g Mono, 1.4 g Poly, 13.3 g Sat); 87 mg Cholesterol; 26 g Carbohydrate; 3 g Fibre; 14 g Protein; 380 mg Sodium

Pictured on page 25.

Antipasto Platter

Put hummus (chickpea dip) or baba ghanoush (eggplant dip) into small bowl and place in centre of platter. Arrange marinated artichokes, sliced salami and whole green and black pitted olives around dip. Serve with ciabatta bread that has been sliced diagonally, lightly brushed with olive (or cooking) oil and baked until lightly golden. Pictured above and on page 25.

Tomato Salad

A fresh, Mediterranean salad with a wonderful basil flavour. Use ripe tomatoes for the best taste and colour.

Medium tomatoes, sliced 1/4 inch (6 mm) thick	4	4
Small red onion, thinly sliced	1	1
Fresh sweet basil leaves, cut chiffonade (see Note)	3 tbsp.	50 mL
HONEY VINEGAR DRESSING		
Olive (or cooking) oil	2 tbsp.	30 mL
Balsamic (or red wine) vinegar	2 tbsp.	30 mL
Liquid honey	2 tsp.	10 mL
Lemon juice	2 tsp.	10 mL
Garlic clove, minced (or 1/4 tsp., 1 mL, powder)	1	1
Crumbled feta cheese (about 1/2 cup, 125 mL)	2 1/2 oz.	70 g

Arrange tomato and onion slices, slightly overlapping, on platter. Sprinkle with basil.

Honey Vinegar Dressing: Combine first 5 ingredients in jar with tight-fitting lid. Shake well. Makes about 1/3 cup (75 mL) dressing. Drizzle over tomato mixture. Cover. Chill for 1 hour.

Just before serving, sprinkle with feta cheese. Serves 6.

1 serving: 115 Calories; 8.3 g Total Fat (4.2 g Mono, 0.6 g Poly, 3.1 g Sat); 9 mg Cholesterol; 8 g Carbohydrate; 1 g Fibre; 3 g Protein; 68 mg Sodium

Pictured on page 23 and on page 25.

Note: To cut chiffonade, stack a few basil leaves at a time and roll up tightly. Slice crosswise into very thin strips.

Lemon Syrup Cake

A lovely, moist cake with a hint of lemon. Serve with whipped cream and fresh berries for an extra special treat.

Hard margarine (or butter), softened	3/4 cup	175 mL
Granulated sugar	1 1/2 cups	375 mL
Egg yolks (large)	6	6
Finely grated lemon zest	2 tbsp.	30 mL
Plain yogurt	1 cup	250 mL
All-purpose flour	2 1/3 cups	575 mL
Baking powder	1 tbsp.	15 mL
Finely chopped almonds	1/2 cup	125 mL
Salt	1/4 tsp.	1 mL
Egg whites (large), room temperature	6	6
LEMON SYRUP		
Granulated sugar	1 cup	250 mL
Water	1/2 cup	125 mL
Liquid honey	2 tbsp.	30 mL
Cinnamon stick (4 inch, 10 cm, length)	1	1
Lemon juice	1/2 cup	125 mL
Dark rum (or 3/4 tsp., 4 mL, rum flavouring)	1 tbsp.	15 mL

Beat margarine and sugar in large bowl until pale and creamy. Add egg yolks, 1 at a time, beating well after each addition.

Add lemon zest and yogurt. Stir.

Add next 4 ingredients. Mix well.

Beat egg whites in medium bowl until soft peaks form. Fold egg whites into cake batter in 2 batches. Pour into greased and lightly floured 12 cup (2.7 L) bundt pan. Bake in 350°F (175°C) oven for about 50 minutes until wooden pick inserted near centre comes out clean. Using skewer, carefully poke about 30 holes in cake ensuring pick goes through to cake pan. Let stand in pan for 10 minutes. Turn out onto wire rack. Put cake back into pan. This ensures cake does not stick to pan after syrup has been poured over it.

Lemon Syrup: Combine first 4 ingredients in medium saucepan. Heat and stir on medium-low for about 8 minutes until sugar is dissolved. Boil on high, without stirring, for 6 to 8 minutes until syrup has thickened slightly. Remove from heat.

Add lemon juice and rum. Stir. Remove and discard cinnamon stick. Slowly pour hot syrup over warm cake. Let stand in pan for about 10 minutes until syrup soaks into cake. Invert onto serving plate. Cuts into 12 slices.

1 slice: 474 Calories; 18.2 g Total Fat (10.9 g Mono, 2.3 g Poly, 3.8 g Sat); 109 mg Cholesterol; 71 g Carbohydrate; 1 g Fibre; 8 g Protein; 332 mg Sodium

Pictured on page 25.

Top Left: Lemon Syrup Cake, this page
Centre Left: Tomato Salad, this page
Centre Right: Antipasto Platter, page 23
Bottom: Tuna And Lemon Pasta, page 23

Patio Party

When warm weather beckons, we are instinctively lured outside. Take your party to the patio with these simple and fresh recipes. With a lot of preparation done the night before, this is a perfect way to entertain on the weekend.

serves 8

Sangria Punch

Crab Patties

Orange And Romaine Salad

Bean And Cashew Salad

Crispy Potato Wedges

Shrimp Quiche

Curry Drumsticks

Chocolate Hazelnut Torte

Top: Sangria Punch, below   Bottom: Crab Patties, page 27

Sangria Punch

A deep ruby red, lightly carbonated punch with a tart, dry wine flavour. Use a lighter style wine such as Pinot Noir or Grenache for best results.

Dry red (or alcohol-free) wine	3 cups	750 mL
Cinnamon stick (4 inch, 10 cm, length)	1	1
Granulated sugar	3 tbsp.	50 mL
Brandy	1/3 cup	75 mL
Grenadine syrup	3 tbsp.	50 mL
Seedless green grapes	1 cup	250 mL
Large orange, quartered and thinly sliced	1	1
Sparkling white (or alcohol-free) wine	3 cups	750 mL

Combine red wine, cinnamon stick and sugar in medium saucepan. Heat and stir on medium-low for about 5 minutes, without boiling, until sugar is dissolved. Cool. Remove and discard cinnamon stick. Pour into large pitcher.

Add next 4 ingredients. Stir. Cover. Chill for at least 6 hours or overnight.

Add white wine. Stir. Makes about 9 cups (2.25 L). Serves 8.

1 serving: 196 Calories; 0.1 g Total Fat (trace Mono, trace Poly, trace Sat);
0 mg Cholesterol; 23 g Carbohydrate; trace Fibre; 1 g Protein; 18 mg Sodium

Pictured above.

Crab Patties

Crunchy on the outside with a soft, even texture on the inside. These patties have a delicate crab flavour with a hint of dill. Serve with a dipping sauce made with equal amounts of sweet chili sauce and mayonnaise.

Cans of crabmeat (6 oz., 170 g, each), drained and cartilage removed	2	2
Mayonnaise (not salad dressing)	1/4 cup	60 mL
Sour cream	1/4 cup	60 mL
Chopped fresh dill (or 1 1/2 tsp., 7 mL, dill weed)	2 tbsp.	30 mL
Finely chopped green onion	6 tbsp.	100 mL
Fine dry bread crumbs	1 1/2 cups	375 mL
Large eggs, fork-beaten	2	2
All-purpose flour	6 tbsp.	100 mL
Cooking oil	3 – 6 tbsp.	50 – 100 mL

Combine first 7 ingredients in medium bowl. Mix well. Shape into patties, using 1 tbsp. (15 mL) each.

Toss lightly in flour.

Heat cooking oil in large frying pan on medium. Add patties. Cook in 2 to 3 batches, until golden. Remove to paper towels to drain. Makes 40 patties. Serves 8.

1 serving: 270 Calories; 15.5 g Total Fat (7.9 g Mono, 4.2 g Poly, 2.3 g Sat); 61 mg Cholesterol; 21 g Carbohydrate; 1 g Fibre; 11 g Protein; 517 mg Sodium

Pictured on page 26.

Orange And Romaine Salad

A fresh summer salad with a wonderful combination of colours and textures.

Head of romaine lettuce, cut or torn	1	1
Large oranges, peeled and divided into segments	2 – 3	2 – 3
Crumbled blue cheese (about 2/3 cup, 150 mL)	3 1/2 oz.	100 g
Sliced almonds, toasted (see Note)	1 cup	250 mL
RED WINE VINAIGRETTE		
Olive (or cooking) oil	1/3 cup	75 mL
Red wine vinegar	3 tbsp.	50 mL
Grainy mustard	1 tbsp.	15 mL
Brown sugar, packed	2 tsp.	10 mL
Salt	1/4 tsp.	1 mL

Combine first 4 ingredients in large bowl. Toss.

Red Wine Vinaigrette: Combine all 5 ingredients in jar with tight-fitting lid. Shake well. Makes 2/3 cup (150 mL) vinaigrette. Drizzle over lettuce mixture. Toss. Makes about 11 cups (2.75 L). Serves 8.

1 serving: 240 Calories; 20.6 g Total Fat (12.7 g Mono, 2.6 g Poly, 4.3 g Sat); 9 mg Cholesterol; 9 g Carbohydrate; 3 g Fibre; 7 g Protein; 281 mg Sodium

Pictured on page 29.

Note: To toast almonds, place in single layer in ungreased shallow pan. Bake in 350°F (175°C) oven for 5 to 10 minutes, stirring or shaking often, until desired doneness.

Bean And Cashew Salad

This mild-flavoured salad is a delightful addition to this menu. Increase the amount of chili paste in the dressing for a little more heat if desired.

Fresh whole green beans, trimmed	1/2 lb.	225 g
Boiling water		
Ice water		
Cashews, toasted (see Note)	1 cup	250 mL
Cherry tomatoes, halved	2 cups	500 mL
Thinly sliced red onion	3/4 cup	175 mL
LEMON DILL DRESSING		
Olive (or cooking) oil	1/3 cup	75 mL
Lemon juice	3 tbsp.	50 mL
Chopped fresh dill (or 1/2 tsp., 2 mL, dill weed)	2 tsp.	10 mL
Garlic clove, minced (or 1/4 tsp., 1 mL, powder)	1	1
Chili paste (sambal oelek)	1/2 tsp.	2 mL
Salt	1/4 tsp.	1 mL

Blanch beans in boiling water in large saucepan for 1 to 3 minutes until bright green. Drain. Plunge into ice water in large bowl. Let stand for about 10 minutes until beans are cold. Drain. Put into large bowl.

Add cashews, tomatoes and onion.

Lemon Dill Dressing: Combine all 6 ingredients in jar with tight-fitting lid. Shake well. Makes 1/2 cup (125 mL) dressing. Drizzle over bean mixture. Toss. Makes 6 cups (1.5 L). Serves 8.

1 serving: 211 Calories; 18 g Total Fat (11.9 g Mono, 2.3 g Poly, 3 g Sat); 0 mg Cholesterol; 11 g Carbohydrate; 1 g Fibre; 4 g Protein; 82 mg Sodium

Pictured on page 29.

Note: To toast cashews, place in single layer in ungreased shallow pan. Bake in 350°F (175°C) oven for 5 to 10 minutes, stirring or shaking often, until desired doneness.

Crispy Potato Wedges

Perfectly browned potato wedges flavoured with rosemary and served with a tangy mustard and bacon dipping sauce.

Large potatoes (with peel), about 3 lbs. (1.4 kg)	6	6
Olive (or cooking) oil	2 tbsp.	30 mL
Dried rosemary, crushed	1 tbsp.	15 mL
Garlic salt	1 tsp.	5 mL
Coarsely ground pepper (or 1/2 tsp., 2 mL, pepper)	1 tsp.	5 mL
DIP		
Sour cream	1/2 cup	125 mL
Grainy mustard	2 tbsp.	30 mL
Bacon slices, cooked crisp and crumbled	3	3
Green onions, finely sliced	2	2

Cut potatoes in half lengthwise. Cut each half into 4 wedges. Put into large bowl.

Add next 4 ingredients. Toss. Arrange in single layer on greased baking sheet. Bake in 400°F (205°C) oven for about 50 minutes, stirring once or twice, until browned.

Dip: Combine all 4 ingredients in small bowl. Makes 3/4 cup (175 mL) dip. Serve with potato wedges. Serves 8.

1 serving: 199 Calories; 7.2 g Total Fat (3.8 g Mono, 0.7 g Poly, 2.3 g Sat); 8 mg Cholesterol; 30 g Carbohydrate; 3 g Fibre; 5 g Protein; 258 mg Sodium

Pictured on page 29.

Shrimp Quiche

A golden, flaky crust with a rich, creamy shrimp filling. Delicious!

Pastry for 1 crust 10 inch (25 cm) pie	1	1
Cooked shrimp, coarsely chopped	1 1/2 cups	375 mL
Block of cream cheese, finely chopped	4 oz.	125 g
Large eggs	6	6
Whipping cream (or whole milk)	2 cups	500 mL
Chopped fresh dill (or 1/2 – 3/4 tsp., 2 – 4 mL, dill weed)	2 – 3 tsp.	10 – 15 mL
Salt	1/4 tsp.	1 mL
Pepper, sprinkle		

Roll out pastry on lightly floured surface to fit 10 inch (25 cm) tart pan with removable bottom or pie plate. Press in bottom and up side. Trim edge.

Scatter shrimp and cream cheese in pastry shell.

Combine remaining 5 ingredients in medium bowl. Pour over shrimp mixture. Bake on bottom rack in 375°F (190°C) oven for 50 to 55 minutes until knife inserted in centre comes out clean. Let stand for 10 minutes before serving. Serves 8.

1 serving: 411 Calories; 34.9 g Total Fat (11.4 g Mono, 2.1 g Poly, 19 g Sat); 308 mg Cholesterol; 11 g Carbohydrate; 0 g Fibre; 14 g Protein; 357 mg Sodium

Pictured on page 29.

Curry Drumsticks

A tasty finger food, perfect for sitting out on the patio. These tender, curry-flavoured drumettes are very quick and easy to prepare.

Ketchup	1/3 cup	75 mL
Dry sherry	1/3 cup	75 mL
Worcestershire sauce	2 tbsp.	30 mL
Curry powder	2 tbsp.	30 mL
Garlic cloves, minced (or 1/2 tsp., 2 mL, powder)	2	2
Salt	3/4 tsp.	4 mL
Coarsely ground pepper (or 1/2 tsp., 2 mL, pepper)	1 tsp.	5 mL
Chicken drumettes (or whole wings, split in half, tips discarded)	2 1/2 lbs.	1.1 kg

Combine first 7 ingredients in large bowl or resealable freezer bag.

Add drumettes. Cover or seal. Toss until well coated. Marinate in refrigerator for at least 8 hours or overnight. Drain and discard marinade. Preheat gas barbecue to medium-low. Cook chicken on greased grill for about 20 minutes, turning occasionally, until no longer pink inside. Makes about 20 drumettes or 30 wing pieces. Serves 8.

1 serving: 343 Calories; 22.9 g Total Fat (9 g Mono, 4.8 g Poly, 6.4 g Sat); 109 mg Cholesterol; 5 g Carbohydrate; trace Fibre; 27 g Protein; 498 mg Sodium

Pictured on page 29.

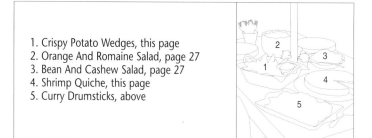

1. Crispy Potato Wedges, this page
2. Orange And Romaine Salad, page 27
3. Bean And Cashew Salad, page 27
4. Shrimp Quiche, this page
5. Curry Drumsticks, above

Chocolate Hazelnut Torte

Fresh strawberries paired with a rich chocolate mousse. Irresistible! Top with whipped cream, strawberries and chocolate curls for an extra special treat.

MERINGUES

Egg whites (large), room temperature	6	6
Granulated sugar	1 1/2 cups	375 mL
White vinegar	1 1/2 tsp.	7 mL
Flaked hazelnuts (filberts), finely chopped	1 1/2 cups	375 mL

CHOCOLATE MOUSSE

Semi-sweet chocolate baking squares (1 oz., 28 g, each), chopped	8	8
Hard margarine (or butter)	2 tbsp.	30 mL
Whipping cream	1 1/2 cups	375 mL
Fresh strawberries (16 oz., 454 g, basket), halved lengthwise	3 cups	750 mL

Meringues: Place oven racks on 2 lowest rack positions. Line 2 baking sheets with parchment paper or foil. Trace 2 circles, each 7 inches (18 cm) in diameter and about 1/3 inch (1 cm) apart, on each sheet. Beat egg whites in large bowl until soft peaks form. Add sugar, 1 tbsp. (15 mL) at a time, beating well after each addition, until sugar is dissolved and stiff peaks form.

Fold in vinegar and hazelnuts. Divide and spoon onto greased circles, smoothing tops. Bake in 250°F (120°C) oven for about 1 hour until dry. You do not need to switch pans at halftime. Turn oven off. Let stand in oven until cool.

Chocolate Mousse: Heat chocolate and margarine in small heavy saucepan on lowest heat, stirring often, until almost melted. Do not overheat. Remove from heat. Stir until smooth. Pour into separate large bowl. Cool.

Beat whipping cream in small bowl until soft peaks form. Fold into chocolate mixture. Makes 3 1/2 cups (875 mL) mousse.

Place 1 meringue disc on large serving plate. Spread with 1/3 of mousse. Top with 1/3 of strawberries. Place another meringue disc over strawberries. Repeat, layering with mousse, strawberries and meringue discs, finishing with meringue disc. Cover. Chill for at least 8 hours or overnight. Cuts into 10 wedges.

1 wedge: 504 Calories; 32.7 g Total Fat (16.3 g Mono, 2 g Poly, 12.9 g Sat); 44 mg Cholesterol; 53 g Carbohydrate; 3 g Fibre; 6 g Protein; 77 mg Sodium

Pictured below.

Chocolate Hazelnut Torte, above

Afternoon Grill

The neighbours will be peering over the fence to see what's cooking. You might want to eat this meal inside!

serves 4

Watermelon Punch

❧

Grilled Steak Sandwiches

❧

Seasoned Corn On The Cob

❧

Raspberry Freeze

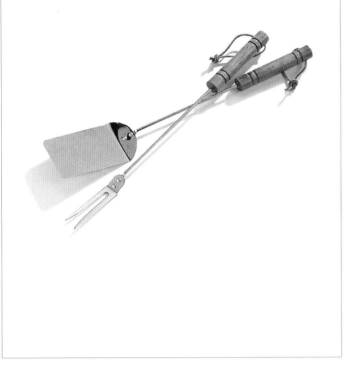

Watermelon Punch, below

Watermelon Punch

This oh-so-refreshing beverage looks pretty served in martini-type glasses or wine goblets. This is an "adults only" drink!

Coarsely chopped seedless watermelon (or seeds removed)	3 cups	750 mL
White rum	1/2 cup	125 mL
Melon-flavoured liqueur (such as Midori)	1/2 cup	125 mL
Diced seedless watermelon (or seeds removed)	2 cups	500 mL
Lemon lime soft drink, chilled	2 cups	500 mL

Process first amount of watermelon in food processor or blender until smooth. Pour into 2 quart (2 L) pitcher.

Add rum, liqueur and second amount of watermelon. Stir. Cover. Chill.

Just before serving, stir soft drink into watermelon mixture. Makes 6 1/2 cups (1.6 L). Serves 4.

1 serving: 319 Calories; 1 g Total Fat (trace Mono, trace Poly, 0 g Sat); 0 mg Cholesterol; 43 g Carbohydrate; 1 g Fibre; 1 g Protein; 21 mg Sodium

Pictured above.

Grilled Steak Sandwiches

These juicy steak sandwiches are perfect for an afternoon meal. The sweet soy sauce and ginger marinade will leave your taste buds wanting more!

FAVOURITE STEAK MARINADE

Lemon juice	2 tbsp.	30 mL
Water	2 tbsp.	30 mL
Brown sugar, packed	3 tbsp.	50 mL
Soy sauce	2 tbsp.	30 mL
Ketchup	1 tbsp.	15 mL
Ground ginger	1/4 tsp.	1 mL
Garlic clove, minced (or 1/4 tsp., 1 mL, powder)	1	1
Rib-eye steaks (about 8 oz., 225 g, each), cut 1/2 – 3/4 inch (1.2 – 2 cm) thick and trimmed of fat	2	2
Kaiser rolls, cut in half	4	4
Hard margarine (or butter), softened	2 tbsp.	30 mL
Cooking oil	1 tbsp.	15 mL
Sliced onion	2 cups	500 mL
Sliced fresh small mushrooms	2 cups	500 mL
Light sour cream	1/2 cup	125 mL
Grainy mustard	2 tbsp.	30 mL
Spinach, stems removed	2 cups	500 mL
Medium yellow pepper, thinly sliced	1	1
Swiss cheese slices	4	4

Favourite Steak Marinade: Combine first 7 ingredients in small bowl. Stir until brown sugar is dissolved. Makes 1/2 cup (125 mL) marinade.

Place steaks in shallow dish or resealable freezer bag. Pour marinade over steaks. Stir or turn until coated. Cover or seal. Marinate in refrigerator for at least 6 hours or overnight, turning several times. Drain and discard marinade. Preheat gas barbecue to medium. Cook steaks on greased grill for about 5 minutes per side until desired doneness. Let stand for 10 minutes. Slice thinly across grain on diagonal.

Spread cut side of rolls with margarine. Heat on grill, cut side down, over medium heat for about 3 minutes until soft and lightly browned. Keep warm.

Heat cooking oil in large frying pan on medium. Add onion. Cook for about 10 minutes, stirring occasionally, until soft and golden.

Add mushrooms. Cook on medium-high for about 5 minutes, stirring occasionally, until golden and liquid is evaporated.

Combine sour cream and mustard in separate small bowl. Divide and spread on bottom half of each roll.

Divide and layer spinach, yellow pepper, cheese slices, steak and mushroom mixture over sour cream mixture. Cover with top half of rolls. Makes 4 sandwiches.

1 sandwich: 606 Calories; 28.6 g Total Fat (12.5 g Mono, 3.6 g Poly, 12 g Sat); 79 mg Cholesterol; 49 g Carbohydrate; 3 g Fibre; 39 g Protein; 1283 mg Sodium

Pictured on page 33.

Seasoned Corn On The Cob

With a mild, peppery heat and the flavour of dried thyme, the seasoning on these cobs is a nice change from traditional salt.

Hard margarine (or butter), softened	3 tbsp.	50 mL
Seasoned salt	1 tsp.	5 mL
Onion powder	1/4 tsp.	1 mL
Dried thyme, crushed	1/4 tsp.	1 mL
Garlic powder (optional)	1/8 tsp.	0.5 mL
Pepper	1/8 tsp.	0.5 mL
Cayenne pepper	1/8 tsp.	0.5 mL
Corncobs	4	4
Water	1/4 cup	60 mL

Combine first 7 ingredients in small bowl.

Spread over corncobs. Place each cob on large piece of foil. Sprinkle each with 1 tbsp. (15 mL) water. Wrap tightly, twisting ends to prevent leakage. Preheat gas barbecue to medium. Cook cobs on ungreased grill for about 30 minutes, turning several times, until tender. Carefully remove foil, reserving liquid. Place cobs on serving plate. Drizzle any reserved liquid over top. Serves 4.

1 serving: 210 Calories; 10.3 g Total Fat (6.1 g Mono, 1.6 g Poly, 2 g Sat); 0 mg Cholesterol; 31 g Carbohydrate; 5 g Fibre; 4 g Protein; 419 mg Sodium

Pictured on page 33.

Raspberry Freeze

An icy-cool dessert with a delicate raspberry flavour.

Granulated sugar	1 cup	250 mL
Envelope of unflavoured gelatin	1/4 oz.	7 g
Salt, sprinkle		
Homogenized (or 2%) milk	2 1/2 cups	625 mL
Frozen raspberries in syrup, thawed	15 oz.	425 g
Lemon juice	1 tbsp.	15 mL
Egg whites (large), room temperature	2	2
Fresh raspberries (optional)	3/4 cup	175 mL

Combine sugar, gelatin and salt in medium saucepan. Stir in milk. Heat on medium for about 5 minutes, stirring occasionally, until sugar is dissolved. Remove from heat. Cool.

Put raspberries with syrup into blender. Add lemon juice. Purée. Strain through sieve. Discard solids. Stir into cooled milk mixture. Pour into 9 x 13 inch (22 x 33 cm) dish. Freeze for about 2 hours, stirring once or twice, until slushy. Scrape into large mixing bowl. Beat on high until foamy.

Beat egg whites with clean beaters in small bowl until soft peaks form. Fold into raspberry mixture. Return to 9 x 13 inch (22 x 33 cm) dish. Freeze for at least 8 hours or overnight until firm.

Serve with raspberries. Makes 6 cups (1.5 L).

1/2 cup (125 mL): 143 Calories; 1.9 g Total Fat (0.5 g Mono, 0.1 g Poly, 1.1 g Sat); 7 mg Cholesterol; 30 g Carbohydrate; 2 g Fibre; 3 g Protein; 37 mg Sodium

Pictured below.

Top Left: Raspberry Freeze, above   Bottom Centre: Grilled Steak Sandwiches, page 32   Top Right: Seasoned Corn On The Cob, page 32

Aussie Barbie

*When it's time to "fire up the barbie,"
you'll appreciate the authenticity
of these wonderful recipes
from Down Under.*

serves 6

Barbecued Shrimp

Herbed Garlic Bread

Butternut Squash Salad

Roasted Beet Salad

Minted Lamb Chops

Pavlova

Barbecued Shrimp

Perfectly barbecued shrimp served with a delicious garlic and lemon mayonnaise. The mayonnaise can easily be made a day or two ahead and stored in a sealed container in the refrigerator.

GARLIC MAYONNAISE

Garlic clove (or 1/4 tsp., 1 mL, powder)	1	1
Large egg	1	1
Egg yolk (large)	1	1
Lemon juice	1 tbsp.	15 mL
Salt	1/8 tsp.	0.5 mL
Olive (or cooking) oil	3/4 cup	175 mL
Cooking oil	2 tbsp.	30 mL
Chopped fresh parsley (or 2 1/4 tsp., 11 mL, flakes)	3 tbsp.	50 mL
Finely grated lemon zest	1/2 tsp.	2 mL
Salt	1/2 tsp.	2 mL
Coarsely ground pepper (or 1/2 tsp., 2 mL, pepper)	1 tsp.	5 mL
Jumbo shrimp (tails intact), peeled and deveined	18	18

Garlic Mayonnaise: Process first 5 ingredients in food processor for about 2 minutes until well combined and creamy.

With motor running, slowly pour olive oil in thin stream through feed chute until pale and thickened. Cover. Chill for 1 to 2 hours. Makes about 1 cup (250 mL) mayonnaise.

Combine next 5 ingredients in medium bowl.

Add shrimp. Toss until coated. Cover. Marinate in refrigerator for 1 hour, stirring occasionally. Drain and discard any remaining marinade. Preheat gas barbecue to medium. Cook shrimp on greased grill for about 2 minutes per side until pink. Do not overcook. Serve with mayonnaise. Serves 6.

1 serving: 409 Calories; 36.4 g Total Fat (24.7 g Mono, 4.6 g Poly, 5 g Sat); 201 mg Cholesterol; 2 g Carbohydrate; trace Fibre; 19 g Protein; 388 mg Sodium

Pictured on page 35.

Herbed Garlic Bread

Crispy garlic bread flavoured with rosemary. Yum!

Hard margarine (or butter), softened	1/2 cup	125 mL
Finely grated fresh Parmesan cheese	3 tbsp.	50 mL
Garlic clove, minced (or 1/4 tsp., 1 mL, powder)	1	1
Dried rosemary, crushed	1/2 tsp.	2 mL
French bread loaf	1	1

Combine first 4 ingredients in small bowl. Mix well.

Cut bread loaf into 3/4 inch (2 cm) slices almost through to bottom crust. Spread both sides of each slice with margarine mixture. Wrap loaf tightly in heavy-duty foil (or double layer of regular foil). Preheat gas barbecue to medium. Heat bread on ungreased grill for 10 to 15 minutes, turning occasionally, until heated through and crust is crisp. Cuts into 18 slices. Serves 6.

1 serving: 366 Calories; 19.5 g Total Fat (5.9 g Mono, 1.2 g Poly, 11.2 g Sat); 46 mg Cholesterol; 40 g Carbohydrate; 2 g Fibre; 8 g Protein; 685 mg Sodium

Pictured on page 36.

Butternut Squash Salad

This bright, colourful salad is sure to be a hit!

Small butternut squash, peeled and cut into 1/2 inch (12 mm) cubes	1	1
Cooking oil	1 tbsp.	15 mL
Salt	1/4 tsp.	1 mL
Pepper, sprinkle		
Fresh asparagus, trimmed of tough ends, each spear cut into 3 pieces	1/2 lb.	225 g
Boiling water		
Ice water		
Bag of baby spinach (about 5 cups, 1.25 L, lightly packed)	6 oz.	170 g
Macadamia nuts, toasted (see Note) and coarsely chopped	2/3 cup	150 mL
HONEY GARLIC VINAIGRETTE		
Olive (or cooking) oil	3 tbsp.	50 mL
Red wine vinegar	2 tbsp.	30 mL
Liquid honey	1 tbsp.	15 mL
Garlic clove, minced (or 1/4 tsp., 1 mL, powder)	1	1
Salt	1/4 tsp.	1 mL
Pepper, just a pinch		

Barbecued Shrimp, page 34

Combine first 4 ingredients in large bowl. Mix well. Arrange in single layer on ungreased baking sheet. Bake in 375°F (190°C) oven for about 50 minutes, turning once, until tender and lightly browned. Cool.

Blanch asparagus in boiling water for about 2 minutes until bright green. Drain. Plunge into ice water in large bowl. Let stand for about 10 minutes until cold. Drain.

Combine squash, asparagus, spinach and macadamia nuts in salad bowl. Toss gently.

Honey Garlic Vinaigrette: Combine all 6 ingredients in jar with tight-fitting lid. Shake well. Makes 1/2 cup (125 mL) vinaigrette. Drizzle over squash mixture. Toss gently. Makes 12 cups (3 L). Serves 6.

1 serving: 304 Calories; 21.1 g Total Fat (15.6 g Mono, 1.6 g Poly, 2.9 g Sat); 0 mg Cholesterol; 31 g Carbohydrate; 6 g Fibre; 5 g Protein; 231 mg Sodium

Pictured on page 36.

Note: To toast macadamia nuts, place in single layer in ungreased shallow pan. Bake in 350°F (175°C) oven for 5 to 10 minutes, stirring or shaking often, until desired doneness.

Roasted Beet Salad

The unique apple cider vinaigrette and crunchy bacon are a pleasing contrast to the sweet roasted beets.

Medium beets (see Note)	6	6
APPLE CIDER VINAIGRETTE		
Olive (or cooking) oil	1/4 cup	60 mL
Apple cider vinegar	2 tbsp.	30 mL
Grainy mustard	1 tbsp.	15 mL
Brown sugar, packed	1 tsp.	5 mL
Salt	1/4 tsp.	1 mL
Bacon slices, cooked crisp and crumbled	6	6
Chopped fresh chives (or 3/4 tsp., 4 mL, dried)	1 tbsp.	15 mL

Wrap beets individually in foil. Bake directly on centre rack in 375°F (190°C) oven for about 1 hour until tender. Remove foil. Let beets stand until cool enough to handle. Peel beets. Cut into quarters. Put into medium bowl.

Apple Cider Vinaigrette: Combine first 5 ingredients in jar with tight-fitting lid. Shake well. Makes 1/2 cup (125 mL) vinaigrette. Drizzle over beets. Toss. Chill for at least 1 hour, stirring occasionally.

Just before serving, sprinkle with bacon and chives. Serves 6.

1 serving: 162 Calories; 13 g Total Fat (8.6 g Mono, 1.3 g Poly, 2.5 g Sat); 5 mg Cholesterol; 9 g Carbohydrate; 2 g Fibre; 3 g Protein; 299 mg Sodium

Pictured below.

Note: Two 14 oz. (398 mL) cans of beets may be used to save time.

Minted Lamb Chops

Tender lamb with a subtle red wine flavour and a hint of mint. Use your favourite cut of lamb chops and adjust cooking time to suit.

Dry red (or alcohol-free) wine	1/2 cup	125 mL
Mint jelly	1/3 cup	75 mL
Lemon juice	3 tbsp.	50 mL
Finely grated peeled gingerroot	1/2 tsp.	2 mL
Salt	1/2 tsp.	2 mL
Coarsely ground pepper (or 1/2 tsp., 2 mL, pepper)	1 tsp.	5 mL
Lamb chops	12	12

Combine first 6 ingredients in medium saucepan. Heat and stir on medium for about 5 minutes until jelly is liquid. Cool.

Place lamb chops in shallow dish. Add red wine mixture. Turn until coated. Cover. Marinate in refrigerator for at least 6 hours or overnight. Drain and discard marinade. Preheat gas barbecue to medium. Cook chops on greased grill for 5 to 7 minutes per side until tender. Makes 12. Serves 6.

1 serving: 386 Calories; 27.8 g Total Fat (11.4 g Mono, 2.2 g Poly, 12.3 g Sat); 77 mg Cholesterol; 13 g Carbohydrate; trace Fibre; 17 g Protein; 265 mg Sodium

Pictured below.

Top Left: Roasted Beet Salad, above
Bottom Centre Left: Minted Lamb Chops, this page

Top Right: Herbed Garlic Bread, page 35
Bottom Centre Right: Butternut Squash Salad, page 35

Pavlova, below

Pavlova

A sweet outer crust with a moist, spongy inside layer. Best made on the day of serving. Don't panic if the top collapses a little—you will have to "collapse" it anyway.

Egg whites (large), room temperature	4	4
Granulated sugar	1 cup	250 mL
White vinegar	1 tsp.	5 mL
Whipping cream	1 1/2 cups	375 mL
Kiwifruit, peeled, halved lengthwise and sliced	2	2
Fresh strawberries (about 4 oz., 113 g), halved lengthwise	1 1/2 cups	375 mL

Line baking sheet with parchment paper or foil. Trace circle, 7 inches (18 cm) in diameter. Beat egg whites in large bowl until soft peaks form. Add sugar, 1 tbsp. (15 mL) at a time, beating well after each addition, until sugar is dissolved and stiff peaks form.

Fold in vinegar. Spoon meringue onto greased circle. Shape side up towards centre with knife. Bake on bottom rack in 225°F (110°C) oven for about 2 hours until dry. Turn oven off. Let stand in oven until cool.

Beat whipping cream in medium bowl until soft peaks form. Carefully cut circle in top of meringue, 1 inch (2.5 cm) from edge, using small sharp knife. Lightly press circle down to sink top slightly. Spoon whipped cream onto meringue.

Arrange kiwifruit and strawberries over whipped cream. Cuts into 10 wedges.

1 wedge: 216 Calories; 12.2 g Total Fat (3.6 g Mono, 0.4 g Poly, 7.6 g Sat); 44 mg Cholesterol; 25 g Carbohydrate; 1 g Fibre; 2 g Protein; 36 mg Sodium

Pictured above.

Beach Party

It's perfect beach weather so pack up the sunscreen, towels and umbrella, along with this portable make-ahead menu, and head for the sand! Lay out this spread, put your sunglasses on, sit back and relax.

serves 10

Orange Pineapple Cocktail

∽

Pecan Cabbage Salad

∽

Pesto Potato Salad

∽

Honey Mustard Rolls

∽

Lemon Garlic Chicken

∽

Sausage-On-A-Stick

∽

Drunken Watermelon

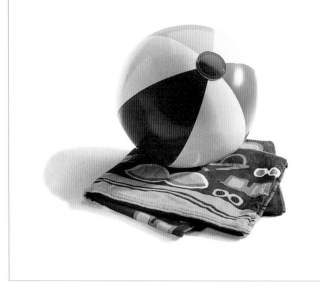

Orange Pineapple Cocktail

Enjoy the taste of the tropics with this attractive citrus beverage. Use fresh pineapple for extra zing.

Coconut-flavoured rum (such as Malibu)	1 2/3 cups	400 mL
Melon-flavoured liqueur (such as Midori)	2/3 cup	150 mL
Orange juice	4 cups	1 L
Pineapple juice	4 cups	1 L
Can of pineapple chunks (with juice)	14 oz.	398 mL
Medium orange, thinly sliced	1	1
Ice cubes		

Combine first 4 ingredients in large pitcher.

Add pineapple with juice and orange slices. Stir. Makes about 13 cups (3.25 L). Just before serving, add ice cubes. Serves 10.

1 serving: 285 Calories; 1.1 g Total Fat (0.1 g Mono, 0.2 g Poly, 0.4 g Sat); 0 mg Cholesterol; 53 g Carbohydrate; 1 g Fibre; 1 g Protein; 6 mg Sodium

Pictured on page 39.

Pecan Cabbage Salad

A colourful, attractive salad with a delightful combination of flavours and textures.

Small head of red cabbage, shredded	1/2	1/2
Head of suey choy (Chinese cabbage), shredded	1/2	1/2
Coarsely chopped pecans	2 cups	500 mL
Sliced green onion	1 1/2 cups	375 mL
Finely chopped yellow pepper	2 cups	500 mL
TANGY DRESSING		
Olive (or cooking) oil	2/3 cup	150 mL
White wine vinegar	1/2 cup	125 mL
Orange juice	1/4 cup	60 mL
Liquid honey	3 tbsp.	50 mL
Garlic cloves, minced (or 1/2 tsp., 2 mL, powder)	2	2
Chili paste (sambal oelek)	1 tsp.	5 mL
Salt	1/2 tsp.	2 mL

Toss first 5 ingredients in very large bowl.

Tangy Dressing: Combine all 7 ingredients in jar with tight-fitting lid. Shake well. Makes 1 3/4 cups (425 mL) dressing. Drizzle over cabbage mixture. Toss. Makes about 16 cups (4 L). Serves 10.

1 serving: 376 Calories; 32.5 g Total Fat (21.7 g Mono, 5.6 g Poly, 3.5 g Sat); 0 mg Cholesterol; 23 g Carbohydrate; 5 g Fibre; 5 g Protein; 139 mg Sodium

Pictured on page 41.

Pesto Potato Salad

Not your ordinary potato salad. Creamy basil dressing combined with crispy bacon and Parmesan cheese. This will be a hit at any party!

Red baby potatoes (with peel), halved	3 1/2 lbs.	1.6 kg
Water		
Salt	1/2 tsp.	2 mL
Sour cream	1/2 cup	125 mL
Basil pesto	1/3 cup	75 mL
Mayonnaise (not salad dressing)	1/3 cup	75 mL
Bacon slices, cooked crisp and crumbled	12	12
Finely chopped red onion	1 1/2 cups	375 mL
Shaved fresh Parmesan cheese (see Note)	1/2 cup	125 mL
Fresh chives, cut into 1/4 inch (6 mm) lengths (or 1 tbsp., 15 mL, dried)	1/4 cup	60 mL

Cook potatoes in water and salt until just tender. Drain. Rinse well with cold water. Drain well.

Combine sour cream, pesto and mayonnaise in large bowl.

Add potatoes, bacon and red onion. Toss.

Sprinkle with Parmesan cheese and chives. Makes about 12 cups (3 L). Serves 10.

1 serving: 294 Calories; 15.9 g Total Fat (8 g Mono, 2.9 g Poly, 4.4 g Sat); 20 mg Cholesterol; 30 g Carbohydrate; 3 g Fibre; 9 g Protein; 277 mg Sodium

Pictured on page 41.

Note: Use vegetable peeler to peel very thin slices from block of Parmesan cheese.

Honey Mustard Rolls

Combine equal amounts of mayonnaise (or salad dressing) and honey mustard in small bowl. Spread on cut sides of kaiser (or other) rolls. Just before serving, fill rolls with Lemon Garlic Chicken, this page, or Sausage-On-A-Stick (without stick), page 40. Pictured on page 40/41.

Orange Pineapple Cocktail, page 38

Lemon Garlic Chicken

Succulent, tender chicken coated in a subtle herb blend. Make at home and take to the beach. Delicious!

Lemon juice	1 cup	250 mL
Chopped fresh parsley (or 3 tbsp., 50 mL, flakes)	3/4 cup	175 mL
Water	1/2 cup	125 mL
Olive (or cooking) oil	1/3 cup	75 mL
Lemon pepper	1/3 cup	75 mL
Soy sauce	1/3 cup	75 mL
Dried rosemary	2 tbsp.	30 mL
Garlic cloves, minced (or 1 1/2 tsp., 7 mL, powder)	6	6
Whole fresh chickens (about 4 1/2 lbs., 2 kg, each)	2	2

Combine first 8 ingredients in medium bowl. Divide between 2 resealable freezer bags.

Add 1 chicken to each bag. Seal. Turn until coated. Marinate in refrigerator for at least 4 hours or overnight, turning several times. Remove chickens, reserving marinade. Pour marinade into small saucepan. Bring to a boil. Reduce heat. Simmer, uncovered, for 5 minutes. Cool. Place chickens on greased wire racks on baking sheet. Tie legs together. Tuck wings behind. Cook in 350°F (175°C) oven for 1 1/2 to 1 3/4 hours, brushing with reserved marinade during cooking, until meat thermometer registers 185°F (85°C) in thickest part of chicken. Cool. Slice or cut into pieces to serve. Serves 10.

1 serving: 693 Calories; 49.7 g Total Fat (23 g Mono, 9.7 g Poly, 13 g Sat); 208 mg Cholesterol; 7 g Carbohydrate; 1 g Fibre; 53 g Protein; 777 mg Sodium

Pictured on page 40 and on page 41.

Sausage-On-A-Stick

Insert pre-soaked 10 inch (25 cm) bamboo skewers into your choice of beef or pork sausages or smokies, from 1 end to other end. Cook on greased barbecue grill or over hot coals for 12 to 15 minutes, turning several times, until desired doneness. Pictured on this page.

Drunken Watermelon

A refreshing summer dessert with a pleasant, lingering liqueur taste. Leave a few slices of watermelon aside for those who don't enjoy alcohol.

Bottles of lemon vodka cooler (11 1/2 oz., 330 mL, each)	4	4
Orange-flavoured liqueur (such as Grand Marnier)	2/3 cup	150 mL
Small to medium watermelon	1/2	1/2

Combine vodka cooler and liqueur in very large bowl.

Cut watermelon into 3/4 inch (2 cm) thick slices. Cut each slice into 8 wedges. Layer wedges in liqueur mixture. Cover. Turn gently until coated. Chill for at least 3 hours or overnight, turning occasionally. Serves 10.

1 serving: 200 Calories; 1 g Total Fat (0 g Mono, trace Poly, trace Sat); 0 mg Cholesterol; 30 g Carbohydrate; 1 g Fibre; 1 g Protein; 16 mg Sodium

Pictured on page 40/41.

1. Honey Mustard Rolls, page 39
2. Pecan Cabbage Salad, page 38
3. Pesto Potato Salad, page 39
4. Lemon Garlic Chicken, page 39
5. Sausage-On-A-Stick, above
6. Drunken Watermelon, above

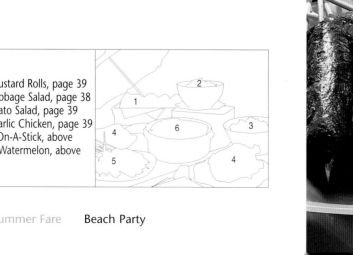

Boating Fare

After a day of fun and frolic in and on the water, take this menu out of the cooler and prepare for a flavourful feast! These delightful dishes will keep everyone's cravings on an even keel.

serves 6

Sparkling Iced Tea

Onion And Brie Tartlets

Shrimp Pasta Salad

Salmon-Wrapped Scallops

Deli Focaccia

Strawberry Shortcakes

Sparkling Iced Tea

A cooling summer beverage with a hint of lime. Can easily be doubled.

Sparkling bottled water (such as Perrier)	4 cups	1 L
Lime juice	1/3 cup	75 mL
Powdered iced tea mix (plain or lemon-flavoured)	1/2 cup	125 mL
Ice cubes	20	20
Medium lime, thinly sliced	1	1

Combine water, lime juice and iced tea mix in 8 cup (2 L) pitcher. Stir until iced tea mix is dissolved.

Just before serving, add ice cubes and lime slices. Makes about 6 cups (1.5 L). Serves 6.

1 serving: 85 Calories; 0.1 g Total Fat (0 g Mono, trace Poly, trace Sat); 0 mg Cholesterol; 22 g Carbohydrate; trace Fibre; trace Protein; 3 mg Sodium

Pictured on page 43.

Onion And Brie Tartlets

The sweet taste of the onions is a nice complement to the Brie cheese.

Olive (or cooking) oil	2 tsp.	10 mL
Finely chopped onion	2/3 cup	150 mL
Granulated sugar	2 tsp.	10 mL
Red wine vinegar	2 tsp.	10 mL
Large eggs	2	2
Half-and-half cream	1/3 cup	75 mL
Ground nutmeg	1/2 tsp.	2 mL
Brie cheese, chopped	4 oz.	113 g
Frozen mini tart shells, thawed	24	24

Heat olive oil in small frying pan on medium-low. Add onion. Cook for about 10 minutes, stirring occasionally, until soft.

Add sugar and vinegar. Heat and stir until sugar is dissolved. Remove from heat.

Process next 4 ingredients in blender until smooth.

Place tart shells (in foil cups) on baking sheet. Divide onion mixture among shells. Fill each tart with cream mixture until about 3/4 full. Bake in 375°F (190°C) oven for about 25 minutes until set. Let stand in foil cups for 10 minutes before removing to serving plate. Serves 6.

1 serving: 327 Calories; 22 g Total Fat (9.8 g Mono, 2.2 g Poly, 8.3 g Sat); 89 mg Cholesterol; 25 g Carbohydrate; trace Fibre; 7 g Protein; 380 mg Sodium

Pictured on page 43.

Shrimp Pasta Salad

A light, creamy dressing over crunchy pine nuts and colourful vegetables. Enjoy the wonderful flavour of fresh dill.

Medium bow pasta (about 6 oz., 170 g)	2 1/2 cups	625 mL
Boiling water	8 cups	2 L
Salt	1 tsp.	5 mL
Cooked medium shrimp, peeled and deveined	13 oz.	375 g
Finely chopped red pepper	1/2 cup	125 mL
Pine nuts, toasted (see Note)	1/2 cup	125 mL
Finely chopped celery	1/3 cup	75 mL
Finely chopped green onion	1/4 cup	60 mL
BUTTERMILK DRESSING		
Buttermilk (or reconstituted from powder)	1/2 cup	125 mL
Sour cream	1/4 cup	60 mL
White wine vinegar	1 tbsp.	15 mL
Granulated sugar	2 tsp.	10 mL
Chopped fresh dill (or 1 1/4 tsp., 6 mL, dill weed)	1 1/2 tbsp.	25 mL
Creamed horseradish	2 tsp.	10 mL
Salt	1/4 tsp.	1 mL
Pepper, just a pinch		

Cook pasta in boiling water and salt in large uncovered pot or Dutch oven for 8 to 10 minutes, stirring occasionally, until tender but firm. Drain. Rinse under cold water. Drain well. Turn into large bowl.

Add next 5 ingredients. Toss.

Buttermilk Dressing: Process all 8 ingredients in blender until smooth. Makes about 1 cup (250 mL) dressing. Drizzle over pasta mixture. Toss. Makes about 6 cups (1.5 L). Serves 6.

1 serving: 308 Calories; 10.1 g Total Fat (3.4 g Mono, 3.6 g Poly, 2.4 g Sat); 127 mg Cholesterol; 34 g Carbohydrate; 4 g Fibre; 22 g Protein; 278 mg Sodium

Pictured on page 45.

Note: To toast pine nuts, place in single layer in ungreased shallow pan. Bake in 350°F (175°C) oven for 5 to 10 minutes, stirring or shaking often, until desired doneness.

Salmon-Wrapped Scallops

Tender, juicy scallops wrapped in smoked salmon and grilled to perfection. Pricey—but delicious!

Thin slices of smoked salmon (about 1/2 lb., 225 g)	24	24
Fresh (or frozen, thawed) large scallops	24	24
Bamboo skewers (8 inch, 20 cm, length), soaked in water for 10 minutes	12	12
White wine vinegar	3 tbsp.	50 mL
Basil pesto	2 tbsp.	30 mL
Granulated sugar	2 tsp.	10 mL

Wrap 1 piece of salmon, 1 inch (2.5 cm) wide and about 6 inches (15 cm) long, around each scallop.

Thread 2 wrapped scallops, from edge to edge through diameter, onto each skewer.

Combine remaining 3 ingredients in small bowl. Brush onto scallops. Preheat gas barbecue to medium. Cook scallops on greased grill for about 2 minutes per side, brushing with pesto mixture, until scallops are opaque. Discard any remaining pesto mixture. Serve warm or cold. Serves 6.

1 serving: 139 Calories; 3.8 g Total Fat (1.9 g Mono, 0.7 g Poly, 0.6 g Sat); 36 mg Cholesterol; 4 g Carbohydrate; trace Fibre; 21 g Protein; 428 mg Sodium

Pictured below.

Top: Sparkling Iced Tea, page 42
Centre: Onion And Brie Tartlets, page 42
Bottom: Salmon-Wrapped Scallops, above

Deli Focaccia

Colourful, attractive sandwich wedges with the distinctive flavour of goat cheese.

Soft goat (chèvre) cheese (about 1 cup, 250 mL), room temperature	5 1/3 oz.	150 g
Sun-dried tomato pesto	1/4 cup	60 mL
Round focaccia bread (about 10 inches, 25 cm, in diameter), cut horizontally into 2 layers	1	1
Can of artichoke hearts, drained and chopped	14 oz.	398 mL
Salami slices (about 12)	3 oz.	85 g
Pastrami slices (about 7)	4 oz.	113 g
Mixed salad greens, loosely packed	2 cups	500 mL

Combine cheese and pesto in small bowl. Spread on cut sides of bread.

Layer remaining 4 ingredients on bottom half of bread. Top with remaining half of bread. Gently press down. Cuts into 6 wedges.

1 wedge: 464 Calories; 14.6 g Total Fat (5.2 g Mono, 1.1 g Poly, 7.2 g Sat); 46 mg Cholesterol; 63 g Carbohydrate; 4 g Fibre; 20 g Protein; 1040 mg Sodium

Pictured on page 45.

Strawberry Shortcakes

A delightful dessert that is delicious and easy to make. The sweet taste of strawberries is complemented by the savoury hint of cinnamon.

All-purpose flour	2 cups	500 mL
Baking powder	1 tbsp.	15 mL
Salt	1/8 tsp.	0.5 mL
Granulated sugar	2 tbsp.	30 mL
Hard margarine (or butter), cut up	2 tbsp.	30 mL
Buttermilk (or reconstituted from powder)	1 cup	250 mL

TOPPING

Sliced fresh strawberries	4 cups	1 L
Granulated sugar	1/3 cup	75 mL
Orange-flavoured liqueur (such as Grand Marnier)	2 tbsp.	30 mL
Whipping cream (or frozen whipped topping, thawed)	1 cup	250 mL
Granulated sugar	1 tbsp.	15 mL
Ground cinnamon	1/4 tsp.	1 mL

Measure first 4 ingredients into large bowl. Cut in margarine until mixture is crumbly.

Stir in buttermilk until mixture just comes together. Turn out onto lightly floured surface. Roll or pat out to 3/4 inch (2 cm) thickness. Cut out six 2 3/4 inch (7 cm) circles with floured cutter. Place, almost touching, in lightly greased 9 × 9 inch (22 × 22 cm) pan. Bake in 450°F (230°C) oven for 12 to 15 minutes until lightly golden. Cool in pan for 5 minutes. Remove to wire rack to cool.

Topping: Combine strawberries, first amount of sugar and liqueur in medium bowl. Cover. Chill.

Beat whipping cream in small bowl until soft peaks form. Add second amount of sugar and cinnamon. Mix. Split shortcakes in half horizontally. Top each bottom half with about 1/4 cup (60 mL) whipped cream mixture and about 1/2 cup (125 mL) strawberry mixture. Cover with top halves. Makes 6 shortcakes.

1 shortcake: 466 Calories; 18.6 g Total Fat (6.7 g Mono, 1.2 g Poly, 9.5 g Sat); 50 mg Cholesterol; 66 g Carbohydrate; 4 g Fibre; 8 g Protein; 345 mg Sodium

Pictured on page 45.

1. Deli Focaccia, this page
2. Strawberry Shortcakes, this page
3. Shrimp Pasta Salad, page 43

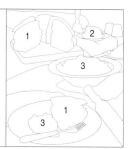

Pool Party

Hot sun, cold drinks and a cool dip in the pool are ingredients for a wonderful summer day. Produce your own splash with this refreshing choice of summertime recipes that can be made ahead.

serves 8

Watermelon Cooler

Ham And Melon Bites

Pistachio Cheese

Crispy Tortilla Wedges

Shrimp And Dip

Mango Beef Salad

Chicken Wraps

Chocolate Raspberry Cheesecake

Watermelon Cooler

A cool, refreshing beverage with the taste of fresh watermelon and orange liqueur. Be ready with a second batch!

Chopped seedless watermelon (or seeds removed)	8 cups	2 L
Orange juice	2 cups	500 mL
Granulated sugar	1 cup	250 mL
Orange-flavoured liqueur (such as Grand Marnier)	1 1/4 cups	300 mL

Orange slices, for garnish
Fresh strawberries, for garnish

Process first 4 ingredients, in 2 batches, in blender until smooth. Pour into glasses.

Garnish with orange slices and strawberries. Makes 10 cups (2.5 L). Serves 8.

1 serving: 351 Calories; 0.9 g Total Fat (trace Mono, 0.1 g Poly, trace Sat); 0 mg Cholesterol; 64 g Carbohydrate; 1 g Fibre; 2 g Protein; 7 mg Sodium

Pictured on page 47 and on page 49.

Ham And Melon Bites

The salty flavour of the glazed ham is a wonderful complement to the sweet, juicy cantaloupe. Serve immediately for the best flavour.

Medium cantaloupe, seeds removed	1	1
Maple (or maple-flavoured) syrup	3 tbsp.	50 mL
Dry mustard	1/2 tsp.	2 mL
Cooked ham, cut into 1 inch (2.5 cm) cubes (about 24)	12 oz.	340 g
Round wooden picks (4 inch, 10 cm, length)	24	24

Shape cantaloupe into 1 inch (2.5 cm) balls with melon baller. You will need 24 balls.

Heat maple syrup and mustard in large frying pan on medium. Add ham. Cook for about 10 minutes, stirring occasionally, until ham is lightly browned and glazed. Cool.

Thread 1 piece of ham and 1 cantaloupe ball onto each wooden pick. Makes 24 appetizers.

3 appetizers: 92 Calories; 3.3 g Total Fat (1.5 g Mono, 0.4 g Poly, 1 g Sat); 20 mg Cholesterol; 9 g Carbohydrate; trace Fibre; 7 g Protein; 476 mg Sodium

Pictured on page 47.

Pistachio Cheese

Serve this soft, tangy cheese mixture with Crispy Tortilla Wedges, below, and salsa. Yum!

Block of cream cheese, softened	8 oz.	250 g
Finely chopped green onion	2 tbsp.	30 mL
Sweet (or regular) chili sauce	1 1/2 tbsp.	25 mL
Lime juice	1 tbsp.	15 mL
Soy sauce	1 tsp.	5 mL
Garlic clove, minced (or 1/4 tsp., 1 mL, powder)	1	1
Pistachios, toasted (see Note) and finely chopped	3 tbsp.	50 mL
Finely chopped fresh parsley (not dried)	2 tbsp.	30 mL

Beat cream cheese in medium bowl until soft and creamy.

Add next 5 ingredients. Beat until well combined. Place mixture on sheet of waxed paper. Shape into circle, 4 inches (10 cm) in diameter and about 1 1/4 inches (3 cm) thick. Cover. Chill for at least 2 hours.

Combine pistachios and parsley in small bowl. Press mixture on top and side of cheese round. Makes 1 1/4 cups (300 mL).

2 tbsp. (30 mL): 105 Calories; 9.9 g Total Fat (3.2 g Mono, 0.5 g Poly, 5.6 g Sat); 27 mg Cholesterol; 2 g Carbohydrate; trace Fibre; 2 g Protein; 144 mg Sodium

Pictured on page 49.

Note: To toast pistachios, place in single layer in ungreased shallow pan. Bake in 350°F (175°C) oven for 5 to 10 minutes, stirring or shaking often, until desired doneness.

Crispy Tortilla Wedges

Cut large flour tortillas into 12 wedges each. Heat 1/4 to 1/3 cup (60 to 75 mL) cooking oil in large frying pan on medium. Cook tortillas, in 3 or 4 batches, for 2 to 3 minutes until golden and crispy. Spread out on paper towels to cool completely before serving. For variety, use different flavours of tortillas. Pictured on page 49.

Shrimp And Dip

The creamy horseradish dip adds a lip-smacking tang to the plump, juicy shrimp.

Large shrimp (tails intact), peeled and deveined	24	24
Boiling water, to cover		
Salt	2 tsp.	10 mL
Ice water		
CREAMY DIP		
Sour cream	1/2 cup	125 mL
Mayonnaise (not salad dressing)	1/4 cup	60 mL
Creamed horseradish	1 1/2 – 2 tsp.	7 – 10 mL
Chopped fresh chives (or 3/4 tsp., 4 mL, dried)	1 tbsp.	15 mL
Lemon juice	2 tsp.	10 mL
Granulated sugar	1/2 tsp.	2 mL

Cook shrimp in boiling water and salt in large uncovered pot or Dutch oven for 3 to 4 minutes until pink. Do not overcook.

Immediately plunge shrimp into ice water in large bowl. Let stand for 15 minutes. Drain well.

Creamy Dip: Combine all 6 ingredients in small bowl. Makes about 3/4 cup (175 mL) dip. Serve with shrimp. Serves 8.

3 shrimp plus 1 1/2 tbsp. (25 mL) dip: 139 Calories; 9 g Total Fat (4 g Mono, 2.4 g Poly, 2.1 g Sat); 97 mg Cholesterol; 2 g Carbohydrate; trace Fibre; 12 g Protein; 129 mg Sodium

Pictured on page 49.

Top: Watermelon Cooler, page 46   Bottom: Ham And Melon Bites, page 46

Mango Beef Salad

An attractive salad with a delicious blend of flavours. The smoky bacon is a nice addition to the tangy mangoes, crisp vegetables and juicy steak. This will become a favourite!

Lemon pepper	1 tbsp.	15 mL
Garlic clove, minced (or 1/4 tsp., 1 mL, powder)	1	1
Olive (or cooking) oil	2 tsp.	10 mL
New York cut steaks (about 2)	1 1/4 lbs.	560 g
Bag of mixed baby salad greens (about 5 cups, 1.25 L)	10 oz.	285 g
Can of sliced mango, drained and coarsely chopped	14 oz.	398 mL
Cashews, toasted (see Note) and coarsely chopped	1/2 cup	125 mL
Bacon slices, cooked crisp and crumbled	8	8

PEANUT OIL DRESSING

Peanut (or cooking) oil	1/3 cup	75 mL
Red wine vinegar	2 tbsp.	30 mL
Maple (or maple-flavoured) syrup	2 tbsp.	30 mL
Soy sauce	2 tsp.	10 mL
Salt	1/4 tsp.	1 mL

Combine first 3 ingredients in small bowl. Spread on both sides of each steak. Preheat gas barbecue to medium-high. Cook steaks on greased grill for about 5 minutes per side until desired doneness. Let stand for 10 minutes. Slice into 1/8 inch (3 mm) thick slices.

Combine steak and next 4 ingredients in large bowl.

Peanut Oil Dressing: Combine all 5 ingredients in jar with tight-fitting lid. Shake well. Makes 2/3 cup (150 mL) dressing. Pour over steak mixture. Toss. Makes 11 cups (2.75 L). Serves 8.

1 serving: 379 Calories; 28.9 g Total Fat (13.8 g Mono, 4.6 g Poly, 8.3 g Sat); 43 mg Cholesterol; 13 g Carbohydrate; 1 g Fibre; 18 g Protein; 313 mg Sodium

Pictured on page 49.

Note: To toast cashews, place in single layer in ungreased shallow pan. Bake in 350°F (175°C) oven for 5 to 10 minutes, stirring or shaking often, until desired doneness.

Chicken Wraps

Tender, moist chicken with a hint of lime and just the right amount of spice.

Lime juice	1/4 cup	60 mL
Chopped fresh cilantro (or fresh parsley)	1/4 cup	60 mL
Cooking oil	3 tbsp.	50 mL
Dried crushed chilies (optional)	2 tsp.	10 mL
Ground cumin	1 tsp.	5 mL
Garlic cloves, minced (or 1/2 tsp., 2 mL, powder)	2	2
Boneless, skinless chicken breast halves (about 4)	1 lb.	454 g
Corn relish	1/4 cup	60 mL
Sour cream	1/4 cup	60 mL
Large flour tortillas (10 inch, 25 cm, diameter)	4	4
Large avocado, sliced	1	1
Medium red pepper, thinly sliced	1	1
Grated Cheddar cheese	1 cup	250 mL

Combine first 6 ingredients in medium bowl. Add chicken. Mix well. Cover. Chill for at least 1 hour. Drain and discard marinade. Preheat gas barbecue to medium. Cook chicken on greased grill for about 5 minutes per side until no longer pink. Slice thinly across grain on diagonal. Keep warm.

Combine corn relish and sour cream in small bowl. Spread 2 tbsp. (30 mL) on each tortilla.

Divide and layer chicken, avocado, red pepper and cheese down centre of each tortilla to within 2 inches (5 cm) of top and bottom. Fold top and bottom edges over filling. Roll up to enclose filling. Slice in half diagonally. Serves 8.

1 serving: 306 Calories; 17.7 g Total Fat (8 g Mono, 3.1 g Poly, 5.3 g Sat); 52 mg Cholesterol; 18 g Carbohydrate; 2 g Fibre; 20 g Protein; 227 mg Sodium

Pictured on page 49.

Variation: Brush wraps with 1 tbsp. (15 mL) cooking oil. Cook on greased grill over medium heat for 5 to 7 minutes, turning occasionally, until lightly browned.

1. Shrimp And Dip, page 47
2. Mango Beef Salad, this page
3. Watermelon Cooler, page 46
4. Chicken Wraps, above
5. Crispy Tortilla Wedges, page 47
6. Pistachio Cheese, page 47

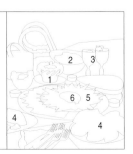

Chocolate Raspberry Cheesecake

This beautiful chilled dessert combines a crunchy chocolate crust with a filling that is rich and creamy. What a treat!

Hard margarine (or butter), softened	1/2 cup	125 mL
Chocolate wafer crumbs	2 cups	500 mL
WHITE CHOCOLATE FILLING		
Envelopes of unflavoured gelatin (1/4 oz., 7 g, each)	2	2
Cold water	1/3 cup	75 mL
White chocolate baking squares (1 oz., 28 g, each), cut up (2 boxes)	12	12
Blocks of cream cheese (8 oz., 250 g, each), softened	2	2
Granulated sugar	1/2 cup	125 mL
Finely grated lemon zest	1 tsp.	5 mL
Lemon juice	1 tbsp.	15 mL
RASPBERRY TOPPING		
Apple juice	3/4 cup	175 mL
Cornstarch	1 1/2 tbsp.	25 mL
Granulated sugar	1 tbsp.	15 mL
Brandy (optional)	1 tbsp.	15 mL
Fresh raspberries	2 cups	500 mL

Chocolate Raspberry Cheesecake, above

Melt margarine in medium saucepan. Add wafer crumbs. Stir until mixed well. Press firmly in bottom and halfway up side of ungreased 9 inch (22 cm) springform pan. Chill for 1 hour.

White Chocolate Filling: Sprinkle gelatin over cold water in small saucepan. Let stand for 3 to 5 minutes until softened. Heat and stir on low until gelatin is dissolved. Cool.

Heat chocolate in small heavy saucepan on lowest heat, stirring often, until almost melted. Do not overheat. Remove from heat. Stir until smooth.

Beat next 4 ingredients in large bowl until smooth. Stir in gelatin mixture and chocolate. Pour over crust. Cover. Chill for about 3 hours until set.

Raspberry Topping: Combine first 3 ingredients in separate medium saucepan. Stir until smooth. Heat and stir on medium-high for about 2 minutes until boiling and thickened.

Stir in brandy. Cool for 1 minute. Gently spread over cheesecake.

Arrange raspberries over top in single layer, just touching, with open end facing down. Chill for about 1 hour until topping is set. Cuts into 12 wedges.

1 wedge: 518 Calories; 34.1 g Total Fat (13.6 g Mono, 2 g Poly, 16.6 g Sat); 52 mg Cholesterol; 48 g Carbohydrate; 1 g Fibre; 7 g Protein; 360 mg Sodium

Pictured below.

Seafood Barbecue

Enjoy a change from traditional barbecue fare with this taste-of-the-sea menu. Succulent, zesty and full of flavour—nothing beats the taste of seafood gently grilled over an open flame.

serves 8

Limeonade Refresher

Shrimp And Mango Salad

Grilled Peppers

Tuna Skewers

Salmon Burgers

Grilled Asparagus

Brown Sugar Meringues

Limeonade Refresher, below

Limeonade Refresher

A sweet, bubbly beverage with a bit of a sparkle. Perfect for a summer barbecue!

Can of frozen concentrated limeonade	12 oz.	341 mL
Bottle of lemon lime soft drink	4 cups	1 L
Club soda	2 cups	500 mL

Lime slices, for garnish
Ice cubes

Combine first 3 ingredients in large pitcher. Makes about 9 cups (2.25 L).

Just before serving, add lime slices and ice cubes. Serves 8.

1 serving: 150 Calories; 0.1 g Total Fat (trace Mono, trace Poly, trace Sat); 0 mg Cholesterol; 39 g Carbohydrate; 0 g Fibre; trace Protein; 28 mg Sodium

Pictured above.

Shrimp And Mango Salad

*A pretty salad with a wonderful roasted peanut flavour.
The delicious combination of mango and shrimp will have
your guests coming back for seconds.*

Fresh (or frozen, thawed) raw large shrimp (tails intact), peeled and deveined	1/2 lb.	225 g
Hard margarine (or butter), melted	3 tbsp.	50 mL
Garlic clove, minced (or 1/4 tsp., 1 mL, powder)	1	1
Salt	1/4 tsp.	1 mL
Pepper, sprinkle		
Bag of baby spinach (about 5 cups, 1.25 L, lightly packed)	6 oz.	170 g
Can of sliced mango in syrup, drained and coarsely chopped	14 oz.	398 mL
Roasted salted peanuts	1/2 cup	125 mL
PEANUT OIL VINAIGRETTE		
Peanut (or cooking) oil	3 tbsp.	50 mL
White wine vinegar	2 tbsp.	30 mL
Brown sugar, packed	2 tsp.	10 mL
Salt	1/4 tsp.	1 mL
Pepper, just a pinch		

Split shrimp along back, halfway through to other side. Put into large bowl.

Add next 4 ingredients. Toss. Preheat gas barbecue to medium. Cook shrimp on greased grill for 3 to 5 minutes, turning occasionally, until pink. Do not overcook.

Combine shrimp, spinach, mango and peanuts in separate large bowl. Toss.

Peanut Oil Vinaigrette: Combine all 5 ingredients in jar with tight-fitting lid. Shake well. Makes 1/2 cup (125 mL) vinaigrette. Drizzle over shrimp mixture. Makes 8 cups (2 L). Serves 8.

1 serving: 196 Calories; 14.8 g Total Fat (7.7 g Mono, 3.8 g Poly, 2.5 g Sat); 32 mg Cholesterol; 10 g Carbohydrate; 2 g Fibre; 7 g Protein; 327 mg Sodium

Pictured on page 53.

1. Salmon Burgers, page 54
2. Shrimp And Mango Salad, above
3. Tuna Skewers, page 54
4. Grilled Asparagus, page 54
5. Grilled Peppers, page 54

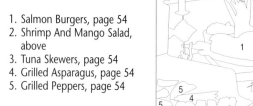

Grilled Peppers

Cut peppers (your choice of colours) into eighths. Brush both sides with peanut (or cooking) oil. Sprinkle both sides with salt and pepper. Place on greased grill over medium heat. Cook, turning occasionally, until grill marks appear and peppers are tender-crisp. Pictured on page 52.

Tuna Skewers

Lightly browned tuna served with fresh, colourful Cantaloupe Salsa. Cook the tuna to your liking, but avoid overcooking to prevent dryness.

CANTALOUPE SALSA

Finely chopped cantaloupe	1 cup	250 mL
Finely chopped green onion	2 tbsp.	30 mL
Chopped fresh sweet basil (not dried)	1 tbsp.	15 mL
Lemon juice	1 1/2 tbsp.	25 mL
Cooking oil	1 tbsp.	15 mL
Salt	1/4 tsp.	1 mL
Pepper, just a pinch		
Lemon juice	1/4 cup	60 mL
Soy sauce	2 tbsp.	30 mL
Brown sugar, packed	2 tbsp.	30 mL
Garlic clove, minced (or 1/4 tsp., 1 mL, powder)	1	1
Tuna steaks (or fillets), cut into 1 inch (2.5 cm) cubes	1 3/4 lbs.	790 g
Bamboo skewers (8 inch, 20 cm, length), soaked in water for 10 minutes	8	8

Cantaloupe Salsa: Combine first 7 ingredients in medium bowl. Chill for up to 3 hours until ready to serve. Drain. Makes 1 cup (250 mL) salsa.

Combine next 4 ingredients in small bowl.

Thread tuna onto skewers. Brush with lemon juice mixture. Preheat gas barbecue to medium. Cook skewers on greased grill for about 5 minutes, brushing with lemon juice mixture and turning occasionally, until firm and no longer opaque. Do not overcook. Serve with salsa. Serves 8.

1 serving: 187 Calories; 6.7 g Total Fat (2.4 g Mono, 2.2 g Poly, 1.4 g Sat); 38 mg Cholesterol; 7 g Carbohydrate; trace Fibre; 24 g Protein; 378 mg Sodium

Pictured on page 52 and on page 53.

Salmon Burgers

Thick, delicious grilled salmon burgers that are a bit messy to eat—but messy is good!

Peanut (or cooking) oil	1 tbsp.	15 mL
Medium onions, thinly sliced	2	2
Salt	1/8 tsp.	0.5 mL
Pepper	1/8 tsp.	0.5 mL
Salmon fillets, skin removed and salmon cut into 8 equal pieces (see Note)	2 lbs.	900 g
Peanut (or cooking) oil	1 tbsp.	15 mL
Lemon pepper	2 tbsp.	30 mL
Buns (your choice), split	8	8
Sour cream	1/2 cup	125 mL
Sweet (or regular) chili sauce	3 tbsp.	50 mL
Medium tomatoes, sliced	2	2

Heat first amount of peanut oil in large frying pan on medium-low. Add onion, salt and pepper. Cook for about 15 minutes, stirring occasionally, until onion is golden.

Brush fillets with second amount of peanut oil. Sprinkle with lemon pepper. Preheat gas barbecue to medium. Cook fillets on greased grill for about 5 minutes per side, depending on thickness, until salmon flakes easily when tested with fork.

Toast cut sides of each bun on grill for 2 minutes.

Combine sour cream and chili sauce in small bowl. Spread on toasted sides of each bun.

Layer bottom half of each bun with salmon, onion mixture and tomato. Cover with top half of each bun. Serves 8.

1 serving: 360 Calories; 17.2 g Total Fat (6.6 g Mono, 5 g Poly, 4.3 g Sat); 56 mg Cholesterol; 29 g Carbohydrate; 1 g Fibre; 22 g Protein; 427 mg Sodium

Pictured on page 52/53.

Note: For even cooking, choose fillets from the thicker centre of the salmon, rather than from the thinner tail end.

Grilled Asparagus

Brush trimmed asparagus spears with melted margarine or butter. Sprinkle with salt and pepper. Place asparagus on greased grill over medium heat. Cook, turning occasionally, until grill marks appear and asparagus is tender-crisp. Pictured on page 52.

Brown Sugar Meringues, below

Brown Sugar Meringues

These luscious caramel meringues are topped with sweet White Chocolate Sauce, wonderful fresh raspberries and whipped cream. A truly delicious dessert!

Egg whites (large), room temperature	4	4
Cream of tartar	1 tsp.	5 mL
Brown sugar, packed	2/3 cup	150 mL
Icing (confectioner's) sugar, sifted	2/3 cup	150 mL
Fresh raspberries (about two 5 2/3 oz., 160 g, baskets)	2 cups	500 mL
Licorice-flavoured liqueur (such as Sambuca)	1/4 cup	60 mL
Icing (confectioner's) sugar	1/4 cup	60 mL
WHITE CHOCOLATE SAUCE		
Whipping cream	1/2 cup	125 mL
White chocolate baking squares (1 oz., 28 g, each), chopped	5 1/2	5 1/2
Large marshmallows, quartered	6	6
Vanilla	1/2 tsp.	2 mL
Whipping cream (or frozen whipped topping, thawed)	1 cup	250 mL

Place oven racks on 2 lowest rack positions. Line 2 baking sheets with parchment paper. Trace 4 circles, 3 inches (7.5 cm) in diameter each and about 2 inches (5 cm) apart, on each sheet. Beat egg whites and cream of tartar in large bowl until soft peaks form. Add brown sugar, 1 tbsp. (15 mL) at a time, beating well after each addition, until stiff peaks form and brown sugar is dissolved.

Fold in first amount of icing sugar. Divide and spoon into greased circles. Do not smooth tops. Bake in 225°F (110°C) oven for about 1 1/2 hours until dry. You do not need to switch pans at halftime. Turn oven off. Let stand in oven until cool.

Combine raspberries, liqueur and second amount of icing sugar in medium bowl. Cover. Chill for up to 24 hours.

White Chocolate Sauce: Combine first 4 ingredients in heavy medium saucepan. Heat and stir on medium-low for 8 to 10 minutes until chocolate is melted and marshmallows are dissolved. Makes 1 cup (250 mL) sauce.

Beat second amount of whipping cream in separate medium bowl until soft peaks form. Drizzle meringues with warm sauce. Divide and spoon raspberry mixture and whipped cream over sauce. Serves 8.

1 serving: 442 Calories; 21.2 g Total Fat (6.3 g Mono, 0.7 g Poly, 12.9 g Sat); 59 mg Cholesterol; 57 g Carbohydrate; 2 g Fibre; 4 g Protein; 72 mg Sodium

Pictured above.

Tailgate Party

Gather the gang and head out to the nearest field. Then put down the tailgate, turn up the music and lay out the food. Or take the kids out for an afternoon adventure. They'll love this down-home, hearty menu—and cleanup will be a breeze!

serves 8

Grape Lemonade

Cold Dressed Beans

Hero Club Sandwiches

Garlic Sausage And Dijon Dip

Pickle Condiments

Big Chip Cookies

Grape Lemonade

A beautiful cranberry red, sweet yet tart, beverage that is oh-so-refreshing.

Water	6 cups	1.5 L
Granulated sugar	2/3 cup	150 mL
Grape juice	4 cups	1 L
Lemon juice	1 1/2 cups	375 mL

Measure water and sugar into 4 quart (4 L) container. Stir until sugar is dissolved.

Add grape juice and lemon juice. Stir. Add more sugar if desired. Chill. Makes about 12 cups (3 L). Serves 8.

1 serving: 162 Calories; 0.1 g Total Fat (0 g Mono, trace Poly, trace Sat); 0 mg Cholesterol; 42 g Carbohydrate; trace Fibre; 1 g Protein; 5 mg Sodium

Pictured on page 57.

Cold Dressed Beans

This hearty mixed bean dish is accented with fresh herbs and spices. You'll love the wonderful combination of textures.

Olive (or cooking) oil	1/2 cup	125 mL
Diced onion	1 cup	250 mL
Garlic cloves, minced (or 1 tsp., 5 mL, powder)	4	4
Plain yogurt	1 cup	250 mL
Chopped fresh mint leaves (or fresh sweet basil) or 1 1/2 tsp. (7 mL) dried	1/4 cup	60 mL
Lemon juice	1 tbsp.	15 mL
Diced English cucumber (with peel)	2 cups	500 mL
Salt	1 tsp.	5 mL
Pepper, sprinkle		
Cans of mixed (or small white) beans (19 oz., 540 mL, each), rinsed and drained	2	2

Heat olive oil in non-stick frying pan on medium-low. Add onion and garlic. Cook for about 20 minutes, stirring occasionally, until golden. Remove from heat. Cool. Strain olive oil, discarding solids.

Combine next 6 ingredients in medium bowl. Add strained olive oil. Stir.

Add beans. Mix. Chill for 1 to 2 hours to blend flavours. Stir. Serve cold or at room temperature. Makes about 5 cups (1.25 L). Serves 8.

1 serving: 241 Calories; 15.5 g Total Fat (10.8 g Mono, 1.5 g Poly, 2.4 g Sat); 2 mg Cholesterol; 20 g Carbohydrate; 3 g Fibre; 7 g Protein; 468 mg Sodium

Pictured on page 59.

Hero Club Sandwiches

These satisfying sandwiches with smoky bacon, deli meats, cheese and a delicious homemade dressing are utterly irresistible! The perfect outdoor meal as they can be very messy to eat!

Multi-grain European bread loaves (10 – 12 inch, 25 – 30 cm, length)	2	2

CLUB DRESSING

Salad dressing (or mayonnaise)	3/4 cup	175 mL
Olive (or cooking) oil	3 tbsp.	50 mL
Finely diced ripe olives	3 tbsp.	50 mL
Finely diced pimiento (or roasted pepper), drained	3 tbsp.	50 mL
Dill pickle liquid	1 tbsp.	15 mL
Chopped capers (optional)	1 tbsp.	15 mL
Medium tomatoes, thinly sliced	3	3
Salt, sprinkle		
Pepper, sprinkle		
Thin provolone cheese slices (about 6 oz., 170 g)	8	8
Bacon slices, cooked crisp and chilled	16	16
Thinly sliced deli white turkey meat	7 oz.	200 g
Thinly sliced green pepper rings	1/2 cup	125 mL
Thinly sliced red onion	1/2 cup	125 mL
Thinly sliced ham	1/3 lb.	150 g
Havarti cheese slices (about 8 oz., 225 g)	8	8
Green leaf lettuce leaves	6	6

Cut each loaf in half horizontally to make 2 layers. Pull out small amount of soft bread from centre of loaves, making shallow indentation and leaving thick shell.

Club Dressing: Combine first 6 ingredients in small dish. Makes about 7/8 cup (200 mL). Divide and spread on cut sides of bread right to edges.

Divide and layer remaining 11 ingredients, in order given, onto bottom halves of bread. Cover with top halves. Press down firmly. Wrap tightly in plastic wrap. Chill for at least 1 hour or up to 8 hours. Just before serving, cut into 2 inch (5 cm) thick slices. Serves 8.

1 serving: 831 Calories; 43.5 g Total Fat (19.9 g Mono, 7 g Poly, 13.9 g Sat); 92 mg Cholesterol; 72 g Carbohydrate; 11 g Fibre; 41 g Protein; 1797 mg Sodium

Pictured on this page and on page 58/59.

Garlic Sausage And Dijon Dip

A tangy, all-purpose dip with a sweet hint of honey.

DIJON DIP

Dijon mustard	2/3 cup	150 mL
Liquid honey	1/4 cup	60 mL
Creamed horseradish	4 tsp.	20 mL
Salt	1/4 tsp.	1 mL
Garlic sausage, sliced	1 lb.	454 g

Dijon Dip: Combine first 4 ingredients in small dish. Let stand at room temperature for 1 hour to blend flavours. Makes about 1 cup (250 mL) dip.

Pack sausage and dip in airtight containers. Serves 8.

1 serving: 167 Calories; 7.9 g Total Fat (0.2 g Mono, 0.9 g Poly, 0.2 g Sat); 0 mg Cholesterol; 14 g Carbohydrate; trace Fibre; 11 g Protein; 899 mg Sodium

Pictured on page 59.

Pickle Condiments

Pack small pickled beets, big dill pickles (quartered lengthwise) and pepper rings (variety of colours) in airtight containers. Pictured on page 59.

Top Left: Big Chip Cookies, page 58
Centre Left: Hero Club Sandwiches, this page
Right: Grape Lemonade, page 56

Big Chip Cookies

Huge, dense, chocolatey cookies that everyone will absolutely love! The perfect finish to a delicious outdoor meal.

Hard margarine (or butter), softened	2/3 cup	150 mL
Granulated sugar	2/3 cup	150 mL
Brown sugar, packed	2/3 cup	150 mL
Large eggs	2	2
Vanilla	2 tsp.	10 mL
Unsweetened chocolate baking squares (1 oz., 28 g, each), chopped	6	6
All-purpose flour	2 cups	500 mL
Baking powder	2 tsp.	10 mL
Salt	1/2 tsp.	2 mL
Semi-sweet chocolate chips	1 1/3 cups	325 mL
Slivered almonds, toasted (see Note)	1 cup	250 mL

Cream margarine, granulated sugar and brown sugar in medium bowl until fluffy. Beat in eggs and vanilla until smooth.

Heat chocolate in small heavy saucepan on lowest heat, stirring often, until almost melted. Do not overheat. Remove from heat. Stir until smooth. Let cool to room temperature. Add to margarine mixture. Stir.

Add flour, baking powder and salt. Stir until just moistened.

Mix in chocolate chips and almonds. Divide dough in half. Form each half into log shape, about 3 inches (7.5 cm) in diameter. Cover in plastic wrap or waxed paper. Chill for 1 hour. Divide each log into 8 portions. Place portions 3 inches (7.5 cm) apart on greased cookie sheets. Bake in 375°F (190°C) oven for about 10 minutes until edges are golden. Do not overbake or cookies will be hard. Let stand on cookie sheets for 5 minutes before removing to wire racks to cool. Makes 16 cookies.

1 cookie: 386 Calories; 23.3 g Total Fat (11.8 g Mono, 2.2 g Poly, 8.2 g Sat); 27 mg Cholesterol; 45 g Carbohydrate; 3 g Fibre; 6 g Protein; 231 mg Sodium

Pictured on page 57 and on page 59.

Note: To toast almonds, place in single layer in ungreased shallow pan. Bake in 350°F (175°C) oven for 5 to 10 minutes, stirring or shaking often, until desired doneness.

1. Hero Club Sandwiches, page 57
2. Big Chip Cookies, above
3. Pickle Condiments, page 57
4. Garlic Sausage And Dijon Dip, page 57
5. Cold Dressed Beans, page 56

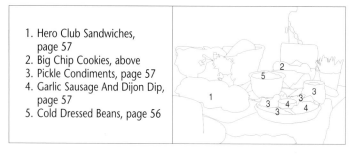

Tropical Barbecue

Imagine yourself surrounded by fragrant bouquets of flowers and sultry Caribbean music. Now settle back to enjoy the fruity flavours of the tropics when you serve these exotic recipes.

serves 6

Tropical Rum Cocktail

Coconut Rice Salad

Buttered Yams

Grilled Lemon And Lime

Mango-Stuffed Chicken

Coconut Banana Cheesecake

Tropical Rum Cocktail, below

Tropical Rum Cocktail

The pineapple and coconut really come through in this rich, frothy cocktail.

Dark (or spice) rum	2/3 cup	150 mL
Coconut-flavoured rum (such as Malibu)	2/3 cup	150 mL
Pineapple juice	4 cups	1 L
Lime juice	1/3 cup	75 mL
Whipping cream	1 cup	250 mL
Ice cubes		
Lime wedges, for garnish	6	6
Pineapple chunks, for garnish	12	12

Process first 5 ingredients in blender until well combined. Makes 7 cups (1.75 L). Immediately pour into 6 individual glasses.

Add ice cubes. Garnish with lime and pineapple. Serves 6.

1 serving: 352 Calories; 13.6 g Total Fat (4 g Mono, 0.5 g Poly, 8.4 g Sat); 49 mg Cholesterol; 28 g Carbohydrate; trace Fibre; 2 g Protein; 18 mg Sodium

Pictured above.

Coconut Rice Salad

A colourful salad with a nice combination of mint and citrus flavours. This is sure to become one of your favourites! Use less mint if desired.

Cooked jasmine (or white) rice (1 cup, 250 mL, uncooked)	3 cups	750 mL
Frozen peas, thawed	1/2 cup	125 mL
Flake coconut, toasted (see Note)	1/2 cup	125 mL
Can of mandarin orange segments, drained	10 oz.	284 mL
Chopped fresh mint leaves (not dried)	3 tbsp.	50 mL
Finely chopped fresh (or canned, drained) pineapple	1 cup	250 mL
Salted peanuts, coarsely chopped	1/2 cup	125 mL
COCONUT LIME DRESSING		
Canned coconut milk	1/2 cup	125 mL
Lime juice	1/4 cup	60 mL
Cooking oil	2 tbsp.	30 mL
Honey mustard	1 1/2 tbsp.	25 mL
Salt	1/4 tsp.	1 mL
Cayenne pepper	1/8 – 1/4 tsp.	0.5 – 1 mL

Combine first 7 ingredients in large bowl.

Coconut Lime Dressing: Combine all 6 ingredients in jar with tight-fitting lid. Shake well. Makes 1 cup (250 mL) dressing. Drizzle over rice mixture. Toss. Makes 8 cups (2 L). Serves 6.

1 serving: 377 Calories; 20.9 g Total Fat (6.5 g Mono, 3.6 g Poly, 9.6 g Sat); 0 mg Cholesterol; 43 g Carbohydrate; 3 g Fibre; 7 g Protein; 258 mg Sodium

Pictured on page 2 and on page 62.

Note: To toast coconut, place in single layer in ungreased shallow pan. Bake in 350°F (175°C) oven for 5 to 10 minutes, stirring or shaking often, until desired doneness.

Buttered Yams

Tender, buttery yam coated in a tasty, sweet, orange glaze.

Medium to large yam (or sweet potato), about 1 1/2 lbs. (680 g), cut into 2 inch (5 cm) pieces	1	1
Water		
Salt	1/2 tsp.	2 mL
Butter (or hard margarine), cut up	1/4 cup	60 mL
Brown sugar, packed	2 tbsp.	30 mL

Cook yam in water and salt in large saucepan on medium-high for about 10 minutes until slightly soft. Drain. Place yam on large piece of heavy-duty foil (or double layers of regular foil).

Sprinkle butter and brown sugar over yam. Wrap to enclose yam mixture. Preheat gas barbecue to medium. Place packet on ungreased grill. Cook for about 15 minutes, carefully turning occasionally, until yam is tender. Serves 6.

1 serving: 224 Calories; 8.4 g Total Fat (2.4 g Mono, 0.4 g Poly, 5.1 g Sat); 22 mg Cholesterol; 36 g Carbohydrate; 5 g Fibre; 2 g Protein; 95 mg Sodium

Pictured on page 63.

Grilled Lemon And Lime

Choose lemons and limes that have smooth skins and small, shallow indentations for juicier fruit. Cut into wedges lengthwise. Place on greased gas barbecue grill over medium heat. Cook, turning occasionally, until grill marks appear. Serve with Mango-Stuffed Chicken, page 62. Pictured on page 2/3 and on page 62/63.

Mango-Stuffed Chicken

Chicken with a wonderful tropical taste. Garnish with Grilled Lemon And Lime, page 61.

Finely chopped mango (or 14 oz., 398 mL, can of sliced mangoes, drained and finely chopped)	1 cup	250 mL
Finely chopped salted macadamia nuts (or almonds)	1/2 cup	125 mL
Thinly sliced green onion	2 tbsp.	30 mL
Finely grated lime (or lemon) zest	1/2 tsp.	2 mL
Curry powder	1/2 tsp.	2 mL
Whole chicken	4 lbs.	1.8 kg
MARINADE		
Plain yogurt	1 1/2 cups	375 mL
Lime (or lemon) juice	1/4 cup	60 mL
Ground coriander	1 tbsp.	15 mL
Curry powder	1 tbsp.	15 mL
Finely grated peeled gingerroot	2 tsp.	10 mL
Garlic cloves, minced (or 1 tsp., 5 mL, powder)	4	4
Salt	1 tsp.	5 mL

Combine first 5 ingredients in medium bowl.

Place chicken, backbone up, on cutting board. Using sharp knife, cut down both sides of backbone to remove. Turn chicken over. Press chicken out flat. Carefully loosen, but do not remove, skin of chicken. Stuff mango mixture between meat and skin, spreading mixture as evenly as possible. Secure opening with wooden picks. Place stuffed chicken in large shallow dish.

Marinade: Combine all 7 ingredients in small bowl. Pour marinade over chicken. Stir until coated. Cover. Marinate in refrigerator for at least 3 hours or overnight. Drain and discard marinade. Preheat gas barbecue to medium. Place chicken, stuffed side down, on greased grill over drip pan. Close lid. Cook, using indirect cooking method, for 45 minutes. Turn over. Cook for 45 to 50 minutes until meat thermometer inserted in breast (not in stuffing) reads 180°F (82°C). Cut into serving-size pieces. Serves 6.

1 serving: 427 Calories; 25 g Total Fat (12.6 g Mono, 3.7 g Poly, 6.3 g Sat); 108 mg Cholesterol; 14 g Carbohydrate; 2 g Fibre; 37 g Protein; 566 mg Sodium

Pictured on page 2/3 and on page 62/63.

Top: Grilled Lemon And Lime, page 61
Centre Left: Coconut Rice Salad, page 61
Centre Right: Buttered Yams, page 61
Bottom: Mango-Stuffed Chicken, above

Coconut Banana Cheesecake

A delicious tropical dessert! With a sweet banana filling and a golden graham cracker and coconut crust, this rich, creamy cheesecake is sure to please.

GRAHAM COCONUT CRUST

Hard margarine (or butter), softened	2/3 cup	150 mL
Graham cracker crumbs	1 2/3 cups	400 mL
Medium coconut, toasted (see Note)	2/3 cup	150 mL

FILLING

Blocks of cream cheese (8 oz., 250 g, each), softened	2	2
Brown sugar, packed	1/2 cup	125 mL
Mashed banana (about 3 medium)	1 1/2 cups	375 mL
Large eggs	3	3
Medium coconut, toasted	2/3 cup	150 mL
Dark rum	3 tbsp.	50 mL
Lime juice	2 tbsp.	30 mL

TOPPING

Whipping cream (or frozen whipped topping, thawed)	1 cup	250 mL
Flake coconut, toasted (see Note)	2 – 3 tbsp.	30 – 50 mL
Thin lime slices	12	12

Coconut Banana Cheesecake, above

Graham Coconut Crust: Melt margarine in medium saucepan. Add graham crumbs and coconut. Stir until well mixed. Press in bottom and 3/4 up side of greased 9 inch (22 cm) springform pan lined with parchment (or waxed) paper. Chill for 1 hour.

Filling: Beat cream cheese and brown sugar in large bowl until smooth.

Add next 5 ingredients. Beat until well combined. Pour mixture over crust. Place pan on baking sheet. Bake in 350°F (175°C) oven for about 50 minutes until set. Turn oven off. Cool in oven with door ajar for 1 hour. Chill for at least 4 hours or overnight.

Topping: Beat whipping cream in medium bowl until soft peaks form. Spread over top of cheesecake. Sprinkle with coconut. Arrange lime slices around outside edge. Cuts into 12 wedges.

1 wedge: 504 Calories; 38.8 g Total Fat (14.4 g Mono, 2.2 g Poly, 20 g Sat); 124 mg Cholesterol; 34 g Carbohydrate; 1 g Fibre; 7 g Protein; 382 mg Sodium

Pictured below.

Note: To toast coconut, place in single layer in ungreased shallow pan. Bake in 350°F (175°C) oven for 5 to 10 minutes, stirring or shaking often, until desired doneness.

Après-Toboggan Party

The ageless fun of sliding down a snowy hillside will always bring hungry adventurers to the table at the end of the day. This hearty, soul-warming menu is certain to keep a smile on those rosy cheeks.

serves 4

French Onion Soup

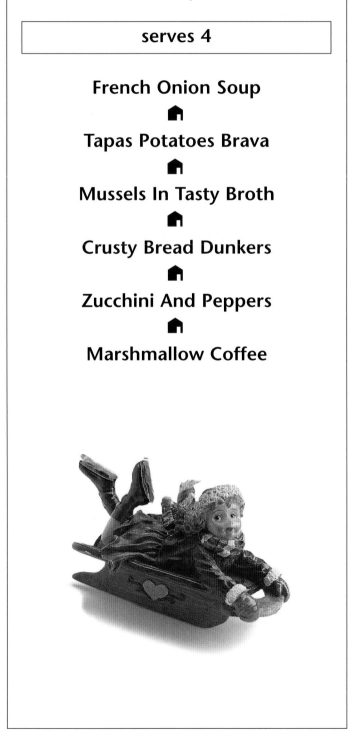

Tapas Potatoes Brava

Mussels In Tasty Broth

Crusty Bread Dunkers

Zucchini And Peppers

Marshmallow Coffee

French Onion Soup

This soup has delicious caramelized onions and a definite herb undertone. Remind everyone—the bowls are very hot!

Onions, peeled (about 8 medium)	2 lbs.	900 g
Hard margarine (or butter)	2 tbsp.	30 mL
Salt	1 tsp.	5 mL
Garlic cloves, minced (or 1 tsp., 5 mL, powder)	4	4
Coarsely ground pepper (or 1/4 tsp., 1 mL, pepper)	1/2 tsp.	2 mL
Dry sherry	1/2 cup	125 mL
Bay leaves	3	3
Fresh thyme sprigs	3	3
Prepared beef broth	4 cups	1 L
Multi-grain rye bread slices, cut about 1/3 inch (1 cm) thick and lightly toasted or air-dried	8	8
Grated Gruyère cheese	1 1/3 cups	325 mL

Cut each onion in half lengthwise. Lay flat side on cutting board. Cut crosswise into 1/8 inch (3 mm) slices.

Melt margarine in large pot or Dutch oven on medium-low. Add onion and salt. Stir. Cover. Cook for about 45 minutes, stirring occasionally, until onion is soft, but still white.

Add garlic and pepper. Stir. Cook, uncovered, on medium-high, stirring frequently and scraping bottom of pot, until onion is deep caramel brown.

Add sherry. Stir well, scraping any browning from pot and blending with liquid.

Add bay leaves, thyme sprigs and broth. Bring to a boil. Reduce heat to medium-low. Cover. Simmer for 30 minutes, without stirring. Remove and discard bay leaves and thyme sprigs. Makes about 5 cups (1.25 L) soup.

Arrange 4 ovenproof serving bowls on baking sheet with sides. Place 2 slices of dried bread in each. Ladle soup over bread, allowing 1 to 2 minutes for bread to soak up liquid.

Sprinkle each with cheese. Broil until cheese is browned and bubbly. Let stand for 5 minutes. Carefully transfer hot soup bowls to plates. Serves 4.

1 serving: 503 Calories; 21.1 g Total Fat (8.7 g Mono, 1.9 g Poly, 9.1 g Sat); 42 mg Cholesterol; 52 g Carbohydrate; 8 g Fibre; 22 g Protein; 1964 mg Sodium

Pictured on page 66.

French Onion Soup, page 65

Tapas Potatoes Brava

These spicy, Spanish-style potatoes are often served as an appetizer. They are deliciously coated in a hot, red sauce.

Olive (or cooking) oil	3 tbsp.	50 mL
Red baby potatoes (with peel), halved	1 lb.	454 g
All-purpose flour	1 tsp.	5 mL
Paprika	1 tsp.	5 mL
Brown sugar, packed	1/2 tsp.	2 mL
Cayenne pepper	1/4 – 1/2 tsp.	1 – 2 mL
Can of tomato sauce	7 1/2 oz.	213 mL
Green onions, sliced	2	2
Red wine vinegar	1 tbsp.	15 mL

Heat olive oil in large frying pan on medium-high. Add potatoes. Cook for about 2 minutes, stirring constantly, until browned.

Combine flour, paprika, brown sugar and cayenne pepper in small cup. Sprinkle over potatoes. Toss well.

Add tomato sauce, green onion and red wine vinegar. Bring to a boil. Reduce heat to medium-low. Cover. Simmer for about 15 minutes until potatoes are tender. Simmer, uncovered, for about 4 minutes until sauce is thickened slightly and coats potatoes. Serve warm or at room temperature. Makes 4 cups (1 L). Serves 4.

1 serving: 199 Calories; 10.6 g Total Fat (7.6 g Mono, 1 g Poly, 1.5 g Sat); 0 mg Cholesterol; 25 g Carbohydrate; 3 g Fibre; 3 g Protein; 342 mg Sodium

Pictured on page 67.

Mussels In Tasty Broth

Tender mussels in a richly flavoured broth. Serve with slices of bread to soak up any extra juices.

Hard margarine (or butter)	2 tbsp.	30 mL
Green onions, sliced	2	2
Garlic cloves, minced (or 1/2 tsp., 2 mL, powder)	2	2
Dry white (or alcohol-free) wine	1/4 cup	60 mL
Prepared chicken broth	1 cup	250 mL
Louisiana hot sauce	1 tbsp.	15 mL
Sprigs of fresh thyme	3	3
Mussels, scrubbed and "beards" removed	2 lbs.	900 g

Melt margarine in large pot or Dutch oven on medium. Add green onion and garlic. Heat and stir for 1 minute.

Add wine, broth, hot sauce and thyme sprigs. Bring to a boil on medium-high.

Add mussels. Stir until coated. Cover tightly. Cook for about 4 minutes until mussels are opened. Discard any that do not open. Transfer mussels to large serving bowl, using slotted spoon. Remove and discard thyme sprigs from broth. Pour broth over mussels. Serves 4.

1 serving: 221 Calories; 10 g Total Fat (4.8 g Mono, 1.7 g Poly, 2 g Sat); 47 mg Cholesterol; 7 g Carbohydrate; trace Fibre; 22 g Protein; 850 mg Sodium

Pictured on page 67.

Crusty Bread Dunkers

Cut 1 1/4 inch (3 cm) thick slices of multi-grain, rye or sourdough bread. Cut into quarters (if the circumference of loaf is quite large, cut each slice into sixths, ensuring that each piece has some crust). Pile in a basket to serve. Pictured on page 67.

Top Left: Mussels In Tasty Broth, above
Top Right: Crusty Bread Dunkers, above
Centre Right: Tapas Potatoes Brava, this page
Bottom: Zucchini And Peppers, page 68

Zucchini And Peppers

A beautiful contrast of shapes and colours. The tangy dressing complements the perfectly roasted zucchini and red peppers.

Zucchini (about 4 medium, with peel), quartered lengthwise and cut crosswise into bite-size pieces	1 lb.	454 g
Olive (or cooking) oil	1 tbsp.	15 mL
Jar of roasted red peppers, drained, blotted dry and cut into strips (see Note)	12 oz.	340 mL
OLIVE DRESSING		
Can of sliced ripe olives, drained	4 1/2 oz.	125 mL
Olive (or cooking) oil	3 tbsp.	50 mL
Balsamic vinegar	3 tbsp.	50 mL
Salt	1/4 tsp.	1 mL
Garlic clove, minced (or 1/4 tsp., 1 mL, powder), optional	1	1

Toss zucchini in olive oil in medium bowl. Arrange in single layer on large greased baking sheet. Cook, uncovered, in 425°F (220°C) oven for 15 minutes. Stir. Cook for about 10 minutes until zucchini is starting to brown and liquid is evaporated.

Combine zucchini and red pepper in large bowl.

Olive Dressing: Combine all 5 ingredients in small jar with tight-fitting lid. Shake well. Pour over zucchini mixture. Toss. Best served warm or at room temperature. Makes 3 cups (750 mL). Serves 4.

1 serving: 209 Calories; 19.1 g Total Fat (13.9 g Mono, 1.7 g Poly, 2.6 g Sat); 0 mg Cholesterol; 10 g Carbohydrate; 4 g Fibre; 2 g Protein; 575 mg Sodium

Pictured on page 67.

Note: To make your own roasted peppers, cut peppers into quarters. Arrange, skin-side up, on ungreased baking sheet. Broil 5 inches (12.5 cm) from heat for about 10 minutes, rearranging as necessary, until skins are blistered and blackened. Remove to bowl. Cover with plastic wrap. Let sweat for 10 to 15 minutes until cool enough to handle. Remove and discard skins. 1 medium pepper = about 4 oz. (113 g) roasted pepper.

Marshmallow Coffee, this page

Marshmallow Coffee

A mellow coffee with a satisfying Irish cream taste. Perfect for a cold winter night by the fire.

Prepared strong coffee	4 cups	1 L
Irish cream-flavoured liqueur (such as Baileys)	1/2 cup	125 mL
Miniature multi-coloured marshmallows	40	40
Miniature multi-coloured marshmallows, for garnish		

Combine first 3 ingredients in medium saucepan. Heat and stir on medium for 5 to 7 minutes until marshmallows are melted. Makes about 4 2/3 cups (1.15 L). Pour into warmed mugs.

Garnish with marshmallows. Serves 4.

1 serving: 232 Calories; 5.2 g Total Fat (1.5 g Mono, 0.2 g Poly, 3.2 g Sat); 5 mg Cholesterol; 38 g Carbohydrate; 0 g Fibre; 2 g Protein; 62 mg Sodium

Pictured on this page.

Cabin Cooking

Tossed Salad, below

Spend a weekend relaxing amidst the rustic surroundings of the family cabin. This easy-to-prepare menu was created for such an event, remembering that not all cabin kitchens are well stocked.

serves 6

Tossed Salad

🏠

Cheese Biscuits

🏠

Steak Strip Dish

🏠

Apple Rhubarb Crumble

Tossed Salad

You don't need to get fancy when cooking at the cabin. This salad will suffice with crisp lettuce and cucumber tossed in a creamy sweet and sour dressing.

Large head of iceberg lettuce, cut up or torn	1	1
Medium tomatoes, cut into wedges	2	2
Diced English cucumber (with peel)	1/2 cup	125 mL
SWEET AND SOUR DRESSING		
Salad dressing (or mayonnaise)	1/3 cup	75 mL
Ketchup	2 tbsp.	30 mL
Granulated sugar	2 tbsp.	30 mL
Salt	1/4 tsp.	1 mL
White vinegar	1/4 cup	60 mL

Combine lettuce, tomato and cucumber in medium bowl. Chill.

Sweet And Sour Dressing: Mix first 4 ingredients in small bowl. Gradually stir in vinegar until well blended. Makes about 3/4 cup (175 mL) dressing. Just before serving, pour over lettuce mixture. Toss well. Makes about 7 1/2 cups (1.9 L). Serves 6.

1 serving: 113 Calories; 7.1 g Total Fat (3.8 g Mono, 2.4 g Poly, 0.5 g Sat); 4 mg Cholesterol; 12 g Carbohydrate; 1 g Fibre; 2 g Protein; 257 mg Sodium

Pictured above.

Cheese Biscuits

Toss 2 cups (500 mL) biscuit mix with 3/4 cup (175 mL) grated sharp or medium Cheddar cheese in medium bowl. Add 1/2 cup (125 mL) milk or water. Stir with fork until ball forms. Knead 6 to 8 times on surface dusted lightly with more biscuit mix. Pat out to 8 inch (20 cm) circle. Cut into 6 wedges. Place on greased baking sheet. Bake in 425°F (220°C) oven according to package directions until nicely browned. Split in half to butter and serve with salad. Pictured on page 71.

Steak Strip Dish

This simple-to-make casserole has tender beef with hearty flavour.

Sirloin (or round) steak, cut into thin strips	1 lb.	454 g
Medium onion, sliced	1	1
Medium carrots, sliced	3	3
Medium potatoes, sliced	4	4
Frozen cut green beans	1 1/2 cups	375 mL
Can of condensed tomato soup (see Note)	10 oz.	284 mL
Beef bouillon powder	2 tsp.	10 mL
Salt	1/2 tsp.	2 mL
Pepper	1/4 tsp.	1 mL

Layer first 5 ingredients, in order given, in ungreased 3 quart (3 L) casserole.

Stir soup, bouillon powder, salt and pepper in small bowl. Pour over steak mixture. Cover. Bake in 350°F (175°C) oven for about 1 1/2 hours until meat and vegetables are tender. Serves 6.

1 serving: 254 Calories; 7.8 g Total Fat (3.1 g Mono, 0.8 g Poly, 2.9 g Sat); 38 mg Cholesterol; 29 g Carbohydrate; 3 g Fibre; 18 g Protein; 806 mg Sodium

Pictured on page 71.

Note: For more flavour use 1 can (10 oz., 284 mL) Tomato Basil or Zesty Tomato Soup.

Apple Rhubarb Crumble

An old-fashioned favourite just like Grandma used to make. Delicious served hot with ice cream.

Large tart cooking apples (such as Granny Smith), peeled, cored and cut into eighths	4	4
Water	1/4 cup	60 mL
Granulated sugar	1/4 cup	60 mL
Chopped fresh (or frozen, thawed) rhubarb	2 cups	500 mL
CRUMBLE TOPPING		
All-purpose flour	1 cup	250 mL
Brown sugar, packed	2/3 cup	150 mL
Baking powder	2 tsp.	10 mL
Ground cinnamon	1/2 tsp.	2 mL
Ground cloves	1/4 tsp.	1 mL
Hard margarine (or butter), cut up	1/2 cup	125 mL

Combine apple, water and granulated sugar in large saucepan. Cover. Cook on low for about 10 minutes until apple is just tender. Drain.

Add rhubarb. Stir. Spoon into greased 1 1/2 quart (1.5 L) casserole.

Crumble Topping: Combine first 5 ingredients in medium bowl. Cut in margarine until mixture is crumbly. Sprinkle over apple mixture. Bake, uncovered, in 350°F (175°C) oven for about 30 minutes until top is browned. Serves 6.

1 serving: 382 Calories; 16.6 g Total Fat (10.5 g Mono, 1.8 g Poly, 3.4 g Sat); 0 mg Cholesterol; 58 g Carbohydrate; 3 g Fibre; 3 g Protein; 324 mg Sodium

Pictured on page 71.

Top Centre: Apple Rhubarb Crumble, above
Left: Cheese Biscuits, this page
Bottom Right: Steak Strip Dish, this page

Campfire Cookout

The enchanting glow of embers is what draws us together around the campfire. Plan a special cookout with this campfire menu—then sit back and enjoy the fire, conversation and evening stars.

serves 4

Pineapple Veggie Skewers

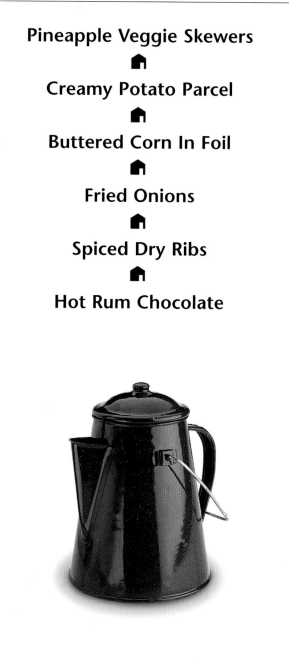

Creamy Potato Parcel

Buttered Corn In Foil

Fried Onions

Spiced Dry Ribs

Hot Rum Chocolate

Pineapple Veggie Skewers

These appetizers are very colourful and delicious. Cooking over a campfire gives them a truly outdoor flavour.

Cubed fresh pineapple, about 3/4 inch (2 cm) each	2 cups	500 mL
Large red peppers, cut into 3/4 inch (2 cm) pieces	2	2
Small zucchini (with peel), cut into 1/2 – 3/4 inch (1.2 – 2 cm) thick slices	2	2
Bamboo skewers (8 inch, 20 cm, length), soaked in water for 10 minutes	8	8
Hard margarine (or butter)	1/2 cup	125 mL
Brown sugar, packed	1 tbsp.	15 mL
Garlic powder	1 tsp.	5 mL
Pepper	1/2 tsp.	2 mL

Alternately thread pineapple, red pepper and zucchini onto skewers.

Combine remaining 4 ingredients in small bowl. Brush onto skewers. Set skewers on greased grill placed over hot coals in fire pit. Cook for 15 to 20 minutes, turning and brushing occasionally with margarine mixture, until browned. Serves 4.

1 serving: 293 Calories; 24.7 g Total Fat (15.8 g Mono, 2.6 g Poly, 5 g Sat); 0 mg Cholesterol; 19 g Carbohydrate; 3 g Fibre; 2 g Protein; 288 mg Sodium

Pictured on page 75.

Tip

To prevent food from sticking to grill and to sear in flavours, make sure grill is hot before you begin cooking. To achieve this, set grill over fire while flames are still evident. Wait until coals are covered with thin coating of light grey ash before cooking.

Creamy Potato Parcel

Use oven mitts instead of tongs to turn this to avoid tearing the foil and losing all the wonderful juices.

Medium potatoes, thinly sliced	4	4
Bacon slices, cooked almost crisp and crumbled	6	6
Grated medium Cheddar cheese	1 cup	250 mL
Ground nutmeg	1/4 tsp.	1 mL
Salt	1/2 tsp.	2 mL
Pepper	1/4 tsp.	1 mL
Whipping cream (or whole milk)	1 cup	250 mL

Lay out 24 inches (60 cm) of heavy-duty foil (or double layers of regular foil). Layer first 6 ingredients down centre of foil. Bring up all sides of foil around potato mixture to form "dish."

Carefully pour whipping cream over potato mixture. Cover top with another piece of foil. Seal edges. Wrap entire package in another layer of foil. Set on grill placed over hot coals in fire pit. Cook for about 50 minutes, turning carefully several times, until potato is tender. Open package carefully to avoid steam burns. Serves 4.

1 serving: 490 Calories; 36.9 g Total Fat (11.5 g Mono, 1.5 g Poly, 21.9 g Sat); 119 mg Cholesterol; 25 g Carbohydrate; 2 g Fibre; 16 g Protein; 703 mg Sodium

Pictured on page 75.

Buttered Corn In Foil

What is a campfire meal without buttered cobs of corn? Cooking the corn in the husk and foil helps to keep it sweet and moist.

Butter (or hard margarine), softened	1/3 cup	75 mL
Mint jelly	3 tbsp.	50 mL
Grainy mustard	1 tbsp.	15 mL
Garlic powder	1 tsp.	5 mL
Corncobs in husk	4	4

Combine first 4 ingredients in small bowl.

Peel back husk from corn, but do not remove. Remove silk. Spread each cob with 2 tbsp. (30 mL) butter mixture. Pull up husks. Wrap each cob in heavy-duty foil (or double layers of regular foil). Set on grill placed over hot coals in fire pit. Cook for 25 to 30 minutes, turning several times, until tender. Serves 4.

1 serving: 316 Calories; 18 g Total Fat (5.2 g Mono, 1.5 g Poly, 10.3 g Sat); 44 mg Cholesterol; 41 g Carbohydrate; 5 g Fibre; 5 g Protein; 244 mg Sodium

Pictured below.

Buttered Corn In Foil, above

Fried Onions

These onions are soft and sweet with a little heat from the pepper sauce. A heavy cast-iron frying pan is best for cooking over an open fire.

Cooking oil	1 tbsp.	15 mL
Large onions, thinly sliced	2	2
Worcestershire sauce	2 tsp.	10 mL
Hot pepper sauce	1/4 tsp.	1 mL
Brown sugar, packed	2 tsp.	10 mL
Salt	1/4 – 1/2 tsp.	1 – 2 mL

Heat cooking oil in large cast-iron frying pan on grill placed over hot coals in fire pit. Add onion. Cook for 20 to 25 minutes, stirring occasionally, until soft and browned.

Add remaining 4 ingredients. Heat and stir for 2 to 3 minutes until brown sugar is dissolved. Serves 4.

1 serving: 69 Calories; 3.6 g Total Fat (2.1 g Mono, 1.1 g Poly, 0.3 g Sat); 0 mg Cholesterol; 9 g Carbohydrate; 1 g Fibre; 1 g Protein; 190 mg Sodium

Pictured on page 75.

Spiced Dry Ribs

Good camping ribs. Make sure you take lots of napkins. Adjust the amount of spice to suit your taste.

Cajun seasoning	1 tbsp.	15 mL
Brown sugar, packed	1 tbsp.	15 mL
Paprika	1 tbsp.	15 mL
Garlic salt	2 tsp.	10 mL
Seasoned salt	2 tsp.	10 mL
Coarsely ground pepper (or 1 tsp., 5 mL, pepper)	2 tsp.	10 mL
Pork baby back ribs (3 – 4 racks), cut into 2 – 3 bone portions	4 lbs.	1.8 kg

Combine first 6 ingredients in small bowl.

Rub seasoning mixture generously over ribs. Set ribs on greased grill placed over hot coals in fire pit. Cook for about 30 minutes, turning several times, until tender. Serves 4.

1 serving: 839 Calories; 65.3 g Total Fat (29.5 g Mono, 5.2 g Poly, 24.1 g Sat); 259 mg Cholesterol; 6 g Carbohydrate; 1 g Fibre; 54 g Protein; 2310 mg Sodium

Pictured on page 75.

Hot Rum Chocolate

A rich chocolate drink with the warming sensation of rum.

Milk	4 cups	1 L
Milk chocolate caramel-filled candy bars (1 3/4 oz., 50 g, each), chopped	4	4
Dark rum (or 1 tsp., 5 mL, rum flavouring)	2 tbsp.	30 mL
Large marshmallows, toasted (see Note)	8	8

Heat milk in heavy medium saucepan on medium until almost boiling. Add chocolate. Heat and stir until chocolate is melted. Remove from heat.

Add rum. Stir. Makes about 4 3/4 cups (1.2 L). Pour into mugs.

Top with marshmallows. Serves 4.

1 serving: 415 Calories; 15.4 g Total Fat (0.8 g Mono, 0.1 g Poly, 1.7 g Sat); 22 mg Cholesterol; 57 g Carbohydrate; 0 g Fibre; 12 g Protein; 197 mg Sodium

Pictured on page 75.

Note: To toast marshmallows, thread onto green wood stick or metal skewer. Hold over hot coals, turning slowly, until golden.

Top Left: Hot Rum Chocolate, above
Centre Left: Creamy Potato Parcel, page 73
Centre Right: Pineapple Veggie Skewers, page 72
Bottom Left: Spiced Dry Ribs, this page
Bottom Centre: Fried Onions, this page

Make-Ahead Family Supper

Sometimes our lives get so busy that it becomes hard to connect with family for even a few minutes. This special make-ahead menu will help you find time to reunite with everyone—at least for one dinner!

serves 6

Crunchy Day-Before Salad

🏠

Refrigerator Cornmeal Rolls

🏠

Fruity Beans And Sausage

🏠

Minty Couscous

🏠

Frosty Peanut Butter Pie

Crunchy Day-Before Salad

Crisp, colourful vegetables in a sweet, tangy dressing. You'll love the creamy texture and the subtle basil aftertaste. Layering the greens under the vegetables and sealing them with the dressing will keep them crunchy overnight.

Chopped romaine lettuce, lightly packed	1 1/2 cups	375 mL
Chopped spinach, lightly packed	1 cup	250 mL
Small cauliflower florets	3/4 cup	175 mL
Broccoli coleslaw	3/4 cup	175 mL
Medium red onion, thinly sliced	1/2	1/2
Medium carrot, cut into long shreds or ribbons with vegetable peeler	1	1
Frozen tiny peas, thawed and drained	1 cup	250 mL
DRESSING		
Mayonnaise (not salad dressing)	1 cup	250 mL
Lemon juice	2 tbsp.	30 mL
Granulated sugar	1 tbsp.	15 mL
Finely chopped fresh sweet basil (not dried)	1 tbsp.	15 mL
Finely chopped fresh parsley (not dried)	1 tbsp.	15 mL
Chopped pistachios (or peanuts)	1/4 cup	60 mL

Layer first 7 ingredients, in order given, in large deep bowl. Pat down gently, but evenly, with sheet of waxed paper. Discard waxed paper.

Dressing: Combine first 5 ingredients in small bowl. Let stand for about 10 minutes until sugar is dissolved. Stir. Makes about 1 1/4 cups (300 mL) dressing. Spoon onto lettuce mixture. Spread carefully right to side of bowl to seal.

Sprinkle with pistachios. Cover with plastic wrap. Chill overnight or up to 24 hours. Just before serving, toss well. Makes 7 cups (1.75 L). Serves 6.

1 serving: 368 Calories; 34.4 g Total Fat (19.3 g Mono, 11 g Poly, 3.4 g Sat); 23 mg Cholesterol; 12 g Carbohydrate; 3 g Fibre; 4 g Protein; 251 mg Sodium

Pictured on page 77.

Refrigerator Cornmeal Rolls

Good-sized dinner rolls made from dough that has chilled in the refrigerator. The slightly sweet taste and light, airy texture go well with a heavier main dish.

Yellow cornmeal	1/3 cup	75 mL
Boiling water	1 1/3 cups	325 mL
Salt	1 tsp.	5 mL
Hard margarine (or butter)	1/3 cup	75 mL
Granulated sugar	2 tbsp.	30 mL
Milk	1/3 cup	75 mL
Warm water	1/3 cup	75 mL
Granulated sugar	1 tsp.	5 mL
Active dry yeast (or 1/4 oz., 8 g, envelope)	1 tbsp.	15 mL
All-purpose flour, approximately	3 cups	750 mL
Hard margarine (or butter), melted	1 tbsp.	15 mL

Stir cornmeal into boiling water and salt in medium saucepan. Heat and stir on medium-low for 6 to 7 minutes until thickened. Remove from heat.

Add first amounts of margarine and sugar. Add milk. Heat and stir until margarine is melted. Turn into large bowl. Cool for about 10 minutes, stirring occasionally, until almost room temperature (may still be warm).

Stir warm water and second amount of sugar in small dish until sugar is dissolved. Sprinkle yeast over top. Stir. Let stand for 10 minutes. Stir until yeast is dissolved. Stir into cornmeal mixture.

Work in enough flour until stiff dough forms that is no longer sticky. Turn out onto lightly floured surface. Knead for about 10 minutes until smooth and elastic. Place in greased bowl, turning once to grease top. Cover with greased waxed paper. Chill in refrigerator for 8 to 24 hours. Punch dough down. Divide and shape into 24 balls. Arrange 12 balls in single layer in each of 2 greased 9 x 13 inch (22 x 33 cm) pans. Cover. Let stand in oven with light on and door closed for about 1 hour until doubled in size. Bake in 425°F (220°C) oven for about 20 minutes until golden brown.

Brush rolls with second amount of margarine. Let stand in pans for 10 minutes. Turn out of pans onto wire racks to cool. Pull apart to serve. Freeze 1 dozen rolls for later use. Makes 24 rolls.

2 rolls: 207 Calories; 6.8 g Total Fat (4.2 g Mono, 0.8 g Poly, 1.4 g Sat); trace Cholesterol; 32 g Carbohydrate; 2 g Fibre; 4 g Protein; 277 mg Sodium

Pictured on page 77.

Fruity Beans And Sausage

The smoky flavour of the sausage is contrasted by the sweet, fruity aftertaste. This easy-to-make, hearty dish tastes great served over couscous.

Can of baked beans in molasses	14 oz.	398 mL
Can of red kidney beans, drained	14 oz.	398 mL
Can of chickpeas (garbanzo beans), drained	19 oz.	540 mL
Cooked smoked sausages, cut into 1/4 inch (6 mm) slices	1 lb.	454 g
Can of pineapple tidbits, drained and juice reserved	14 oz.	398 mL
Medium cooking apple (such as McIntosh), with peel, diced	1	1
Chopped onion	1/2 cup	125 mL
Apple cider vinegar	2 tbsp.	30 mL
Fancy (mild) molasses	2 tbsp.	30 mL
Dry mustard	1 tsp.	5 mL
Reserved pineapple juice (optional)	2 tbsp.	30 mL
Cornstarch (optional)	1 tbsp.	15 mL

Put first 10 ingredients into 3 1/2 quart (3.5 L) slow cooker. Stir. Cover. Cook on Low for 6 to 7 hours or on High for 3 to 3 1/2 hours.

Turn heat to High. Stir pineapple juice into cornstarch in small cup until smooth. Stir into bean mixture. Cook for about 5 minutes until thickened slightly. Makes about 8 cups (2 L). Serves 6.

1 serving: 515 Calories; 24.8 g Total Fat (11.1 g Mono, 3.3 g Poly, 8.3 g Sat); 54 mg Cholesterol; 56 g Carbohydrate; 11 g Fibre; 21 g Protein; 1186 mg Sodium

Pictured on page 77.

Minty Couscous

Couscous is wonderfully easy and quick to prepare. It's actually a granular pasta that looks like rice. The possibilities are endless for unique and flavourful ways to serve this side dish. Count on couscous almost tripling in volume.

Water	1 3/4 cups	425 mL
Chicken (or vegetable) bouillon powder	2 tsp.	10 mL
Salt	1/2 tsp.	2 mL
Hard margarine (or butter)	1 tbsp.	15 mL
Couscous	1 1/2 cups	375 mL
Finely chopped fresh mint leaves (or 3/4 – 2 1/4 tsp., 4 – 11 mL, dried)	1 – 3 tbsp.	15 – 50 mL

Bring first 4 ingredients to a boil in large saucepan.

Add couscous and mint. Stir. Cover. Remove from heat. Let stand for about 10 minutes until water is absorbed. Fluff with fork just before serving. Makes 4 cups (1 L). Serves 6.

1 serving: 203 Calories; 2.4 g Total Fat (1.4 g Mono, 0.4 g Poly, 0.5 g Sat); trace Cholesterol; 38 g Carbohydrate; 2 g Fibre; 6 g Protein; 442 mg Sodium

Pictured on page 77.

Frosty Peanut Butter Pie

This delicious dessert can be made several weeks ahead, but even freezing might not save it for when it's needed! It's just too irresistible!

CHOCOLATE CRUST

Hard margarine (or butter)	6 tbsp.	100 mL
Chocolate wafer crumbs	1 1/2 cups	375 mL
Icing (confectioner's) sugar	1 tbsp.	15 mL

FILLING

Vanilla ice cream, softened	2 1/2 cups	625 mL
Smooth peanut butter	1/3 cup	75 mL
Frozen whipped topping, thawed	1 cup	250 mL
Ground (or finely chopped) peanuts	3 tbsp.	50 mL

Chocolate Crust: Melt margarine in medium saucepan. Add wafer crumbs and icing sugar. Stir. Reserve 2 tbsp. (30 mL) for garnish. Press remaining crumbs in bottom and up side of 9 inch (22 cm) pie plate. Bake in 350°F (175°C) oven for 10 minutes. Cool.

Filling: Mash about 1/2 cup (125 mL) ice cream with peanut butter in small bowl. Add to remaining ice cream in large bowl. Gently fold together.

Add whipped topping and peanuts. Fold in. Turn into crust. Smooth top. Sprinkle with reserved crumbs. Freeze until firm. Cover. Let stand at room temperature for 10 minutes before cutting into 8 wedges.

1 wedge: 369 Calories; 25.6 g Total Fat (12.7 g Mono, 3.5 g Poly, 8 g Sat); 26 mg Cholesterol; 31 g Carbohydrate; 1 g Fibre; 7 g Protein; 329 mg Sodium

Pictured below.

Frosty Peanut Butter Pie, this page

Picnic In The Park

The park is a popular place for everyone to gather when warm sunshine is in the weekend forecast. Stock your picnic basket with these wonderful dishes, lay out your blanket and join in this traditional summer activity.

serves 6

Iced Tea/Lemonade

🏠

Macaroni Salad

🏠

Bean And Egg Salad

🏠

Buttered Bread Rolls

🏠

Baked Ham

🏠

Cold Fried Chicken

🏠

Apple Rhubarb Sour Cream Pie

Iced Tea/Lemonade

Fill large insulated drink containers 3/4 full with iced tea or lemonade. Add enough ice cubes to fill container. If you prefer not to dilute the beverages with melting ice, make an extra batch of iced tea or lemonade the day before and freeze in ice cube trays. Serve individual drinks either with lemon or lime slices. Pictured on page 81 and on page 83.

Macaroni Salad

The creamy pasta is perfectly complemented by the crunch of celery and sweet apple chunks.

Elbow macaroni (about 8 oz., 225 g)	2 cups	500 mL
Boiling water	8 cups	2 L
Salt	1 tsp.	5 mL
Can of pineapple chunks, drained	14 oz.	398 mL
Pecans, toasted (see Note) and chopped	1/2 cup	125 mL
Chopped celery	1/2 cup	125 mL
Chopped green onion	1/4 cup	60 mL
Coarsely grated carrot	1/2 cup	125 mL
Chopped peeled green apple	1 cup	250 mL
Raisins	1/2 cup	125 mL
DRESSING		
Mayonnaise (or salad dressing)	1/2 cup	125 mL
Sour cream	1/2 cup	125 mL
Liquid honey	1/4 cup	60 mL
White vinegar	2 tbsp.	30 mL
Garlic salt	1 tsp.	5 mL

Cook macaroni in boiling water and salt in large uncovered pot or Dutch oven for 5 to 7 minutes, stirring occasionally, until tender but firm. Drain. Rinse under cold water. Drain. Put into large bowl.

Add next 7 ingredients. Toss.

Dressing: Combine all 5 ingredients in small bowl. Makes 1 1/3 cups (325 mL) dressing. Spoon over macaroni mixture. Toss until well coated. Makes about 5 cups (1.25 L). Serves 6.

1 serving: 513 Calories; 26.2 g Total Fat (13.9 g Mono, 7.3 g Poly, 3.9 g Sat); 19 mg Cholesterol; 66 g Carbohydrate; 4 g Fibre; 7 g Protein; 326 mg Sodium

Pictured on page 83.

Note: To toast pecans, place in single layer in ungreased shallow pan. Bake in 350°F (175°C) oven for 5 to 10 minutes, stirring or shaking often, until desired doneness.

Bean And Egg Salad

A colourful salad with a delicious, tangy dressing and a wonderful combination of textures. To retain the bright green colour of the beans, toss with dressing just before serving.

Fresh whole green beans, trimmed	1 1/2 lbs.	680 g
Boiling water		
Ice water		
Dried cranberries	1 cup	250 mL
Finely chopped red onion	2/3 cup	150 mL
Hard-boiled eggs, peeled and quartered	6	6
Finely chopped gherkins (or dill pickles)	1/3 cup	75 mL
DRESSING		
Olive (or cooking) oil	1/3 cup	75 mL
Lemon juice	1/4 cup	60 mL
Chopped fresh parsley (or 2 1/4 tsp., 11 mL, flakes)	3 tbsp.	50 mL
Garlic clove, minced (or 1/4 tsp., 1 mL, powder)	1	1
Salt	1/4 tsp.	1 mL
Pepper	1/4 tsp.	1 mL

Blanch green beans in boiling water in large saucepan for about 5 minutes until bright green. Drain.

Immediately plunge beans into ice water in large bowl. Let stand for about 10 minutes until cold. Drain. Put into salad bowl.

Add next 4 ingredients. Stir.

Dressing: Combine all 6 ingredients in jar with tight-fitting lid. Shake well. Makes 1/2 cup (125 mL) dressing. Just before serving, drizzle over bean mixture. Toss gently. Serves 6.

1 serving: 281 Calories; 18.3 g Total Fat (11.4 g Mono, 1.9 g Poly, 3.4 g Sat); 216 mg Cholesterol; 23 g Carbohydrate; 6 g Fibre; 9 g Protein; 225 mg Sodium

Pictured on this page.

Buttered Bread Rolls

To make things easier at your picnic, cut bread rolls in half at home. Spread cut sides with margarine (or butter). Place in container to keep from being crushed. Pack container in cooler. Pictured on page 83.

Baked Ham

Sweet, glazed ham with a hint of spice on the outside and a moist, juicy interior.

Maple (or maple-flavoured) syrup	1/2 cup	125 mL
Sweet (or regular) chili sauce	1/4 cup	60 mL
White vinegar	2 tbsp.	30 mL
Dry mustard	2 tsp.	10 mL
Cooked smoked ham	1 1/2 lbs.	680 g

Combine first 4 ingredients in small bowl.

Place ham on sheet of foil in 9 x 9 inch (22 x 22 cm) pan. Bring foil up around sides of ham to hold in syrup mixture. Leave open. Brush some syrup mixture on top of ham. Bake in 375°F (190°C) oven for 40 to 45 minutes, brushing with syrup mixture 3 to 4 times, until ham is glazed. Let stand in foil until cool. Serves 6.

1 serving: 263 Calories; 9.1 g Total Fat (4.5 g Mono, 1.4 g Poly, 3.1 g Sat); 57 mg Cholesterol; 22 g Carbohydrate; 1 g Fibre; 22 g Protein; 1610 mg Sodium

Pictured below and on page 83.

Top: Iced Tea, page 80
Bottom Left: Baked Ham, above   Bottom Right: Bean And Egg Salad, this page

Cold Fried Chicken

Spicy, seasoned chicken that tastes great cold. The perfect picnic finger food!

Italian salad dressing	2/3 cup	150 mL
All-purpose flour	1/3 cup	75 mL
Salt	1/2 tsp.	2 mL
Chicken parts, with skin	2 1/2 lbs.	1.1 kg
Pancake mix	1 1/2 cups	375 mL
Onion powder	1 tbsp.	15 mL
Paprika	1 tbsp.	15 mL
Garlic salt	2 tsp.	10 mL
Pepper	1 1/2 tsp.	7 mL
Buttermilk (or reconstituted from powder)	1/2 cup	125 mL
Cooking oil	1/3 cup	75 mL

Combine salad dressing, flour and salt in large bowl. Add chicken. Toss. Cover. Marinate in refrigerator for at least 6 hours or overnight, stirring occasionally.

Combine next 5 ingredients in resealable freezer bag.

Measure buttermilk into medium deep bowl. Dip chicken pieces (with clinging marinade), 1 or 2 at a time, into buttermilk. Toss in seasoned pancake mix until well coated. Discard any remaining marinade.

Heat cooking oil in large frying pan on medium-low. Cook chicken, in batches, for 2 to 3 minutes per side until browned. Remove to paper towels to drain. Place chicken on greased wire rack on baking sheet with sides. Bake in 375°F (190°C) oven for 30 to 35 minutes until crispy and no longer pink inside. Chill. Serves 6.

1 serving: 531 Calories; 32.9 g Total Fat (16.3 g Mono, 9.5 g Poly, 4.8 g Sat); 88 mg Cholesterol; 33 g Carbohydrate; 1 g Fibre; 25 g Protein; 1372 mg Sodium

Pictured on page 83.

Apple Rhubarb Sour Cream Pie

Your guests will love the old-fashioned taste of this creamy rhubarb pie. The golden brown crust and the fresh, tart filling are simply irresistible!

Pastry for 2 crust 9 inch (22 cm) pie	1	1
Thinly sliced peeled cooking apple (such as McIntosh)	3 cups	750 mL
Coarsely chopped fresh rhubarb	2 1/2 cups	625 mL
Sour cream	1 cup	250 mL
Brown sugar, packed	3/4 cup	175 mL
Finely grated orange zest	1 tsp.	5 mL
Ground nutmeg	1/2 tsp.	2 mL
Cornstarch	1/4 cup	60 mL
Egg yolk (large), fork-beaten	1	1
Granulated sugar	2 tsp.	10 mL

Roll out 1/2 of pastry on lightly floured surface to about 1/8 inch (3 mm) thickness. Line 9 inch (22 cm) pie plate.

Fill shell with apple and rhubarb.

Combine next 5 ingredients in small bowl. Spread over apple mixture. Roll out remaining pastry on lightly floured surface to about 1/8 inch (3 mm) thickness. Dampen bottom pastry edge with water. Cover with top pastry. Trim and crimp edge to seal. Cover. Chill for 15 minutes. Cut slits in top.

Brush top pastry and edge with egg yolk. Sprinkle with granulated sugar. Bake on bottom rack in 375°F (190°C) oven for about 50 minutes until golden brown. Cool completely before packing in cooler. Cuts into 8 wedges.

1 wedge: 344 Calories; 15.6 g Total Fat (6.5 g Mono, 1.6 g Poly, 6.3 g Sat); 39 mg Cholesterol; 49 g Carbohydrate; 1 g Fibre; 3 g Protein; 228 mg Sodium

Pictured on page 83.

1. Iced Tea, page 80
2. Lemonade, page 80
3. Macaroni Salad, page 80
4. Buttered Bread Rolls, page 81
5. Apple Rhubarb Sour Cream Pie, above
6. Baked Ham, page 81
7. Cold Fried Chicken, this page

Rainy Day Supper

No one can control the weather, and it can seem especially dull and grey when rain falls on your weekend plans. No matter—we've created this menu for just such an occasion and it's guaranteed to put a rainbow back in that cloudy sky. And if your local weatherman is able to forecast the day before, the salad, noodles and stew can be made ahead.

serves 6

Diced Beet Salad

Spaetzle

Beef Carbonnade

Applesauce Rice Pudding

Raspberry Mocha

Diced Beet Salad

A pretty salad with a slightly tangy dressing. Make this the day before for the best flavour.

Diced, cooked fresh beets (or canned, drained)	1 1/3 cups	325 mL
Diced cooked carrot	1 1/3 cups	325 mL
Finely chopped red onion	1/3 cup	75 mL
Finely chopped sweet pickles	2 tbsp.	30 mL
DRESSING		
Olive (or cooking) oil	3 tbsp.	50 mL
White vinegar	2 tbsp.	30 mL
Sweet pickle juice	1 tbsp.	15 mL
Granulated sugar	1 tbsp.	15 mL
Celery seed	1/4 tsp.	1 mL
Salt	1/4 tsp.	1 mL

Combine first 4 ingredients in medium bowl.

Dressing: Whisk all 6 ingredients in small bowl until sugar is dissolved. Makes about 1/3 cup (75 mL) dressing. Add to beet mixture. Stir. Let stand at room temperature for at least 1 hour or up to 24 hours to blend flavours. Makes about 3 cups (750 mL). Serves 6.

1 serving: 109 Calories; 7 g Total Fat (5.1 g Mono, 0.6 g Poly, 1 g Sat); 0 mg Cholesterol; 12 g Carbohydrate; 2 g Fibre; 1 g Protein; 172 mg Sodium

Pictured on page 85.

Top Left and Bottom: Beef Carbonnade, page 86
Centre Left and Bottom: Spaetzle, page 86
Centre Right: Diced Beet Salad, above

Spaetzle

A German egg noodle dish, pronounced SHPEHT-sluh.
Freezes well.

All-purpose flour	3 cups	750 mL
Salt	1 1/4 tsp.	6 mL
Baking powder	1/4 tsp.	1 mL
Large eggs, fork-beaten	4	4
Water, approximately	1 1/4 cups	300 mL
Water		
Hard margarine (or butter)	3 tbsp.	50 mL

Food Processor Method: Measure flour, salt and baking powder into food processor with dough blade. Pulse twice to mix.

Add eggs. Pulse for about 1 minute until combined.

With motor running, slowly add first amount of water through feed chute until very stiff, sticky batter forms.

Hand Method: Stir flour, salt and baking powder in medium bowl.

Stir in eggs.

Add first amount of water, 1/4 cup (60 mL) at a time, until very stiff, sticky batter forms.

To Complete: Fill large pot or Dutch oven 2/3 full with water. Bring to a boil on medium-high. Place colander with large holes (see Note) on pot. Transfer 1/2 of batter into colander. Carefully press batter through holes with flexible spatula. Once spaetzle start to rise to surface of water, boil for 1 to 2 minutes until light and fluffy. Remove with slotted spoon or sieve to serving bowl. Repeat with remaining batter.

Melt margarine in small saucepan. Pour 1/2 over first batch of spaetzle. Stir gently until coated. Keep warm. Repeat with remaining spaetzle and margarine. Add second batch, a little at a time, to first batch, stirring gently. Makes about 5 cups (1.25 L). Serves 6.

1 serving: 342 Calories; 9.8 g Total Fat (5.1 g Mono, 1.3 g Poly, 2.3 g Sat); 144 mg Cholesterol; 51 g Carbohydrate; 2 g Fibre; 11 g Protein; 621 mg Sodium

Pictured on page 85.

Note: A spaetzle maker can be used instead of a colander. The device resembles a ricer with larger holes. The long handles allow it to sit on a pot's edge while the batter is pressed into the boiling water to cook.

Beef Carbonnade

This easy-to-make stew, originating in Belgium, typically contains bacon, beer and lots of onions.

Bacon slices	4	4
Inside round (or boneless chuck) steak, trimmed of fat and cut into 1 inch (2.5 cm) cubes	1 1/2 lbs.	680 g
Pepper, sprinkle		
Medium onions, cut lengthwise and sliced	3	3
Garlic clove, minced (or 1/4 tsp., 1 mL, powder)	1	1
Brown sugar, packed	1 tbsp.	15 mL
Beer (or alcohol-free beer)	12 1/2 oz.	355 mL
Can of condensed beef broth	10 oz.	284 mL
Bay leaf	1	1
Red wine vinegar	1 tbsp.	15 mL
Cornstarch	1 tbsp.	15 mL
Chopped fresh parsley (or 3/4 tsp., 4 mL, flakes)	1 tbsp.	15 mL

Cook bacon in large pot or Dutch oven until crisp. Remove to paper towel with slotted spoon, reserving 2 tsp. (10 mL) drippings in pot. Cool bacon until able to handle. Crumble. Set aside.

Heat reserved bacon drippings in same pot on medium-high. Add beef. Sprinkle with pepper. Cook beef until browned on all sides. Transfer to medium bowl, reserving any drippings in pot.

Add onion to drippings in pot. Cook on medium for about 10 minutes, stirring occasionally, until soft. Add garlic and brown sugar. Stir. Cook on medium-low for about 5 minutes until onion is browned and very soft.

Stir in beer, broth and bay leaf. Bring to a boil. Add beef. Stir. Reduce heat. Cover. Simmer for about 1 1/2 hours, stirring occasionally, until beef is very tender. Remove and discard bay leaf.

Stir wine vinegar into cornstarch in small cup. Stir into beef mixture. Heat and stir until boiling and slightly thickened.

Sprinkle individual servings with reserved bacon and parsley. Serves 6.

1 serving: 240 Calories; 6.2 g Total Fat (2.7 g Mono, 0.6 g Poly, 2.3 g Sat); 54 mg Cholesterol; 11 g Carbohydrate; 1 g Fibre; 29 g Protein; 450 mg Sodium

Pictured on page 85.

Applesauce Rice Pudding

This is a great dessert using leftover rice, and it can be ready in less than 25 minutes!

Granulated sugar	1/2 cup	125 mL
Cornstarch	2 tbsp.	30 mL
Can of evaporated milk (not skim)	13 1/2 oz.	385 mL
Milk	1/2 cup	125 mL
Applesauce	2/3 cup	150 mL
Cooked short grain white rice (not instant), about 7/8 cup (200 mL) uncooked	1 1/2 cups	375 mL
Raisins	1/2 cup	125 mL
Ground cinnamon	1/2 tsp.	2 mL
Large egg	1	1
Milk	1/4 cup	60 mL
Vanilla	1 1/4 tsp.	6 mL

Ground cinnamon, sprinkle

Combine sugar and cornstarch in medium saucepan. Stir in next 6 ingredients, in order given. Heat on medium, stirring occasionally, until boiling. Reduce heat to medium-low. Simmer, uncovered, for 5 minutes, stirring occasionally.

Beat egg and milk with fork in small bowl until frothy. Stir briskly into rice mixture. Heat and stir for about 5 minutes until boiling and thickened.

Stir in vanilla.

Sprinkle individual servings with cinnamon. Serves 6.

1 serving: 322 Calories; 6.7 g Total Fat (2.1 g Mono, 0.4 g Poly, 3.8 g Sat); 57 mg Cholesterol; 57 g Carbohydrate; 1 g Fibre; 9 g Protein; 102 mg Sodium

Pictured on this page.

Raspberry Mocha

Enjoy this comforting beverage in front of the fire on a cold, rainy day.

Skim milk powder	1 1/2 cups	375 mL
Powdered coffee whitener	6 tbsp.	100 mL
Granulated sugar	1/2 cup	125 mL
Cocoa, sifted if lumpy	6 tbsp.	100 mL
Instant coffee granules	5 tsp.	25 mL
Sweetened raspberry-flavoured drink crystals	3 tbsp.	50 mL
Hot water	3 cups	750 mL
Milk	4 1/2 cups	1.1 L
Whipped cream (optional)	6 tbsp.	100 mL
Grated semi-sweet chocolate (optional)	2 tsp.	10 mL

Mix first 6 ingredients in large saucepan. Slowly stir in hot water until well combined.

Stir in milk. Heat on medium, stirring occasionally, until very hot and surface is foamy. Makes about 8 cups (2 L) cocoa.

Garnish individual servings with whipped cream and chocolate. Serves 6.

1 serving: 329 Calories; 5.2 g Total Fat (1 g Mono, 0.1 g Poly, 3.8 g Sat); 14 mg Cholesterol; 54 g Carbohydrate; 2 g Fibre; 19 g Protein; 284 mg Sodium

Pictured below.

Top: Raspberry Mocha, this page
Bottom: Applesauce Rice Pudding, this page

Simple Supper

Busy, busy, busy! That's how some people describe their weekends. Still, you have to eat and that's why this great menu is your perfect solution. Keep it simple, delicious and fun.

serves 4

Veggies 'N' Bread

Pretty Pink Soup

Glazed Carrots

Microwave Supper

Sauced Lemon Pudding Cake

Veggies 'N' Bread

Fill 3 inch (7.5 cm) pieces of celery with your favourite cream cheese spread or dip. Arrange on small plate. Arrange, overlapping, sliced tomato and cucumber on separate small plate. Mix 2 tsp. (10 mL) olive (or cooking) oil, a pinch of crushed dried marjoram or oregano and some crumbled feta cheese. Scatter over tomato and cucumber. Grind pepper over top. Serve with bread sticks. Pictured on page 89.

Pretty Pink Soup

An easy-to-make soup with an attractive coral colour and a pleasant, creamy texture.

Hard margarine (or butter)	2 tsp.	10 mL
Chopped onion	1/2 cup	125 mL
All-purpose flour	1 tbsp.	15 mL
Can of condensed chicken broth	10 oz.	284 mL
Can of sliced beets (with liquid)	14 oz.	398 mL
Can of stewed tomatoes (with juice)	14 oz.	398 mL
Lemon juice	1 tbsp.	15 mL
Bay leaf	1	1
Milk	1 1/2 cups	375 mL

Sour cream, for garnish

Heat margarine in large saucepan on medium. Add onion. Cook for about 10 minutes, stirring occasionally, until very soft and starting to brown.

Sprinkle with flour. Stir well. Stir in broth slowly. Heat and stir until boiling and slightly thickened.

Add next 4 ingredients. Bring to a boil. Reduce heat. Cover. Simmer, without stirring, for 30 minutes. Remove and discard bay leaf. Purée, in batches, in blender. Return to saucepan.

Add milk. Heat and stir on medium for about 5 minutes until hot, but not boiling.

Garnish individual servings with dollop of sour cream. Makes about 5 cups (1.25 L). Serves 4.

1 serving: 155 Calories; 4 g Total Fat (2 g Mono, 0.5 g Poly, 1.3 g Sat); 5 mg Cholesterol; 23 g Carbohydrate; 3 g Fibre; 9 g Protein; 1088 mg Sodium

Pictured on page 89.

Glazed Carrots

Delicious, lightly browned carrots with a sweet, buttery coating.

Water	1/4 cup	60 mL
Hard margarine (or butter)	2 tbsp.	30 mL
Brown sugar, packed	6 tbsp.	100 mL
Baby carrots	1 lb.	454 g
Green onions, sliced (optional)	2	2

Combine water, margarine and brown sugar in medium saucepan. Bring to a boil on medium.

Add carrots. Cover. Cook for 5 minutes. Carrots will not be fully cooked. Cook, uncovered, on medium-high for about 10 minutes, stirring frequently, until liquid is evaporated and carrots are lightly browned and glazed.

Add green onion. Stir. Makes 2 cups (500 mL). Serves 4.

1 serving: 179 Calories; 6 g Total Fat (3.8 g Mono, 0.7 g Poly, 1.2 g Sat); 0 mg Cholesterol; 32 g Carbohydrate; 3 g Fibre; 1 g Protein; 116 mg Sodium

Pictured on page 90 and on page 91.

Microwave Supper

A rich, hearty dish with a colourful variety of vegetables coated in a creamy garlic sauce. Serve with peas.

Chopped cabbage	3 cups	750 mL
Diced potato	2 cups	500 mL
Finely chopped onion	1/2 cup	125 mL
Grated carrot	1/4 cup	60 mL
Water	1/4 cup	60 mL
All-purpose flour	1 tbsp.	15 mL
Milk	1/2 cup	125 mL
Tub of garlic herb spreadable cream cheese	8 oz.	250 g
Dry mustard	1/2 tsp.	2 mL
Salt	1/2 tsp.	2 mL
Pepper	1/4 tsp.	1 mL
Smokies (or other cooked spicy sausage), cut on diagonal into 3/4 inch (2 cm) slices	1 lb.	454 g

Combine first 5 ingredients in ungreased 2 quart (2 L) casserole. Cover. Microwave on high (100%) for about 8 minutes, stirring once halfway through cooking time, until vegetables are tender.

Sprinkle with flour. Stir in milk. Spoon cream cheese, in 8 to 10 pieces, directly onto cabbage mixture. Add mustard, salt and pepper. Stir.

Lay sausage on top of cabbage mixture. Cover. Microwave on high (100%) for about 6 minutes, stirring occasionally, until sausage is plump and cream cheese is melted. Serves 4.

1 serving: 710 Calories; 57 g Total Fat (22.5 g Mono, 4.7 g Poly, 26.1 g Sat); 150 mg Cholesterol; 26 g Carbohydrate; 3 g Fibre; 24 g Protein; 1588 mg Sodium

Pictured on page 90/91.

Top: Veggies 'N' Bread, page 88
Bottom Left and Centre Right: Pretty Pink Soup, page 88

Sauced Lemon Pudding Cake

This pale yellow cake is drizzled with a sweet, lemon-flavoured sauce. The perfect comfort food!

All-purpose flour	1 cup	250 mL
Granulated sugar	2/3 cup	150 mL
Baking powder	2 tsp.	10 mL
Baking soda	1/4 tsp.	1 mL
Salt	1/8 tsp.	0.5 mL
Hard margarine (or butter), softened	2 tbsp.	30 mL
Juice of 1 medium lemon, plus milk to make	1/2 cup	125 mL
Grated lemon peel	1 tbsp.	15 mL
Boiling water	1 3/4 cups	425 mL
Granulated sugar	1 cup	250 mL
Hard margarine (or butter)	1 tbsp.	15 mL
Lemon flavouring	2 tsp.	10 mL

Measure first 8 ingredients into medium bowl. Stir until just moistened. Turn into greased 1 1/2 quart (1.5 L) casserole.

Combine boiling water and second amounts of sugar and margarine in small bowl. Add lemon flavouring. Stir until sugar is dissolved. Pour over batter. Do not stir. Bake, uncovered, in 400°F (205°C) oven for about 30 minutes until top is golden and firm to touch. Let stand for 15 minutes before serving. Serves 4.

1 serving: 549 Calories; 9 g Total Fat (5.7 g Mono, 1 g Poly, 1.8 g Sat);
0 mg Cholesterol; 117 g Carbohydrate; 1 g Fibre; 4 g Protein; 369 mg Sodium

Pictured on page 91.

Centre Left and Bottom Right: Glazed Carrots, page 89
Centre Right: Sauced Lemon Pudding Cake, above
Top and Bottom Centre: Microwave Supper, page 89

Sunday Roast

It's a wonderful tradition for busy families to finish their week by gathering around the dinner table. This charming menu selection can help you prepare without too much fuss or effort—after all, Sunday is your day of rest too!

serves 6

Yorkshire Pudding

Roasted Potatoes

Roast Beef

Maple Mustard Carrots

Creamy Beans

Chocolate Cake

Yorkshire Pudding

Crispy and golden on the outside, soft and tender on the inside. These are very easy to make and are the perfect complement to this roast beef dinner.

All-purpose flour	2 cups	500 mL
Salt	1 tsp.	5 mL
Milk, room temperature	1 cup	250 mL
Water, room temperature	1 cup	250 mL
Large eggs	3	3

Measure flour and salt into large bowl. Stir.

Add milk, water and eggs. Beat until well combined and bubbles start to form. Cover. Let stand at room temperature for 1 hour. Place muffin pan in 450°F (230°C) oven for about 20 minutes until very hot. Working quickly, remove from oven and spray with cooking spray. Immediately fill each cup 3/4 full with batter. Bake on second lowest rack in 450°F (230°C) oven for 15 minutes. Decrease temperature to 350°F (175°C). Bake for 15 to 20 minutes until puffed and golden. Makes 12 Yorkshire puddings. Serves 6.

1 serving: 216 Calories; 3.4 g Total Fat (1.1 g Mono, 0.5 g Poly, 1.1 g Sat); 109 mg Cholesterol; 36 g Carbohydrate; 1 g Fibre; 9 g Protein; 449 mg Sodium

Pictured on page 93.

Roasted Potatoes

Brush peeled small to medium potatoes with melted hard margarine (or butter). Sprinkle with garlic salt and paprika. Bake in 375°F (190°C) oven for about 1 hour until potatoes are golden and tender. Pictured on page 94/95.

Roast Beef

A tender roast filled with a moist horseradish stuffing and served with a succulent wine sauce.

STUFFING

Bacon slices, chopped	4	4
Finely chopped onion	1 cup	250 mL
Fresh bread crumbs	2 cups	500 mL
Creamed horseradish	1 tbsp.	15 mL
Chopped fresh parsley (or 2 1/4 tsp., 11 mL, flakes)	3 tbsp.	50 mL
Salt	1/4 tsp.	1 mL
Pepper, just a pinch		
Top sirloin roast	3 lbs.	1.4 kg
Water	1 cup	250 mL

RED WINE SAUCE

Dry red (or alcohol-free) wine	1 cup	250 mL
Prepared beef broth	1 cup	250 mL
Red currant jelly	1/4 cup	60 mL
Grainy mustard	1 1/2 tbsp.	25 mL
Cornstarch	1 tbsp.	15 mL
Salt, sprinkle		
Pepper, sprinkle		

Stuffing: Cook bacon in frying pan on medium until browned but still soft. Remove to paper towel. Put into medium bowl. Drain and discard all but 1 tbsp. (15 mL) fat from pan.

Add onion. Cook on medium-low for about 10 minutes, stirring occasionally, until onion is soft. Add to bacon.

Add next 5 ingredients. Mix well. Makes 2 1/2 cups (625 mL) stuffing.

Cut deep horizontal pocket in side of roast almost through to other side. Fill with stuffing. Tie with butcher's string at 1 1/2 inch (3.8 cm) intervals. Place on greased wire rack in small roasting pan.

Pour water into bottom of pan. Cook roast, uncovered, in 425°F (220°C) oven for 25 minutes. Reduce heat to 350°F (175°C). Cook, uncovered, for about 1 hour until meat thermometer inserted into meat (not stuffing) reads 140°F (60°C) or until desired doneness. Remove to serving platter, leaving drippings in pan. Tent roast with foil. Let stand for 10 minutes before carving. Carve into 1/4 inch (6 mm) thick slices.

Red Wine Sauce: Heat roasting pan drippings in small saucepan on medium-high. Add wine. Heat and stir for 5 to 7 minutes until reduced by half.

Yorkshire Pudding, page 92

Combine remaining 6 ingredients in small bowl. Add to wine mixture. Heat and stir for about 5 minutes until jelly is liquid and sauce is thickened. Makes about 1 2/3 cups (400 mL) sauce. Serve with roast beef. Makes twelve 3 oz. (85 g) servings.

1 serving: 372 Calories; 16.6 g Total Fat (7.1 g Mono, 1.1 g Poly, 6.4 g Sat); 68 mg Cholesterol; 21 g Carbohydrate; 1 g Fibre; 30 g Protein; 421 mg Sodium

Pictured on page 94/95.

Maple Mustard Carrots

Sweet, glazed carrots with a mild mustard tang.

Bag of baby carrots	2 lbs.	900 g
Water		
Salt, just a pinch		
Maple (or maple-flavoured) syrup	1/4 cup	60 mL
Hard margarine (or butter)	1/4 cup	60 mL
Chopped fresh parsley (or 2 1/4 tsp., 11 mL, flakes)	3 tbsp.	50 mL
Grainy mustard	2 tbsp.	30 mL

Cook carrots in water and salt in large saucepan for about 8 minutes until tender-crisp. Drain. Transfer to medium bowl.

Put remaining 4 ingredients into same large saucepan. Cook on medium for about 5 minutes, stirring occasionally, until boiling and thickened. Add carrots. Heat and stir for about 3 minutes until carrots are hot and glazed. Makes about 5 1/2 cups (1.4 L). Serves 6.

1 serving: 179 Calories; 8.8 g Total Fat (5.4 g Mono, 1.1 g Poly, 1.8 g Sat); 0 mg Cholesterol; 25 g Carbohydrate; 4 g Fibre; 2 g Protein; 220 mg Sodium

Pictured on page 95.

Creamy Beans

Tender beans tossed in a creamy onion, garlic and dill sauce.

Prepared chicken broth	3/4 cup	175 mL
Package of frozen whole green beans	1 3/4 lbs.	750 g
Hard margarine (or butter)	2 tbsp.	30 mL
Finely chopped red onion	1/2 cup	125 mL
Garlic cloves, minced (or 1/2 tsp., 2 mL, powder)	2	2
All-purpose flour	1 tbsp.	15 mL
Dry white (or alcohol-free) wine	1/4 cup	60 mL
Whipping cream (or whole milk)	3/4 cup	175 mL
Chopped fresh dill (or 3/4 tsp., 4 mL, dill weed)	1 tbsp.	15 mL
Salt	1/4 tsp.	1 mL
Pepper	1/4 tsp.	1 mL

Bring broth to a boil in large frying pan. Add beans. Reduce heat to medium. Cover. Cook for about 5 minutes until tender. Drain. Transfer to medium bowl.

Melt margarine in same frying pan on medium-low. Add red onion and garlic. Cook for about 10 minutes, stirring occasionally, until onion is soft.

Add flour. Mix. Heat and stir for 2 minutes to cook flour.

Add wine. Heat and stir for about 2 minutes until boiling and slightly thickened.

Add remaining 4 ingredients. Heat and stir on medium-high for 2 to 3 minutes until heated through. Add beans. Toss until beans are hot and evenly coated. Serves 6.

1 serving: 190 Calories; 14.3 g Total Fat (5.5 g Mono, 0.8 g Poly, 7.2 g Sat); 37 mg Cholesterol; 13 g Carbohydrate; trace Fibre; 3 g Protein; 161 mg Sodium

Pictured on page 95.

Top Left: Roasted Potatoes, page 92
Centre: Creamy Beans, above
Centre Right: Maple Mustard Carrots, page 93
Bottom Left: Roast Beef, page 93

Chocolate Cake, below

Chocolate Cake

A moist chocolate cake with a smooth texture and a rich fudge frosting.

Water	1 cup	250 mL
Granulated sugar	1 1/2 cups	375 mL
Hard margarine (or butter), cut up	1/2 cup	125 mL
Cocoa, sifted if lumpy	3 tbsp.	50 mL
Baking soda	1/2 tsp.	2 mL
All-purpose flour	1 1/2 cups	375 mL
Baking powder	1 tbsp.	15 mL
Large eggs, fork-beaten	2	2

CHOCOLATE FROSTING		
Granulated sugar	1/4 cup	60 mL
Hard margarine (or butter)	1/4 cup	60 mL
Water	1/4 cup	60 mL
Icing (confectioner's) sugar	1 1/2 cups	375 mL
Cocoa, sifted if lumpy	1/4 cup	60 mL

Measure first 5 ingredients into medium saucepan. Heat and stir on medium-low until sugar is dissolved. Simmer, without stirring, for 5 minutes. Transfer to large bowl. Cool slightly.

Add flour, baking powder and eggs. Beat until smooth. Pour mixture into greased and waxed paper-lined 9 x 9 inch (22 x 22 cm) pan. Bake in 350°F (175°C) oven for about 40 minutes until wooden pick inserted in centre comes out clean. Let stand in pan for 10 minutes before removing to wire rack to cool.

Chocolate Frosting: Combine first 3 ingredients in small saucepan. Heat and stir on medium-low until granulated sugar is dissolved. Remove from heat.

Put icing sugar and cocoa into medium bowl. Add margarine mixture. Stir until smooth. Cover. Chill for about 1 hour, stirring occasionally, until thick. Makes 1 cup (250 mL) frosting. Spread on top of cake. Cuts into 8 pieces.

1 piece: 581 Calories; 21.9 g Total Fat (13.1 g Mono, 2.1 g Poly, 5.5 g Sat); 54 mg Cholesterol; 99 g Carbohydrate; 6 g Fibre; 8 g Protein; 452 mg Sodium

Pictured above.

Unexpected Guests!

Your out-of-town friends have phoned and you've convinced them to come for supper. Now what do you do? Make a mad dash to the store to complete your ingredient list for this easy and impressive menu.

serves 6

Bacon And Corn Dip

Bacon And Corn Dip, below, with Veggie Dippers, below

Bacon And Corn Dip

Veggie Dippers

A wonderfully smooth dip with the delicious flavours of bacon, sweet corn and creamy cheese. Perfect for serving with raw vegetables or potato chips.

Tomato Pineapple Salad

Sour cream	1/2 cup	125 mL
Corn relish	1/3 cup	75 mL
Bacon slices, cooked crisp and finely crumbled	4	4
Sliced pickled jalapeño pepper, chopped	1 tbsp.	15 mL
Grated medium Cheddar cheese	1/2 cup	125 mL

Mustard Chicken Pasta

Combine all 5 ingredients in medium microwave-safe bowl. Microwave, uncovered, on medium-high (70%) for 2 to 3 minutes, stirring twice, until cheese is melted. Makes about 1 cup (250 mL).

2 tbsp. (30 mL): 78 Calories; 6 g Total Fat (2 g Mono, 0.3 g Poly, 3.3 g Sat); 16 mg Cholesterol; 3 g Carbohydrate; trace Fibre; 3 g Protein; 164 mg Sodium

Apricot Crisp

Pictured above.

Veggie Dippers

Cut carrots and English cucumber (with peel) into 3 inch (7.5 cm) sticks. Arrange on platter or in basket. Add trimmed radishes. Serve with Bacon And Corn Dip, above. Pictured above.

Tomato Pineapple Salad

A colourful, summery salad with a wonderful combination of fresh tastes.

Roma (plum) tomatoes, quartered	6	6
Thinly sliced red onion	1/4 cup	60 mL
Can of pineapple tidbits, drained	14 oz.	398 mL
Coarsely chopped fresh sweet basil (or 1 1/2 tsp., 7 mL, dried)	2 tbsp.	30 mL
CHILI DRESSING		
Cooking oil	2 tbsp.	30 mL
White (or red) wine vinegar	2 tbsp.	30 mL
Dried crushed chilies	1/4 tsp.	1 mL
Garlic clove, minced (or 1/4 tsp., 1 mL, powder)	1	1
Salt	1/4 tsp.	1 mL
Pepper	1/4 tsp.	1 mL
Pecans, toasted (see Note) and coarsely chopped	1/3 cup	75 mL

Combine first 4 ingredients in medium bowl.

Chili Dressing: Combine first 6 ingredients in jar with tight-fitting lid. Shake well. Makes about 1/4 cup (60 mL) dressing. Drizzle over tomato mixture. Toss.

Sprinkle with pecans. Makes about 7 1/2 cups (1.9 L). Serves 6.

1 serving: 139 Calories; 9.8 g Total Fat (5.7 g Mono, 2.7 g Poly, 0.8 g Sat); 0 mg Cholesterol; 14 g Carbohydrate; 3 g Fibre; 2 g Protein; 112 mg Sodium

Pictured on page 98/99.

Note: To toast pecans, place in single layer in ungreased shallow pan. Bake in 350°F (175°C) oven for 5 to 10 minutes, stirring or shaking often, until desired doneness.

Top Left: Tomato Pineapple Salad, above
Top Right: Apricot Crisp, page 100
Bottom: Mustard Chicken Pasta, page 100

Mustard Chicken Pasta

An attractive pasta dish with a rich, creamy sauce and a lively citrus tang. For something a bit different, substitute chicken breasts with boneless chicken thighs.

Cooking oil	1 tbsp.	15 mL
Boneless, skinless chicken breast halves (about 4)	1 lb.	454 g
Cooking oil	1 tbsp.	15 mL
Finely chopped onion	1 cup	250 mL
Garlic cloves, minced (or 1/2 tsp., 2 mL, powder)	2	2
Dry white (or alcohol-free) wine	1/2 cup	125 mL
Whipping cream (or whole milk)	1 2/3 cups	400 mL
Grainy (or Dijon) mustard	2 tbsp.	30 mL
Liquid honey	2 tbsp.	30 mL
Salt	1/4 tsp.	1 mL
Pepper	1/4 tsp.	1 mL
Frozen peas	2/3 cup	150 mL
Chopped fresh parsley (or 2 1/4 tsp., 11 mL, flakes), optional	3 tbsp.	50 mL
Finely grated lemon zest	1 tsp.	5 mL
Spinach fettuccine (or pasta of your choice)	1/2 lb.	225 g
Boiling water	10 cups	2.5 L
Salt	1 tsp.	5 mL

Chopped fresh parsley, for garnish

Heat first amount of cooking oil in large frying pan on medium. Add chicken. Cook for 3 to 4 minutes per side until almost cooked. Chop coarsely. Set aside.

Heat second amount of cooking oil in same pan on medium-low. Add onion and garlic. Cook for about 10 minutes, stirring occasionally, until onion is soft.

Add wine. Boil on medium-high for about 3 minutes until wine is reduced by half.

Add next 5 ingredients. Stir. Boil gently for about 10 minutes, stirring occasionally, until thickened.

Add chicken and peas. Heat and stir for 5 to 6 minutes until chicken is cooked. Remove from heat.

Add first amount of parsley and lemon zest. Stir.

Cook fettuccine in boiling water and second amount of salt in large uncovered pot or Dutch oven for about 10 minutes, stirring occasionally, until tender but firm. Drain. Return to pot. Add chicken mixture. Stir.

Garnish with second amount of parsley. Makes about 6 cups (1.5 L). Serves 6.

1 serving: 562 Calories; 29.7 g Total Fat (9.8 g Mono, 2.9 g Poly, 15 g Sat); 135 mg Cholesterol; 42 g Carbohydrate; 4 g Fibre; 29 g Protein; 229 mg Sodium

Pictured on page 99.

Apricot Crisp

A sweet, chewy dessert with a delicious, crispy, golden brown topping. Use peaches or pears if you don't have any apricots in your pantry. Serve with whipped cream or ice cream for a finishing touch.

Cans of apricot halves in light syrup (14 oz., 398 mL, each), drained and coarsely chopped	2	2
Ground ginger	1/4 tsp.	1 mL
Ground cinnamon	1/4 tsp.	1 mL
Strawberry jam, warmed	2 tbsp.	30 mL
TOPPING		
All-purpose flour	1/2 cup	125 mL
Baking powder	1 tsp.	5 mL
Hard margarine (or butter), cut up	1/2 cup	125 mL
Brown sugar, packed	1/2 cup	125 mL
Rolled oats (not instant)	1/3 cup	75 mL

Combine first 4 ingredients in medium bowl. Place in greased 4 cup (1 L) deep casserole.

Topping: Combine flour and baking powder in separate medium bowl. Cut in margarine until mixture is crumbly.

Add brown sugar and rolled oats. Stir. Sprinkle over apricot mixture. Bake in 350°F (175°C) oven for about 45 minutes until topping is crisp and browned. Serves 6.

1 serving: 333 Calories; 16.8 g Total Fat (10.7 g Mono, 1.8 g Poly, 3.4 g Sat); 0 mg Cholesterol; 45 g Carbohydrate; 3 g Fibre; 3 g Protein; 265 mg Sodium

Pictured on page 99.

Weekend Baking Bee

*Gather friends or neighbours
together for a traditional baking
bee with this selection of recipes.
The reward will be twofold: a great
gab session in the kitchen and
a well-stocked cupboard
for the coming week!*

Orange Yogurt Loaf Cake

🏠

Sour Cherry Cake

🏠

Macadamia Nut Brownies

🏠

Coconut Squares

🏠

White Chocolate Pecan Cookies

🏠

Coffee Crumble Cake

Orange Yogurt Loaf Cake

A delicious poppy seed cake with a fresh orange kick.

Hard margarine (or butter), softened	1/2 cup	125 mL
Granulated sugar	1 cup	250 mL
Finely grated lemon zest	1 tbsp.	15 mL
Large eggs	3	3
All-purpose flour	1 1/4 cups	300 mL
Baking powder	1 tsp.	5 mL
Plain yogurt (not low-fat)	1/2 cup	125 mL
Poppy seeds	3 tbsp.	50 mL
ORANGE ICING		
Block of cream cheese, softened	8 oz.	250 g
Finely grated orange zest	2 tsp.	10 mL
Icing (confectioner's) sugar	1 cup	250 mL

Cream margarine, sugar and lemon zest in medium bowl until light and fluffy. Add eggs, 1 at a time, beating well after each addition.

Add next 4 ingredients. Mix until well combined. Turn into well-greased 8 x 4 x 3 inch (20 x 10 x 7.5 cm) loaf pan. Smooth top. Bake in 350°F (175°C) oven for about 1 hour until wooden pick inserted in centre comes out clean. Let stand in pan for 10 minutes before removing to wire rack to cool.

Orange Icing: Beat cream cheese, orange zest and icing sugar in small bowl until smooth. Spread over top and sides of cooled cake. Cuts into 16 slices.

1 slice: 257 Calories; 13.4 g Total Fat (6 g Mono, 1.5 g Poly, 5.1 g Sat); 58 mg Cholesterol; 31 g Carbohydrate; trace Fibre; 4 g Protein; 158 mg Sodium

Pictured on page 103.

Sour Cherry Cake

A sweet, white cake with a colourful layer of sour cherries. The moist, melt-in-your-mouth texture will leave you wanting more!

Hard margarine (or butter), softened	1/2 cup	125 mL
Granulated sugar	1 cup	250 mL
Finely grated lemon zest	2 tsp.	10 mL
Large eggs	2	2
All-purpose flour	1 1/2 cups	375 mL
Baking powder	1 tbsp.	15 mL
Plain yogurt (not low-fat)	1 cup	250 mL
Milk	1/3 cup	75 mL
Sour cherries, drained on paper towels and coarsely chopped	3 cups	750 mL

Icing (confectioner's) sugar, for dusting

Cream margarine, granulated sugar and lemon zest in medium bowl until light and fluffy. Add eggs, 1 at a time, beating well after each addition.

Add next 4 ingredients. Mix until well combined. Pour 1/2 of batter into well-greased and lightly floured 12 cup (2.7 L) bundt pan.

Scatter cherries evenly over batter. Carefully pour remaining batter over cherries. Bake in 350°F (175°C) oven for about 45 minutes until wooden pick inserted in centre of cake comes out clean. Let stand in pan for 10 minutes before removing to wire rack to cool.

Dust with icing sugar. Cuts into 8 wedges.

1 wedge: 380 Calories; 14.3 g Total Fat (8.6 g Mono, 1.5 g Poly, 3.3 g Sat); 56 mg Cholesterol; 58 g Carbohydrate; 2 g Fibre; 7 g Protein; 332 mg Sodium

Pictured on page 103.

Top: Sour Cherry Cake, above
Top Right: White Chocolate Pecan Cookies, page 104
Centre: Macadamia Nut Brownies, page 104
Bottom Left: Coconut Squares, page 104
Bottom Right: Orange Yogurt Loaf Cake, page 101

Macadamia Nut Brownies

Soft, chewy brownies with a generous amount of crunchy macadamia nuts. Delicious!

Hard margarine (or butter), cut up	1/2 cup	125 mL
Semi-sweet chocolate baking squares (1 oz., 28 g, each), cut up	4	4
Brown sugar, packed	1 3/4 cups	425 mL
Large eggs, fork-beaten	2	2
All-purpose flour	1 cup	250 mL
Baking powder	1/4 tsp.	1 mL
Salt	1/4 tsp.	1 mL
Macadamia nuts, toasted (see Note) and coarsely chopped	3/4 cup	175 mL

Combine margarine, chocolate and brown sugar in heavy medium saucepan. Heat and stir on medium-low until smooth. Cool.

Add eggs. Stir.

Add remaining 4 ingredients. Stir until well combined. Spread in greased 9 x 9 inch (22 x 22 cm) pan. Bake in 350°F (175°C) oven for about 30 minutes until just set. Cool. Cut into 16 squares. To serve, cut each square in half diagonally. Makes 32 triangles.

1 triangle: 130 Calories; 6.4 g Total Fat (4 g Mono, 0.4 g Poly, 1.7 g Sat); 13 mg Cholesterol; 18 g Carbohydrate; 1 g Fibre; 1 g Protein; 66 mg Sodium

Pictured on page 103.

Note: To toast macadamia nuts, place in single layer in ungreased shallow pan. Bake in 350°F (175°C) oven for 5 to 10 minutes, stirring or shaking often, until desired doneness.

Coconut Squares

Sweet squares with a hint of apricot. You'll love the wonderful shortbread-style base and the tempting coconut topping.

Hard margarine (or butter), softened	1/2 cup	125 mL
Granulated sugar	1/2 cup	125 mL
Large egg	1	1
All-purpose flour	1 cup	250 mL
Baking powder	3/4 tsp.	4 mL
Apricot jam	1/2 cup	125 mL

TOPPING

Large eggs, fork-beaten	2	2
Granulated sugar	1/3 cup	75 mL
Medium coconut	1 1/2 cups	375 mL
Ground almonds	1/2 cup	125 mL

Cream margarine, sugar and egg in medium bowl until light and fluffy.

Add flour and baking powder. Stir until well combined. Spread in greased 9 x 13 inch (22 x 33 cm) pan.

Carefully spread jam over batter.

Topping: Combine all 4 ingredients in small bowl. Spread over jam. Bake in 350°F (175°C) oven for about 30 minutes until lightly browned. Cuts into 48 squares.

1 square: 79 Calories; 4.6 g Total Fat (1.8 g Mono, 0.4 g Poly, 2.3 g Sat); 13 mg Cholesterol; 9 g Carbohydrate; trace Fibre; 1 g Protein; 36 mg Sodium

Pictured on page 102/103.

White Chocolate Pecan Cookies

Crispy, golden cookies with chunks of chocolate and nuts. These make good dunkers for your afternoon tea.

Brown sugar, packed	3/4 cup	175 mL
Vanilla	1 tsp.	5 mL
Large egg	1	1
Cooking oil	1/2 cup	125 mL
All-purpose flour	3/4 cup	175 mL
Baking powder	1/2 tsp.	2 mL
Ground cinnamon	1/4 tsp.	1 mL
Medium coconut	1/2 cup	125 mL
Pecans, toasted (see Note) and coarsely chopped	1 1/2 cups	375 mL
White chocolate chips	1 cup	250 mL

Beat brown sugar, vanilla and egg in medium bowl until light and fluffy.

Add remaining 7 ingredients. Mix well. Cover. Chill for 30 minutes. Roll rounded tablespoonfuls into balls. Place on greased cookie sheets, about 2 inches (5 cm) apart. Bake in 350°F (175°C) oven for 12 to 15 minutes until edges are golden. Let stand on cookie sheets for 5 minutes before removing to wire racks to cool. Makes 32 cookies.

1 cookie: 145 Calories; 10.4 g Total Fat (5.2 g Mono, 2.1 g Poly, 2.5 g Sat); 8 mg Cholesterol; 13 g Carbohydrate; 1 g Fibre; 1 g Protein; 16 mg Sodium

Pictured on page 103.

Note: To toast pecans, place in single layer in ungreased shallow pan. Bake in 350°F (175°C) oven for 5 to 10 minutes, stirring or shaking often, until desired doneness.

Coffee Crumble Cake

A moist, coffee-coloured cake with a sweet topping and a subtle walnut flavour. The delightful array of spices goes well with a cup of coffee.

Hard margarine (or butter), softened	1/2 cup	125 mL
Granulated sugar	3/4 cup	175 mL
Large eggs	2	2
Milk	1/2 cup	125 mL
Instant coffee granules	1 tbsp.	15 mL
Vanilla	1 tsp.	5 mL
All-purpose flour	1 1/2 cups	375 mL
Baking powder	1 tbsp.	15 mL
Ground nutmeg	1/2 tsp.	2 mL
Ground cinnamon	1 tsp.	5 mL
Chopped walnuts	2/3 cup	150 mL
CRUMBLE LAYER		
Chopped walnuts	1/3 cup	75 mL
Brown sugar, packed	3/4 cup	175 mL
Ground cinnamon	1 tsp.	5 mL
All-purpose flour	1/3 cup	75 mL
Medium coconut	1/3 cup	75 mL
Hard margarine (or butter), softened	1/4 cup	60 mL

Cream margarine and sugar in large bowl until well combined. Add eggs, 1 at a time, beating well after each addition.

Combine milk, instant coffee and vanilla in small bowl. Add to margarine mixture. Stir.

Add next 5 ingredients. Mix well. Spread 1/3 of batter in greased 8 × 8 inch (20 × 20 cm) pan.

Crumble Layer: Put all 6 ingredients into medium bowl. Mix well. Sprinkle 1/3 of crumble mixture over batter. Put dabs of 1/2 of remaining batter over crumble mixture. Spread carefully. Sprinkle with 1/2 of remaining crumble mixture. Repeat with remaining batter and crumble mixture. Bake in 350°F (175°C) oven for about 40 minutes until wooden pick inserted in centre comes out clean. Cuts into 16 pieces.

1 piece: 297 Calories; 16.3 g Total Fat (7.4 g Mono, 4.3 g Poly, 3.7 g Sat); 27 mg Cholesterol; 35 g Carbohydrate; 1 g Fibre; 4 g Protein; 194 mg Sodium

Pictured below.

Coffee Crumble Cake, above

A Taste Of Italy

The hearty flavours of this classic Italian feast will become a favourite among your guests. Include a bottle of wine and a little background opera music to complement the dishes as they arrive at the table.

serves 6

Zuppa d'Aglio

Hot Garlic Bread Sticks

Tangy Mixed Salad

Balsamic Vegetables

Pasta Pronto

Italian Colours

Amaretti

Zuppa d'Aglio

. . . or Garlic Soup in plain English! Mellow, roasted garlic flavour is almost sweet. A thinner consistency than most creamy soups.

Large garlic bulb	1	1
Olive (or cooking) oil	2 tbsp.	30 mL
Small onion, chopped	1	1
Large celery rib, chopped	1	1
Dry white (or alcohol-free) wine	1/2 cup	125 mL
Chicken stock	8 cups	2 L
All-purpose flour	2 tbsp.	30 mL
Water	2 cups	500 mL
Small potato, peeled and cut into 6 pieces	1	1
Whipping cream (or whole milk)	1/2 cup	125 mL
Chopped fresh sweet basil (or 3/4 tsp., 4 mL, dried)	1 tbsp.	15 mL
Chopped fresh thyme leaves (or 1/4 tsp., 1 mL, dried)	1 tsp.	5 mL
Salt	1 tsp.	5 mL
Hot pepper sauce	1/2 tsp.	2 mL

Chopped fresh parsley, for garnish
Coarsely ground pepper, for garnish

Cut garlic bulb in half horizontally. Remove any loose, papery outer skins. Preheat gas barbecue or frying pan to medium. Cook bulb halves, cut sides down, on greased grill or in small greased frying pan until exposed garlic is very brown. Cool until able to handle. Peel and separate garlic cloves.

Heat olive oil in large pot or Dutch oven on medium-high. Cook onion, celery and garlic cloves, stirring constantly, until all are golden.

Add wine. Boil, uncovered, for 2 minutes.

Stir 1/3 cup (75 mL) stock into flour in small cup until smooth. Add to onion mixture. Add remaining stock and water. Stir. Add potato. Bring to a boil, stirring constantly. Reduce heat to medium. Cover. Boil gently for 1 hour. Strain solids from liquid, returning liquid to pot. Purée solids in blender or food processor. Add purée to liquid. Bring to a boil.

Add whipping cream, basil, thyme, salt and hot pepper sauce. Stir until heated through. Do not boil. Remove from heat.

Sprinkle individual servings with parsley and pepper. Makes 8 cups (2 L). Serves 6.

1 serving: 211 Calories; 13.4 g Total Fat (6.2 g Mono, 1 g Poly, 5.4 g Sat); 24 mg Cholesterol; 11 g Carbohydrate; 1 g Fibre; 9 g Protein; 1516 mg Sodium

Pictured on page 107.

Top: Tangy Mixed Salad, below   Centre: Hot Garlic Bread Sticks, below   Bottom and Top Right: Zuppa d'Aglio, page 106

Hot Garlic Bread Sticks

Melt 1/3 cup (75 mL) hard margarine (or butter) in small saucepan. Add 1 to 3 minced garlic cloves. Heat on low for 2 minutes to infuse flavour. Brush on pre-made, partially baked bread sticks. Arrange on greased baking sheet. Sprinkle with finely grated fresh Parmesan or Romano cheese. Bake in 425°F (220°C) oven for 10 to 12 minutes until lightly browned or as directed on package. Pictured on front cover and above.

Tangy Mixed Salad

Add sliced roma (plum) tomato, sliced red onion, croutons and whole ripe olives to bag of mixed European-style salad greens in large bowl. Drizzle with a mixture of olive oil and balsamic vinegar. Add finely grated fresh Parmesan or Romano cheese. Toss. Pictured on front cover and above.

Balsamic Vegetables

These vegetables are deliciously coated in a tangy balsamic glaze.

Olive (or cooking) oil	2 tbsp.	30 mL
Garlic cloves, halved	2	2
Small zucchini (with peel), cut on diagonal into 1/2 inch (12 mm) slices	3	3
Medium red pepper, cut lengthwise into 1/2 inch (12 mm) slices	1	1
Medium onion, sliced lengthwise into wedges	1	1
Fresh small mushrooms (or medium mushrooms, cut in half)	2 cups	500 mL
Balsamic vinegar	1/3 cup	75 mL
Water	1/3 cup	75 mL
Cornstarch	1 tbsp.	15 mL
Granulated sugar	1 tsp.	5 mL
Salt	1/2 tsp.	2 mL

Chopped fresh sweet basil, for garnish

Heat olive oil in large frying pan on medium. Add garlic. Cook until golden. Remove and discard garlic.

Add zucchini, red pepper, onion and mushrooms to same frying pan. Cook for about 3 minutes, stirring constantly, until almost tender-crisp.

Stir vinegar and water into cornstarch in small cup until smooth. Add sugar and salt. Stir. Add to zucchini mixture. Heat and stir for about 2 minutes until sauce is thickened and vegetables are glazed.

Sprinkle with basil. Makes 4 1/2 cups (1.1 L). Serves 6.

1 serving: 82 Calories; 4.9 g Total Fat (3.4 g Mono, 0.5 g Poly, 0.7 g Sat); 0 mg Cholesterol; 10 g Carbohydrate; 2 g Fibre; 2 g Protein; 202 mg Sodium

Pictured on front cover and on page 109.

Pasta Pronto

Toss chopped fresh parsley, if desired, and olive oil with your favourite pasta for a simple side dish. Pictured on front cover, on page 109 and on back cover.

Italian Colours

A pretty presentation of Chicken Parmigiana. Tender white chicken and creamy cheese, with a splash of red tomato and green basil. All the colours of the Italian flag!

All-purpose flour	1/3 cup	75 mL
Seasoned (or garlic) salt	1 tsp.	5 mL
Pepper, generous sprinkle		
Large egg	1	1
Olive (or cooking) oil	2 tbsp.	30 mL
Milk	1 tbsp.	15 mL
Fine dry bread crumbs	2/3 cup	150 mL
Chopped fresh parsley (or 1 tbsp., 15 mL, flakes)	1/4 cup	60 mL
Grated Parmesan cheese	3 tbsp.	50 mL
Boneless, skinless chicken breast halves (about 1 1/2 lbs., 680 g)	6	6
Provolone (or mozzarella) cheese slices (about 4 oz., 113 g)	6	6
Tomato slices	6	6
Finely chopped fresh sweet basil (or 1 1/2 tsp., 7 mL, dried)	2 tbsp.	30 mL

Combine flour, seasoned salt and pepper in shallow dish.

Beat egg, olive oil and milk in small bowl with fork.

Mix bread crumbs, parsley and Parmesan cheese in separate shallow dish.

Dredge chicken in flour mixture. Dip into egg mixture. Coat well in crumb mixture. Arrange on greased baking sheet. Bake, uncovered, in 375°F (190°C) oven for about 25 minutes until golden brown and no longer pink inside.

Place 1 slice of provolone cheese, 1 slice of tomato and a sprinkle of basil on top of each chicken breast. Heat in oven for about 5 minutes until cheese is melted. Serves 6.

1 serving: 343 Calories; 14.2 g Total Fat (6.1 g Mono, 1.4 g Poly, 5.4 g Sat); 117 mg Cholesterol; 17 g Carbohydrate; 1 g Fibre; 35 g Protein; 546 mg Sodium

Pictured on front cover, on page 109 and on back cover.

Amaretti

Serve these crispy almond cookies with fresh fruit, Italian gelato and coffee. Such a nice finish to a great meal!

Ground almonds	3/4 cup	175 mL
Icing (confectioner's) sugar	1/2 cup	125 mL
Egg white (large)	1	1
Vanilla	1/2 tsp.	2 mL
Almond flavouring	1/2 tsp.	2 mL

Mix almonds and icing sugar in small bowl.

Beat egg white in medium bowl with vanilla and almond flavouring until stiff peaks form. Fold almond mixture into egg white mixture. Drop by rounded teaspoonfuls (about 1/2 tbsp., 7 mL, each) onto parchment paper-lined cookie sheet. Bake in 325°F (160°C) oven for about 15 minutes until lightly browned. Turn oven off. Let stand in oven with door opened until oven is cold and cookies are dry. Makes 2 dozen cookies.

1 cookie: 24 Calories; 1.1 g Total Fat (0.7 g Mono, 0.2 g Poly, 0.1 g Sat); 0 mg Cholesterol; 3 g Carbohydrate; 0 g Fibre; 1 g Protein; 2 mg Sodium

Pictured below.

Note: 3/4 cup (175 mL) blanched whole almonds can be ground in blender or food processor if ground almonds are not available.

Top Left and Bottom Centre: Italian Colours, page 108
Bottom Left: Pasta Pronto, page 108

Top Right: Amaretti, above
Centre Right: Balsamic Vegetables, page 108

African Safari

Take a walk on the wild side with an exciting safari adventure. Included in this menu selection are some distinctive flavours from Africa.

serves 6

Coconut Chicken Soup

Beef And Yam Stew

Buttered Couscous

Rum Fruit Salad

Pistachio Ice Cream

Coconut Chicken Soup

A smooth, creamy soup with a mild curry flavour and the sweet taste of coconut.

Peanut (or cooking) oil	1 tbsp.	15 mL
Boneless, skinless chicken breast halves (about 3)	3/4 lb.	340 g
Peanut (or cooking) oil	1 tbsp.	15 mL
Finely chopped red onion	1 cup	250 mL
Coarsely grated carrot	1/2 cup	125 mL
Finely grated peeled gingerroot	1 tsp.	5 mL
Garlic cloves, minced (or 1/2 tsp., 2 mL, powder)	2	2
Curry powder	2 – 3 tsp.	10 – 15 mL
Chili powder	1/2 – 1 tsp.	2 – 5 mL
Ground allspice	1/4 tsp.	1 mL
Ground nutmeg	1/4 tsp.	1 mL
Cans of coconut milk (14 oz., 398 mL, each)	2	2
Salt	1/2 tsp.	2 mL
Lime (or lemon) juice	1 1/2 tbsp.	25 mL

Heat first amount of peanut oil in large pot or Dutch oven on medium. Add chicken. Cook for about 3 minutes per side until browned. Remove from pot. Chop. Set aside.

Heat second amount of peanut oil in same pot on medium-low. Add next 4 ingredients. Cook for about 10 minutes, stirring occasionally, until onion is soft.

Add next 4 ingredients. Heat and stir for 1 to 2 minutes until fragrant.

Add coconut milk and salt. Stir. Bring to a gentle boil. Reduce heat to medium-low. Simmer, uncovered, for 5 minutes to blend flavours. Remove from heat. Cool slightly. Process in blender, in 2 batches, until smooth. Return to same pot.

Add chicken and lime juice. Heat and stir for 2 to 3 minutes until hot. Makes about 5 cups (1.25 L). Serves 6.

1 serving: 389 Calories; 33 g Total Fat (3.6 g Mono, 2.1 g Poly, 25.1 g Sat); 41 mg Cholesterol; 8 g Carbohydrate; 1 g Fibre; 19 g Protein; 221 mg Sodium

Pictured on page 111.

Top: Rum Fruit Salad, page 112
Centre Left: Beef And Yam Stew, page 112
Centre Right: Buttered Couscous, page 112
Bottom: Coconut Chicken Soup, above

Beef And Yam Stew

The sweetness of the raisins and yam complements the nutty flavour of peanut butter sauce.

Peanut (or cooking) oil	1 tbsp.	15 mL
Beef stew meat	2 lbs.	900 g
Peanut (or cooking) oil	1 tbsp.	15 mL
Large onion, chopped	1	1
Garlic powder	1 tsp.	5 mL
Ground coriander	2 – 3 tsp.	10 – 15 mL
Chili powder	1/2 – 1 tsp.	2 – 5 mL
Prepared beef broth	2 cups	500 mL
Tomato paste	1/4 cup	60 mL
Cubed yam (or sweet potato), about 1 inch (2.5 cm) pieces	2 cups	500 mL
Raisins	2/3 cup	150 mL
Salt	1/2 tsp.	2 mL
Pepper	1/2 tsp.	2 mL
Smooth peanut butter	1/3 cup	75 mL
Fresh spinach, stems removed	1 1/2 cups	375 mL

Heat first amount of peanut oil in large pot or Dutch oven on medium-high. Add beef. Cook, in 2 to 3 batches, until browned on all sides. Remove from pot.

Heat second amount of peanut oil in same pot on medium. Add onion. Cook for about 10 minutes, stirring occasionally, until soft.

Add garlic powder, coriander and chili powder. Heat and stir for 1 to 2 minutes until fragrant.

Add beef, broth and tomato paste. Stir. Bring to a boil. Reduce heat to low. Cover. Simmer for 1 hour, stirring occasionally.

Add next 4 ingredients. Cover. Simmer for about 45 minutes, stirring occasionally, until beef and yam are tender.

Add peanut butter and spinach. Stir. Heat and stir for 2 to 3 minutes until combined and spinach is wilted. Makes 6 cups (1.5 L). Serves 6.

1 serving: 531 Calories; 25.9 g Total Fat (11.5 g Mono, 4.2 g Poly, 7.8 g Sat); 83 mg Cholesterol; 37 g Carbohydrate; 5 g Fibre; 40 g Protein; 662 mg Sodium

Pictured on page 111.

Buttered Couscous

Bring 4 cups (1 L) prepared chicken (or vegetable) broth and 2 tbsp. (30 mL) butter (or hard margarine) to a boil in large saucepan. Remove from heat. Add 4 cups (1 L) couscous. Cover. Let stand for about 10 minutes until broth is absorbed. Fluff with fork just before serving. Add some toasted slivered almonds. Pictured on page 111.

Rum Fruit Salad

An attractive, colourful fruit salad with a citrus tang and a hint of rum. For those with a sweet tooth, more sugar may be added.

Lime juice	1/3 cup	75 mL
Granulated sugar	1/3 cup	75 mL
Dark rum	1/4 cup	60 mL
Chopped papaya (about 3/4 inch, 2 cm, cubes)	2 cups	500 mL
Chopped fresh (or canned) pineapple	2 cups	500 mL
Large oranges, peeled and separated into segments	4	4
Flake coconut, toasted (see Note)	3 tbsp.	50 mL

Combine lime juice and sugar in small saucepan. Heat and stir on low for about 5 minutes until sugar is dissolved. Bring to a boil on medium-high. Boil, uncovered, for 3 to 5 minutes until slightly thickened.

Add rum. Stir. Cool.

Put papaya, pineapple and orange into large bowl. Add rum mixture. Stir. Chill for 3 hours, stirring occasionally.

Just before serving, sprinkle with coconut. Makes 8 cups (2 L). Serves 6.

1 serving: 188 Calories; 2.3 g Total Fat (0.1 g Mono, 0.1 g Poly, 1.7 g Sat); 0 mg Cholesterol; 38 g Carbohydrate; 2 g Fibre; 2 g Protein; 5 mg Sodium

Pictured on page 111.

Note: To toast coconut, place in single layer in ungreased shallow pan. Bake in 350°F (175°C) oven for 5 to 10 minutes, stirring or shaking often, until desired doneness.

Pistachio Ice Cream

Add some chopped toasted pistachios to softened vanilla ice cream. Mix well. Freeze until firm. Serve scoops of ice cream with Rum Fruit Salad, above.

Asian Night

This imported menu features a nice balance of flavours to please even the most selective appetite. Think about adding some decorations and traditional cutlery and dinnerware to give your evening a touch of the exotic.

serves 6

Miso Soup

Japanese Salad

Pork Fried Noodles

Spicy Fish

Tea Custard

Exotic Fruit Plate

Miso Soup

A delicate broth surrounds thin mushroom slices and crunchy bean sprouts. Makes a light, healthy starter.

Dried shiitake mushrooms	3	3
Boiling water	1 cup	250 mL
Miso (fermented soybean paste)	1/4 cup	60 mL
Sesame (or cooking) oil	2 tsp.	10 mL
Green onions, sliced	3	3
Coarsely shredded carrot	1/4 cup	60 mL
Water	3 cups	750 mL
Firm tofu, diced into 1/2 inch (12 mm) pieces (about 1 cup, 250 mL)	5 oz.	140 g
Fresh bean sprouts (about 1 cup, 250 mL)	3 oz.	85 g
Green onion, sliced	1	1
Sesame seeds, toasted (see Note)	1 1/2 tsp.	7 mL

Soak mushrooms in boiling water in small bowl for 20 minutes. Strain water through sieve lined with paper towel or several thicknesses of cheesecloth, reserving water. Discard paper towel and stems. Slice mushrooms very thinly. Set aside.

Combine reserved water and miso in separate small bowl. Set aside.

Heat sesame oil in medium saucepan on medium. Add first amount of green onion and carrot. Cook for about 2 minutes until soft.

Add water, mushrooms and miso mixture. Bring to a boil.

Add tofu. Reduce heat to medium-low. Cover. Simmer for 3 minutes.

Just before serving, divide and scatter bean sprouts, second amount of green onion and sesame seeds over individual servings. Serves 6.

1 serving: 90 Calories; 4.8 g Total Fat (1.4 g Mono, 2.4 g Poly, 0.7 g Sat); 0 mg Cholesterol; 8 g Carbohydrate; 2 g Fibre; 6 g Protein; 452 mg Sodium

Pictured on page 115.

Note: To toast sesame seeds, place in single layer in ungreased shallow pan. Bake in 350°F (175°C) oven for 5 to 10 minutes, stirring or shaking often, until desired doneness.

Japanese Salad

The creamy dressing, with a hint of sweetness, complements the crisp, cold vegetables.

GINGER DRESSING

Slice of peeled gingerroot, 1/2 inch (12 mm) thick	1	1
Garlic clove, halved (or 1/4 tsp., 1 mL, powder)	1	1
Green onion, cut into 4 pieces	1	1
Baby carrot, halved	1	1
Cooking oil	1/2 cup	125 mL
Rice vinegar	1/3 cup	75 mL
Soy sauce	1 tbsp.	15 mL
Sesame (or cooking) oil (optional)	2 tsp.	10 mL
Dry mustard	1/2 tsp.	2 mL
Cut or torn iceberg lettuce	3 cups	750 mL
Medium roma (plum) tomato, cut into wedges	1	1
English cucumber slices (with peel), cut 1/4 inch (6 mm) thick on diagonal and halved	6	6
Long carrot shreds	1/4 cup	60 mL
Medium radish, thinly sliced	1	1

Ginger Dressing: Process first 9 ingredients in blender for about 1 minute, scraping down sides if necessary, until smooth. Pour into jar or container. Cover. Chill for at least 1 hour to blend flavours. Makes about 1 cup (250 mL) dressing.

Combine remaining 5 ingredients in large salad bowl. Drizzle dressing over top. Serves 6.

1 serving: 189 Calories; 19.4 g Total Fat (11.4 g Mono, 5.8 g Poly, 1.4 g Sat); 0 mg Cholesterol; 4 g Carbohydrate; 1 g Fibre; 1 g Protein; 182 mg Sodium

Pictured on page 115.

Top: Japanese Salad, above
Centre Left: Pork Fried Noodles, page 116
Centre Right: Miso Soup, page 113
Bottom: Spicy Fish, page 116

Pork Fried Noodles

A very attractive dish with an Indonesian influence. The sauce is slightly sweet and goes well with the flavours of the other ingredients.

Packages of instant noodles (3 oz., 85 g, each), flavour packets discarded	2	2
Boiling water	4 cups	1 L
Cooking oil	2 tbsp.	30 mL
Garlic cloves, pressed flat	2	2
Boneless pork loin chops, thinly sliced	1/2 lb.	225 g
Indonesian sweet (or thick) soy sauce	2 tbsp.	30 mL
Medium red onion, cut into 8 wedges	1	1
Bunch of baby bok choy, chopped into 1/2 inch (12 mm) pieces	1	1
Water	1/2 cup	125 mL
Indonesian sweet (or thick) soy sauce	3 tbsp.	50 mL
Cornstarch	1 tbsp.	15 mL
Coarsely chopped cashews	1/4 cup	60 mL

Cook noodles in boiling water in large saucepan for 3 minutes, stirring occasionally. Drain immediately. Keep warm.

Heat cooking oil in wok or large frying pan on medium-high. Add garlic. Stir-fry for about 2 minutes until fragrant. Discard garlic.

Add pork. Stir-fry for 2 minutes. Add first amount of soy sauce. Stir. Add red onion and bok choy. Stir-fry for 2 minutes.

Stir water and second amount of soy sauce into cornstarch in small bowl until smooth. Add to pork mixture. Heat and stir until boiling and thickened.

Transfer noodles to serving plate. Spoon pork mixture over top. Sprinkle cashews over top. Makes 5 1/2 cups (1.4 L). Serves 6.

1 serving: 255 Calories; 10.2 g Total Fat (5.4 g Mono, 2.3 g Poly, 1.7 g Sat); 48 mg Cholesterol; 26 g Carbohydrate; 1 g Fibre; 15 g Protein; 859 mg Sodium

Pictured on page 114.

Spicy Fish

Traditionally in Thailand, a fish is sliced in several places with a sharp knife and the slits are packed with lots of chilies and garlic. We've "Canadianized" this recipe by using more available fish fillets and by cutting down on the chilies and garlic.

Garlic cloves, minced (or 3/4 tsp., 4 mL, powder)	3	3
Small hot chili peppers, seeds removed (see Note)	3	3
Brown sugar, packed	1 tbsp.	15 mL
Finely grated lime zest	3/4 tsp.	4 mL
Fish sauce	1/4 cup	60 mL
Firm fish fillets (or steaks), about 1 1/2 lbs. (680 g)	6	6
Sliced green onion	1/3 cup	75 mL
Prepared chicken broth	3/4 cup	175 mL
Lime juice	3 tbsp.	50 mL
Chopped fresh cilantro (or fresh parsley), optional	1 tbsp.	15 mL

Process first 5 ingredients in blender until smooth.

Brush fillets with 1/2 of garlic mixture. Set in large bamboo steamer or on rack over rapidly boiling water in wok or Dutch oven. Sprinkle with green onion. Cover. Steam for 4 to 8 minutes until fish flakes easily when tested with fork. Remove to serving plate. Keep warm.

Combine remaining garlic mixture and broth in small saucepan. Bring to a boil on medium. Boil, uncovered, for about 5 minutes until sauce is slightly reduced.

Stir in lime juice and cilantro. Makes 1/2 cup (125 mL) sauce. Drizzle over fish. Serves 6.

1 serving: 162 Calories; 2.9 g Total Fat (0.9 g Mono, 1 g Poly, 0.4 g Sat); 36 mg Cholesterol; 7 g Carbohydrate; 1 g Fibre; 26 g Protein; 899 mg Sodium

Pictured on page 114/115.

Note: Wear gloves when chopping chili peppers and avoid touching your eyes.

Tea Custard

This very different, Japanese-influenced custard has a light, smooth texture and a very pleasant tea flavour. Makes a nice, light finish to a stimulating meal.

Large eggs	3	3
Granulated sugar	1/4 cup	60 mL
Skim milk powder	2/3 cup	150 mL
Salt	1/4 tsp.	1 mL
Vanilla	1/2 tsp.	2 mL
Boiling water	1 3/4 cups	425 mL
Orange pekoe tea bag	1	1
Whipped topping, for garnish	2 cups	500 mL
Fresh fruit, for garnish		

Beat eggs and sugar in medium bowl until frothy. Add skim milk powder, salt and vanilla. Beat until mixed.

Pour boiling water over tea bag in 2 cup (500 mL) liquid measure. Press bag with teaspoon for about 6 seconds until water colour is medium brown. Squeeze bag while removing. Beat tea into egg mixture on low speed. Turn into ungreased custard cups or ovenproof Asian tea cups. Set in pan or small roaster. Pour enough hot water into pan to come 1 inch (2.5 cm) up side of custard cups. Bake, uncovered, in 325°F (160°C) oven for about 1 hour until knife inserted halfway between centre and edge of custard comes out clean. Cool. Chill.

Just before serving, garnish with whipped topping and fruit. Serves 6.

1 serving: 198 Calories; 6.1 g Total Fat (1.2 g Mono, 0.4 g Poly, 3.9 g Sat); 113 mg Cholesterol; 22 g Carbohydrate; 0 g Fibre; 9 g Protein; 227 mg Sodium

Pictured below.

Exotic Fruit Plate

Arrange attractively sliced fresh fruit on a small platter. Some suggestions are: star fruit, kiwifruit, cherries, oranges, raspberries, red currants and apples. Serve with Tea Custard, this page. Pictured below.

Top Left: Exotic Fruit Plate, this page

Bottom: Tea Custard, this page

Casual Dinner Party

Don't worry about the jeans or faded T-shirt—this party group will have nothing more serious on their minds than to relax, which is the perfect setting for this casual dinner menu.

serves 8

Crunchy Sweet Salad

Chicken In Wine Sauce

Honey Yams And Potatoes

Yellow Beans And Snap Peas

Lime Poppy Seed Cake

Juicy Berries

Crunchy Sweet Salad

The sweet vinaigrette complements the slightly bitter greens. Serve with crusty rolls.

Small heads of butter lettuce, cut or torn	3	3
Small head of radicchio, cut or torn	1	1
Thinly sliced radish	1/4 cup	60 mL
Thinly sliced red, orange or yellow pepper	1/4 cup	60 mL
Paper-thin sliced onion	1/4 cup	60 mL
Bacon slices, cooked crisp and broken into about 4 pieces each	8	8
SWEET APPLE VINAIGRETTE		
Apple jelly	1/3 cup	75 mL
Olive (or cooking) oil	3 tbsp.	50 mL
Apple cider vinegar	3 tbsp.	50 mL
Dry mustard	1/2 tsp.	2 mL
Salt	1/4 tsp.	1 mL
Pepper, sprinkle		

Combine first 6 ingredients in large salad bowl. Toss. Chill until ready to serve.

Sweet Apple Vinaigrette: Microwave jelly in small microwave-safe bowl on medium (50%) for about 1 minute until warm. (Or warm in small saucepan on low.)

Put next 5 ingredients into blender. Add jelly. Process for about 30 seconds until smooth. Chill. Makes about 1/2 cup (125 mL) vinaigrette. Just before serving, drizzle over lettuce mixture. Toss. Serves 8.

1 serving: 147 Calories; 8.8 g Total Fat (5.4 g Mono, 1 g Poly, 1.9 g Sat); 5 mg Cholesterol; 15 g Carbohydrate; 2 g Fibre; 5 g Protein; 195 mg Sodium

Pictured on page 119.

Chicken In Wine Sauce

Colourful herbs and vegetables in a delicate wine sauce.

Olive (or cooking) oil	1 tbsp.	15 mL
Boneless, skinless chicken breast halves (about 2 lbs., 900 g)	8	8
Olive (or cooking) oil	1 tbsp.	15 mL
Green onion, sliced	1	1
Sliced fresh button mushrooms	1 cup	250 mL
Garlic clove, minced (or 1/4 tsp., 1 mL, powder), optional	1	1
Dry white (or alcohol-free) wine	1 cup	250 mL
Fresh sweet basil, cut chiffonade (see Note) or 3/4 tsp. (4 mL) dried	1 tbsp.	15 mL
Chopped fresh rosemary (or 1/4 tsp., 1 mL, dried)	1 tsp.	5 mL
Chopped firm tomato, seeds removed	1 cup	250 mL
Salt	1/2 tsp.	2 mL
Granulated sugar	1/4 tsp.	1 mL
Water	3 tbsp.	50 mL
Cornstarch	3 tbsp.	50 mL

Heat first amount of olive oil in large frying pan on medium. Add chicken. Cook until browned on both sides. Turn into ungreased 2 quart (2 L) casserole. Cover to keep warm.

Heat second amount of olive oil in same frying pan. Add next 3 ingredients. Cook for 3 to 5 minutes until green onion is soft.

Stir in wine. Bring to a rapid boil. Reduce heat to medium. Boil, uncovered, for 10 to 15 minutes until slightly reduced.

Add next 5 ingredients. Stir. Pour over chicken. Cover. Bake in 350°F (175°C) oven for about 45 minutes until chicken is no longer pink inside. Remove chicken to serving platter. Keep warm. Strain liquid into small saucepan, reserving solids.

Stir water into cornstarch in small cup until smooth. Add to tomato liquid. Heat and stir on medium until boiling and thickened. Add reserved solids. Stir. Pour over chicken. Serves 8.

1 serving: 196 Calories; 5.5 g Total Fat (3 g Mono, 0.8 g Poly, 1 g Sat); 66 mg Cholesterol; 5 g Carbohydrate; trace Fibre; 26 g Protein; 152 mg Sodium

Pictured on page 120 and on page 121.

Note: To cut chiffonade, stack a few basil leaves at a time and roll up tightly. Slice crosswise into very thin strips.

Crunchy Sweet Salad, page 118

Honey Yams And Potatoes

Tender vegetables coated in a sweet glaze.

Hard margarine (or butter)	3 tbsp.	50 mL
Liquid honey	2 tbsp.	30 mL
Dijon mustard	1 tbsp.	15 mL
Salt	1/4 tsp.	1 mL
Pepper, heavy sprinkle		
Large yams (or sweet potatoes), peeled and cubed	1 1/2 lbs.	680 g
Red baby potatoes (with peel), halved	1 1/2 lbs.	680 g
Finely chopped onion	1/2 cup	125 mL
Finely chopped garlic (or 1 1/2 tsp., 7 mL, powder), optional	2 tbsp.	30 mL
Sesame seeds, toasted (see Note)		

Heat first 5 ingredients in small saucepan until bubbling.

Put next 4 ingredients into large bowl. Drizzle with margarine mixture. Toss until well coated. Arrange in single layer on greased 11 × 17 inch (28 × 43 cm) baking sheet with sides. Bake in 375°F (190°C) oven for about 45 minutes, stirring occasionally, until yams and potatoes are tender and lightly browned.

Sprinkle with sesame seeds. Makes 8 cups (2 L). Serves 8.

1 serving: 210 Calories; 4.7 g Total Fat (2.9 g Mono, 0.6 g Poly, 1 g Sat); 0 mg Cholesterol; 40 g Carbohydrate; 5 g Fibre; 3 g Protein; 164 mg Sodium

Pictured on page 121.

Note: To toast sesame seeds, place in single layer in ungreased shallow pan. Bake in 350°F (175°C) oven for 5 to 10 minutes, stirring or shaking often, until desired doneness.

Yellow Beans And Snap Peas

Light-tasting vegetables with a hint of dill.

DILL BUTTER SAUCE

Butter (not margarine)	3 tbsp.	50 mL
Lemon juice	2 tsp.	10 mL
Finely chopped fresh dill (or 3/4 tsp., 4 mL, dill weed)	1 tbsp.	15 mL
Fresh (or frozen, thawed) yellow wax beans	3 cups	750 mL
Boiling water	1 cup	250 mL
Whole sugar snap peas	8 oz.	225 g

Dill Butter Sauce: Melt butter in small saucepan. Simmer, uncovered, on medium for about 3 minutes until butter starts to darken. Remove from heat.

Stir in lemon juice and dill. Makes about 1/4 cup (60 mL) sauce.

Add beans to boiling water in large saucepan. Cover. Cook on medium for 2 minutes. Add peas. Cover. Cook for about 6 minutes until vegetables are tender-crisp. Drain well. Pour sauce over bean mixture. Toss lightly. Makes 4 1/2 cups (1.1 L). Serves 8.

1 serving: 64 Calories; 4.5 g Total Fat (1.3 g Mono, 0.2 g Poly, 2.8 g Sat); 12 mg Cholesterol; 5 g Carbohydrate; 1 g Fibre; 2 g Protein; 48 mg Sodium

Pictured on page 121.

1. Chicken In Wine Sauce, page 119
2. Yellow Beans And Snap Peas, above
3. Honey Yams And Potatoes, page 119

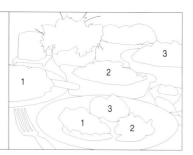

Lime Poppy Seed Cake

Very pretty, moist cake with a tangy lime bite. Serve with Juicy Berries, this page, in the centre for a pretty presentation.

Milk	1 cup	250 mL
Poppy seeds	3 tbsp.	50 mL
Egg whites (large), room temperature	3	3
Almond flavouring	1 tsp.	5 mL
Hard margarine (or butter), softened	1 cup	250 mL
Granulated sugar	1 1/4 cups	300 mL
Egg yolks (large)	3	3
Finely grated lime zest	1 tbsp.	15 mL
All-purpose flour	2 cups	500 mL
Baking powder	1 tbsp.	15 mL
Salt	1/2 tsp.	2 mL
LIME SYRUP		
Hot water	2 tbsp.	30 mL
Icing (confectioner's) sugar	3/4 cup	175 mL
Lime juice	6 tbsp.	100 mL

Heat and stir milk and poppy seeds in small saucepan on medium until very hot, but not boiling. Remove from heat. Cool to room temperature.

Beat egg whites and flavouring in medium bowl until stiff peaks form. Set aside.

With same beaters, cream margarine in large bowl. Gradually add granulated sugar, beating until light and fluffy. Beat in egg yolks, lime zest and milk mixture until combined.

Add flour, baking powder and salt. Beat well. Fold egg white mixture into batter until no streaks remain. Turn into greased and floured 10 inch (25 cm) angel food tube pan or springform pan. Bake in 325°F (160°C) oven for about 1 hour until wooden pick inserted in centre of cake comes out clean. Let stand in pan for 10 minutes before removing to serving plate.

Lime Syrup: Stir hot water and icing sugar in cup until smooth. Stir in lime juice. Remove cake to serving plate. Slowly spoon syrup over hot cake, allowing syrup to soak in. Cool. Cuts into 12 wedges.

1 wedge: 382 Calories; 18.9 g Total Fat (5.4 g Mono, 1.6 g Poly, 10.8 g Sat); 98 mg Cholesterol; 50 g Carbohydrate; 1 g Fibre; 5 g Protein; 385 mg Sodium

Pictured on this page.

Lime Poppy Seed Cake, above   Juicy Berries, this page

Juicy Berries

Combine 2 cups (500 mL) whole fresh berries (such as blackberries, blueberries, raspberries) and sliced strawberries in medium bowl. Add 1 cup (250 mL) white grape juice and 1/2 cup (125 mL) white corn syrup. Stir gently until well combined. Let stand in refrigerator for at least 1 hour to blend flavours. Pile into centre of Lime Poppy Seed Cake, this page. Pictured on this page.

Variation: A slightly more expensive, but quite delightful, alternative is to use ice wine instead of white grape juice and corn syrup. Use 1 or 2 small bottles of ice wine and 1 1/2 to 3 cups (375 to 750 mL) berries.

Curry Night

Put a little spice in your life—a little curry spice, that is. This featured flavour of many countries continues to gain more popularity here at home. Show off your international culinary style with this impressive menu.

serves 8

Creamy Tomato Dahl

Cauliflower And Potato Curry

Condiments

Fish Molee

Pappadums And Naan Bread

Rice

Butter Chicken

Peach Lassi

Creamy Tomato Dahl

Your guests will love this creamy, golden yellow dish with just the right amount of spice. Enjoy the well-blended flavours of curry, cinnamon and chili.

Yellow split peas, rinsed	1 cup	250 mL
Boiling water		
Cooking oil	1 tbsp.	15 mL
Finely chopped onion	1 cup	250 mL
Garlic cloves, minced (or 1/2 tsp., 2 mL, powder)	2	2
Finely grated peeled gingerroot	2 tsp.	10 mL
Curry powder	1 tbsp.	15 mL
Chili powder	1 tsp.	5 mL
Cinnamon stick (4 inch, 10 cm, length)	1	1
Can of diced tomatoes (with juice)	28 oz.	796 mL
Prepared vegetable (or chicken) broth	2 cups	500 mL
Brown sugar, packed	1 1/2 tsp.	7 mL
Dried red lentils, rinsed	1 cup	250 mL
Whipping cream (or whole milk)	1/2 cup	125 mL
Coarsely ground pepper (or 1/4 tsp., 1 mL, pepper)	1/2 tsp.	2 mL
Chopped fresh cilantro (or fresh parsley)	1 tbsp.	15 mL
Salt	1 1/2 tsp.	7 mL

Cover split peas with boiling water in medium bowl. Let stand for 50 minutes. Drain.

Heat cooking oil in large pot or Dutch oven on medium-low. Add onion, garlic and ginger. Cook for about 10 minutes, stirring occasionally, until onion is soft.

Add curry powder, chili powder and cinnamon stick. Heat and stir for 1 to 2 minutes until fragrant.

Add split peas and next 3 ingredients. Stir. Bring to a boil on medium. Reduce heat to medium-low. Cover. Simmer for 1 hour.

Add lentils. Simmer for 30 to 40 minutes until lentils and split peas are tender.

Add remaining 4 ingredients. Heat and stir on medium for 3 to 5 minutes until hot. Remove and discard cinnamon stick. Makes 8 cups (2 L). Serves 8.

1 serving: 285 Calories; 8.2 g Total Fat (2.8 g Mono, 1.1 g Poly, 3.5 g Sat); 18 mg Cholesterol; 39 g Carbohydrate; 6 g Fibre; 17 g Protein; 832 mg Sodium

Pictured on page 125.

Cauliflower And Potato Curry

This mild dish is perfect for those who prefer less spicy foods.

Cooking oil	2 tbsp.	30 mL
Medium onion, cut in half and sliced	1	1
Garlic cloves, minced (or 1/2 tsp., 2 mL, powder)	2	2
Paprika	2 tsp.	10 mL
Ground cumin	1 tsp.	5 mL
Ground coriander	1 tsp.	5 mL
Chili powder	1/2 – 1 tsp.	2 – 5 mL
Whole green cardamom, bruised (see Note)	6	6
Whole cloves	4	4
Medium potatoes, peeled and cut into 1 1/2 inch (3.8 cm) pieces	3	3
Cauliflower florets	2 1/2 cups	625 mL
Can of coconut milk	14 oz.	398 mL
Prepared chicken (or vegetable) broth	1 cup	250 mL
Salt	1 1/2 tsp.	7 mL
Frozen peas	1 cup	250 mL

Heat cooking oil in large pot or Dutch oven on medium-low. Add onion and garlic. Cook for about 15 minutes, stirring occasionally, until onion is soft.

Add next 6 ingredients. Stir. Cook for 1 to 2 minutes until fragrant.

Add next 5 ingredients. Stir. Bring to a boil on medium-high. Reduce heat to medium. Cover. Boil gently for about 15 minutes until potato and cauliflower are tender-crisp.

Stir in peas. Heat for about 2 minutes, stirring occasionally, until peas are hot. Remove and discard cardamom and cloves. Makes 8 cups (2 L). Serves 8.

1 serving: 204 Calories; 14.2 g Total Fat (2.6 g Mono, 1.3 g Poly, 9.3 g Sat); 0 mg Cholesterol; 17 g Carbohydrate; 3 g Fibre; 5 g Protein; 592 mg Sodium

Pictured on page 125.

Note: To bruise cardamom, hit with mallet or flat side of wide knife to "bruise" or crack open slightly.

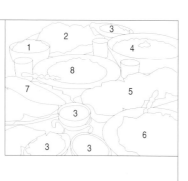

Condiments

East Indian food is often served with condiments and chutneys that help cool the palate. Include one of the following with this menu:

- Sliced banana tossed in medium or shredded coconut.

- Chopped red onion and tomato combined in a small bowl.

- Mix plain yogurt, finely chopped seeded cucumber and finely chopped mint together.

- Mango chutney spooned into small flat bowls makes a sweet and tangy addition to any curry. You might prefer a plain mango chutney or, perhaps, a hot chutney.

Pictured on page 124 and on page 125.

Fish Molee

Delicious rolled snapper fillets served in a vibrant yellow, delicately flavoured sauce.

Cooking oil	1 tbsp.	15 mL
Finely chopped onion	1 cup	250 mL
Garlic cloves, minced (or 1/2 tsp., 2 mL, powder)	2	2
Finely grated peeled gingerroot	1/2 tsp.	2 mL
Ground turmeric	1 tsp.	5 mL
Ground coriander	1 tsp.	5 mL
Ground cumin	1/2 tsp.	2 mL
Whole green cardamom, bruised (see Note)	4	4
Cinnamon stick (4 inch, 10 cm, length)	1	1
Cans of coconut milk (14 oz., 398 mL, each)	2	2
Salt	1 tsp.	5 mL
Snapper fillets (about 4 oz., 113 g, each)	8	8

Heat cooking oil in large saucepan on medium-low. Add onion, garlic and ginger. Cook for about 10 minutes, stirring occasionally, until onion is soft.

Add next 5 ingredients. Heat and stir for 1 to 2 minutes until fragrant.

Add coconut milk and salt. Stir. Simmer, uncovered, for about 20 minutes until sauce is slightly thickened. Remove and discard cardamom and cinnamon stick.

Roll up each fillet, jelly roll-style. Place, seam-side down, in single layer, in coconut milk mixture. Cover. Simmer for about 10 minutes until fish flakes easily when tested with fork. Do not overcook. Serves 8.

1 serving: 332 Calories; 23.7 g Total Fat (2.2 g Mono, 1.3 g Poly, 18.4 g Sat); 44 mg Cholesterol; 5 g Carbohydrate; trace Fibre; 26 g Protein; 386 mg Sodium

Pictured on page 125.

Note: To bruise cardamom, hit with mallet or flat side of wide knife to "bruise" or crack open slightly.

Pappadums And Naan Bread

- Pappadums are made from chickpea flour and are available in Asian section of grocery stores and East Indian spice stores. There are several different flavours. Brush with cooking oil and microwave on high (100%) for about 1 minute until puffed or deep-fry in hot (375°F, 190°C) cooking oil. Read instructions on package. They are perfect for scooping up delicious curries. Pictured on page 124/125.

- You can buy naan bread in bread section of grocery stores or you can make your own. To reheat naan bread, wrap in foil and place in 350°F (175°C) oven for 5 to 10 minutes until hot. Pictured on page 124.

Rice

Serve regular long grain rice with curries, but try basmati rice for a more authentic flavour. Pictured on page 124.

Butter Chicken

Tender chicken in a rich, smooth sauce. Delicious!

Plain yogurt	2/3 cup	150 mL
Tomato paste	1/4 cup	60 mL
Ground coriander	1 1/2 tsp.	7 mL
Garam masala (available in Asian section of grocery store)	1 1/2 tsp.	7 mL
Ground ginger	1 tsp.	5 mL
Paprika	1 tsp.	5 mL
Granulated sugar	1 tsp.	5 mL
Chili powder	1/2 tsp.	2 mL
Garlic cloves, minced (or 1 tsp., 5 mL, powder)	4	4
Boneless, skinless chicken thighs, cut in half	12	12
Butter (or hard margarine)	1/4 cup	60 mL
Finely chopped onion	1 1/2 cups	375 mL
Tomato sauce	1 cup	250 mL
Prepared chicken broth	1 cup	250 mL
Whole green cardamom, bruised (see Note)	6	6
Cinnamon stick (4 inch, 10 cm, length)	1	1
Salt	1/2 – 1 tsp.	2 – 5 mL
Whipping cream (or whole milk)	1 cup	250 mL

Combine first 9 ingredients in large bowl.

Add chicken. Stir until coated. Cover. Marinate in refrigerator for at least 6 hours or overnight, stirring occasionally.

Melt butter in large deep frying pan or Dutch oven on medium-low. Add onion. Cook for about 10 minutes, stirring occasionally, until onion is soft.

Add chicken with marinade and next 5 ingredients. Stir. Cover. Simmer for 10 minutes. Remove and discard cardamom and cinnamon stick.

Add whipping cream. Stir. Simmer, uncovered, for 15 minutes. Boil gently on medium for 30 minutes, stirring occasionally, until chicken is tender and sauce is thickened. Makes 6 cups (1.5 L). Serves 8.

1 serving: 327 Calories; 22.2 g Total Fat (6.6 g Mono, 1.9 g Poly, 11.7 g Sat); 132 mg Cholesterol; 11 g Carbohydrate; 1 g Fibre; 22 g Protein; 545 mg Sodium

Pictured on page 124/125.

Note: To bruise cardamom, hit with mallet or flat side of wide knife to "bruise" or crack open slightly.

Peach Lassi

The perfect palate-cleansing drink to serve with spicy curry dishes.

Plain yogurt	2 1/2 cups	625 mL
Milk	1 cup	250 mL
Ice water	1 cup	250 mL
Cans of sliced peaches in pear juice (14 oz., 398 mL, each)	2	2
Granulated sugar	1/4 – 1/3 cup	60 – 75 mL
Ice cubes	12	12
Ground cinnamon	1/4 tsp.	1 mL
Ground cardamom	1/4 tsp.	1 mL

Process all 8 ingredients in blender, in 2 batches, until smooth. Transfer to punch bowl. Makes about 11 cups (2.75 L). Serves 8.

1 serving: 137 Calories; 1.6 g Total Fat (0.5 g Mono, 0.1 g Poly, 1 g Sat); 6 mg Cholesterol; 26 g Carbohydrate; 1 g Fibre; 6 g Protein; 77 mg Sodium

Pictured below.

Peach Lassi, above

Mexican Fiesta

The weekend was made for fun, and that's exactly what you'll find inside this selection of spicy food from our friends to the South. The colourful, energetic styles of Mexico will turn your party into a real fiesta!

serves 6

Pineapple And Lime Margaritas

Guacamole And Tortilla Chips

Creamy Corn Salad

Fiery Grilled Chicken

Seafood Enchiladas

Confetti Rice

Tropical Trifle

Pineapple And Lime Margaritas

A refreshing, citrusy beverage. Adjust the amount of alcohol to suit your taste.

Coarse sea (or regular) salt	2 tbsp.	30 mL
Lime wedges	1 – 2	1 – 2
Pineapple juice	4 cups	1 L
Lime juice	1 cup	250 mL
Gold tequila	2/3 cup	150 mL
Orange-flavoured liqueur (such as Grand Marnier)	1/3 cup	75 mL
Ice cubes	18	18
Lime wedges, for garnish		

Measure salt into small shallow dish. Run first amount of lime wedges around rims of 6 margarita glasses. Press rims into salt.

Combine next 4 ingredients in large pitcher. Divide among prepared glasses.

Add 3 ice cubes to each glass.

Garnish with second amount of lime wedges. Makes 6 cups (1.5 L). Serves 6.

1 serving: 229 Calories; 0.2 g Total Fat (trace Mono, 0.1 g Poly, trace Sat); 0 mg Cholesterol; 35 g Carbohydrate; trace Fibre; 1 g Protein; 2360 mg Sodium

Pictured on page 129.

Guacamole And Tortilla Chips

Mash ripe avocado with small amount of sour cream, lemon juice, garlic, hot pepper sauce, salt and pepper. Add some finely chopped red onion and tomato. Serve with warmed colourful tortilla chips, such as red, white and green to honour the Mexican national colours. Pictured on page 129.

Left: Pineapple And Lime Margaritas, above
Right: Guacamole And Tortilla Chips, above

Creamy Corn Salad

A wonderful combination of spices and textures. This vibrant salad really brightens this menu!

Can of kernel corn, drained	12 oz.	341 mL
Can of black beans, rinsed and drained	14 oz.	398 mL
Finely chopped red onion	1/2 cup	125 mL
Finely chopped red pepper	1/2 cup	125 mL
Medium tomatoes, quartered, seeded and finely chopped	2	2
Chopped fresh cilantro (or fresh parsley), optional	2 tbsp.	30 mL
Salt	1/4 tsp.	1 mL

SPICY RANCH DRESSING		
Ranch-style dressing	1/4 cup	60 mL
Lime juice	1 tbsp.	15 mL
Ground cumin	1/4 tsp.	1 mL
Chili powder	1/4 tsp.	1 mL
Garlic clove, minced (or 1/4 tsp., 1 mL, powder)	1	1

Combine first 7 ingredients in large bowl.

Spicy Ranch Dressing: Combine all 5 ingredients in small bowl. Stir until well combined. Makes 2/3 cup (150 mL) dressing. Drizzle over corn mixture. Toss well. Makes about 4 cups (1 L). Serves 6.

1 serving: 155 Calories; 4.6 g Total Fat (2.3 g Mono, 1.6 g Poly, 0.4 g Sat); 3 mg Cholesterol; 25 g Carbohydrate; 4 g Fibre; 6 g Protein; 411 mg Sodium

Pictured on page 131.

Fiery Grilled Chicken

The dark, spicy coating adds a lot of pizzazz. This will put everyone in the mood for a Mexican fiesta!

Lime juice	2 tbsp.	30 mL
Cocoa, sifted if lumpy	1 1/2 tbsp.	25 mL
Fresh (or pickled) jalapeño pepper, chopped (see Note)	1 1/2 tbsp.	25 mL
Cooking oil	1 tbsp.	15 mL
Ground cumin	2 tsp.	10 mL
Dried crushed chilies	1 tsp.	5 mL
Granulated sugar	1 tsp.	5 mL
Ground cinnamon	3/4 tsp.	4 mL
Salt	3/4 tsp.	4 mL
Boneless, skinless chicken breast halves (about 1 1/2 lbs., 680 g)	6	6

Process first 9 ingredients in blender until smooth. Turn into large bowl or resealable freezer bag.

Add chicken. Turn until coated. Cover or seal. Marinate in refrigerator for at least 3 hours or overnight, turning several times. Preheat gas barbecue to medium. Cook chicken on greased grill for about 8 minutes per side until no longer pink inside. Serves 6.

1 serving: 158 Calories; 4.6 g Total Fat (1.9 g Mono, 1.1 g Poly, 0.8 g Sat); 66 mg Cholesterol; 3 g Carbohydrate; 1 g Fibre; 26 g Protein; 303 mg Sodium

Pictured on page 131.

Note: Wear gloves when chopping jalapeño peppers and avoid touching your eyes.

Seafood Enchiladas

These soft, creamy tortillas are stuffed with seafood, cheese and spices and topped with a dollop of salsa. Garnish with chopped tomatoes or avocados for a lively twist.

Fresh (or frozen, thawed) scallops	1 lb.	454 g
Fresh (or frozen, thawed) raw medium shrimp, peeled and deveined	3/4 lb.	340 g
Water	1 cup	250 mL
Can of crabmeat, drained, cartilage removed and flaked	4 1/4 oz.	120 g
Block of cream cheese, softened	8 oz.	250 g
Sour cream	1/2 cup	125 mL
Garlic clove, minced (or 1/4 tsp., 1 mL, powder)	1	1
Ground cumin	1/2 tsp.	2 mL
Chopped fresh cilantro (or fresh parsley), optional	2 tbsp.	30 mL
Salt	1/4 tsp.	1 mL
Pepper	1/4 tsp.	1 mL
Chopped yellow pepper	2/3 cup	150 mL
Sliced green onion	2/3 cup	150 mL
Large flour tortillas (10 inch, 25 cm, diameter)	6	6
Mild salsa	2 cups	500 mL
Grated Monterey Jack cheese	1 cup	250 mL
Grated medium Cheddar cheese	1 cup	250 mL

Combine scallops, shrimp and water in medium saucepan. Bring to a boil on medium. Reduce heat to medium-low. Cover. Simmer for about 2 minutes until scallops are opaque and slightly firm and shrimp are pink. Do not overcook. Drain. Chop. Turn into large bowl.

Add next 10 ingredients. Stir until thoroughly combined.

Divide and spread seafood mixture down centre of each tortilla. Fold to enclose filling. Arrange tortillas, seam-side down, in greased 3 quart (3 L) casserole.

Pour salsa over tortillas. Bake, uncovered, in 375°F (190°C) oven for about 20 minutes until heated through.

Sprinkle with Monterey Jack cheese and Cheddar cheese. Bake for 3 to 5 minutes until cheese is melted. Makes 6 enchiladas.

1 enchilada: 825 Calories; 39.1 g Total Fat (11.6 g Mono, 4.5 g Poly, 20.3 g Sat); 203 mg Cholesterol; 67 g Carbohydrate; 5 g Fibre; 51 g Protein; 1514 mg Sodium

Pictured on page 131.

Confetti Rice

The bright colours of the peppers add a festive flair to this sweet rice. The flavour of cumin is a nice complement to many Mexican dishes.

Hard margarine (or butter)	1 tbsp.	15 mL
Medium onion, chopped	1	1
Garlic cloves, minced (or 1/2 tsp., 2 mL, powder)	2	2
Long grain white rice, uncooked	1 cup	250 mL
Ground cumin	1/4 tsp.	1 mL
Chili powder	1/4 tsp.	1 mL
Salt	1/4 tsp.	1 mL
Vegetable bouillon powder	1 tbsp.	15 mL
Water	2 cups	500 mL
Finely chopped red pepper	1/4 cup	60 mL
Finely chopped yellow pepper	1/4 cup	60 mL
Finely chopped green onion	1/4 cup	60 mL

Melt margarine in large saucepan on medium-high. Add onion and garlic. Cook for about 3 minutes, stirring often, until onion is soft.

Add next 4 ingredients. Heat and stir for about 1 minute until rice is coated.

Add bouillon powder and water. Stir. Bring to a boil. Reduce heat to medium-low. Cover. Simmer for about 15 minutes until liquid is absorbed and rice is tender. Remove from heat.

Add both peppers and green onion. Stir until just combined. Cover. Let stand for 5 minutes. Makes 4 cups (1 L). Serves 6.

1 serving: 155 Calories; 2.4 g Total Fat (1.4 g Mono, 0.3 g Poly, 0.5 g Sat); trace Cholesterol; 30 g Carbohydrate; 1 g Fibre; 3 g Protein; 423 mg Sodium

Pictured on page 131.

Top Left: Seafood Enchiladas, this page
Centre Right: Creamy Corn Salad, page 129
Bottom Left: Fiery Grilled Chicken, page 129
Bottom Right: Confetti Rice, above

Tropical Trifle

This fresh, fruity trifle contains beautiful layers of cake, custard, caramel and fruit. Yum!

CUSTARD

Custard powder	1/4 cup	60 mL
Granulated sugar	1/4 cup	60 mL
Milk	2 cups	500 mL
Finely grated orange zest	1 tsp.	5 mL

CARAMEL SAUCE

Hard margarine (or butter), cut up	1/2 cup	125 mL
Whipping cream (or whole milk)	1/2 cup	125 mL
Brown sugar, packed	1/2 cup	125 mL
Lime cordial	1/4 cup	60 mL
Pineapple juice	1/2 cup	125 mL
Tequila	1/4 cup	60 mL
Frozen pound cakes (10 1/2 oz., 298 g, each), thawed and cut into 1/2 inch (12 mm) pieces	2	2
Fresh strawberries, halved lengthwise	9 oz.	255 g
Kiwifruit, peeled and sliced	4	4
Can of mandarin orange segments, drained	10 oz.	284 mL

Tropical Trifle, above

Custard: Combine custard powder and granulated sugar in medium saucepan. Stir in milk. Add orange zest. Heat and stir on medium until custard is just boiling and thickened. Pour into medium bowl. Cover. Chill for about 1 hour, stirring occasionally, until custard is slightly cooled. Makes about 2 cups (500 mL) custard.

Caramel Sauce: Combine margarine, whipping cream and brown sugar in separate medium saucepan. Heat and stir on medium for about 5 minutes until margarine is melted. Bring to a boil. Boil gently, uncovered, for about 5 minutes, without stirring, until slightly thickened. Put into separate medium bowl. Cover. Chill for about 1 hour, stirring occasionally, until sauce is slightly cooled. Makes about 1 1/3 cups (325 mL) sauce.

Combine lime cordial, pineapple juice and tequila in medium shallow dish.

Layer 10 cup (2.5 L) glass trifle bowl as follows:

1. 1/3 of cake dipped into 1/3 of cordial mixture.
2. Stand all of strawberries up around edge, cut side facing out.
3. 1/2 of custard.
4. 1/2 of remaining cake dipped into 1/2 of remaining cordial mixture.
5. All of caramel sauce.
6. All of kiwifruit slices, cut side facing out.
7. Remaining cake dipped into remaining cordial mixture.
8. Remaining custard.
9. All of mandarin orange segments. Chill for at least 8 hours or overnight. Makes 10 cups (2.5 L). Serves 6.

1 serving: 814 Calories; 26.1 g Total Fat (13.2 g Mono, 2.5 g Poly, 8.6 g Sat); 58 mg Cholesterol; 125 g Carbohydrate; 4 g Fibre; 11 g Protein; 655 mg Sodium

Pictured on this page.

Romantic Dinner

Show the love of your life true devotion with this thoughtful selection of intimate recipes, perfectly proportioned for two.

serves 2

Creamy Seafood Soup

Spinach Salad

Beef And Pears In Wine

Chocolate Pots

Creamy Seafood Soup

This thick, creamy soup has a rich, decadent seafood flavour. A very special dish.

Hard margarine (or butter)	1 tbsp.	15 mL
Raw medium shrimp (about 16, 4 with tails intact), peeled and deveined	6 oz.	170 g
Fresh (or frozen, thawed) large scallops (8 – 10)	6 oz.	170 g
Cooking oil	1 tbsp.	15 mL
Chopped onion	1/3 cup	75 mL
Garlic clove, minced (or 1/4 tsp., 1 mL, powder)	1	1
All-purpose flour	2 tsp.	10 mL
Dry white (or alcohol-free) wine	1/4 cup	60 mL
Prepared chicken broth	1 cup	250 mL
Salt	1/8 tsp.	0.5 mL
Pepper, sprinkle		
Whipping cream (or whole milk)	1/2 cup	125 mL

Chopped fresh chives, for garnish

Melt margarine in medium saucepan on medium. Add shrimp and scallops. Cook for about 3 minutes, stirring occasionally, until shrimp are pink and scallops are opaque. Reserve 4 shrimp with tails and 2 scallops for garnish. Keep warm. Transfer remaining shrimp mixture to small plate.

Heat cooking oil in same saucepan on medium-low. Add onion and garlic. Cook for about 10 minutes, stirring occasionally, until onion is soft.

Add flour. Heat and stir for 1 minute. Add wine. Stir for 1 to 2 minutes until boiling and thickened.

Add broth, salt and pepper. Stir. Bring to a boil on medium-high. Reduce heat to medium-low. Heat and stir for 3 to 5 minutes until smooth. Remove from heat.

Add whipping cream. Pour slightly cooled broth mixture into blender. Add shrimp mixture. Process until smooth. Return to same saucepan. Heat and stir on medium-low for 3 to 5 minutes until hot. Makes about 2 1/3 cups (575 mL) soup.

Garnish individual servings with reserved shrimp and scallops. Sprinkle with chives. Serves 2.

1 serving: 504 Calories; 35.4 g Total Fat (14.3 g Mono, 4 g Poly, 14.8 g Sat); 187 mg Cholesterol; 10 g Carbohydrate; 1 g Fibre; 31 g Protein; 881 mg Sodium

Pictured on page 134.

Creamy Seafood Soup, page 133

Spinach Salad

A nicely textured salad with the wonderful tastes of smoky bacon and toasted cashews.

Baby spinach, stems removed	2 1/2 cups	625 mL
Sun-dried tomatoes in oil, drained and chopped	2 tbsp.	30 mL
Cashews, toasted (see Note) and coarsely chopped	1/3 cup	75 mL
Bacon slices, cooked crisp and crumbled	2	2
DRESSING		
Olive (or cooking) oil	2 tbsp.	30 mL
Apple cider vinegar	1 tbsp.	15 mL
Granulated sugar	1 tsp.	5 mL
Salt, sprinkle		

Combine first 4 ingredients in medium bowl.

Dressing: Combine all 4 ingredients in jar with tight-fitting lid. Shake well. Makes 3 tbsp. (50 mL) dressing. Drizzle over spinach mixture. Toss. Makes 4 cups (1 L). Serves 2.

1 serving: 309 Calories; 26.7 g Total Fat (15.2 g Mono, 6.2 g Poly, 4 g Sat); 5 mg Cholesterol; 14 g Carbohydrate; 2 g Fibre; 8 g Protein; 235 mg Sodium

Pictured on page 135.

Note: To toast cashews, place in single layer in ungreased shallow pan. Bake in 350°F (175°C) oven for 5 to 10 minutes, stirring or shaking often, until desired doneness.

Beef And Pears In Wine

Tender, flavourful beef complemented by a fruity wine sauce. To ensure even cooking, remove beef from refrigerator 30 minutes before cooking. Serve with buttered pasta.

Beef tenderloin roast	1/2 – 3/4 lb.	225 – 340 g
Cooking oil	1 tsp.	5 mL
Pepper, sprinkle		
Cooking oil	2 tsp.	10 mL
Finely chopped onion	2 tbsp.	30 mL
Dry red (or alcohol-free) wine	1 cup	250 mL
Red currant jelly	2 tbsp.	30 mL
Dijon mustard	2 tsp.	10 mL
Firm medium pear, peeled, cored and quartered	1	1

Place roast on greased wire rack in small roasting pan. Drizzle with first amount of cooking oil. Sprinkle with pepper. Cook, uncovered, in 350°F (175°C) oven for 40 to 45 minutes until meat thermometer reads 140°F (60°C) for medium doneness or until desired doneness. Cover with foil. Let stand for 10 minutes.

Heat second amount of cooking oil in medium saucepan on medium-low. Add onion. Cook for about 5 minutes, stirring occasionally, until onion is soft.

Add wine, jelly and mustard. Heat and stir on medium until jelly is liquid. Bring to a boil. Reduce heat to medium-low.

Add pear. Simmer, uncovered, for 10 to 15 minutes, stirring occasionally, until pear is soft. Remove pear. Keep warm. Strain wine mixture. Discard solids. Return wine mixture to same saucepan. Boil, uncovered, on medium-high for about 5 minutes, stirring occasionally, until thickened. Makes 1/3 cup (75 mL) sauce. Drizzle sauce over sliced beef and pear on individual plates. Serves 2.

1 serving: 363 Calories; 13.8 g Total Fat (6.7 g Mono, 2.6 g Poly, 3 g Sat); 42 mg Cholesterol; 22 g Carbohydrate; 2 g Fibre; 18 g Protein; 133 mg Sodium

Pictured on page 135.

Centre Left: Spinach Salad, this page
Bottom Right: Beef And Pears In Wine, above

Chocolate Pots, below

Chocolate Pots

A very rich, creamy dessert with a velvety chocolate texture and a subtle, lingering liqueur taste. Make this quick and easy dessert one to two days ahead to improve the already delicious flavour.

Whipping cream	2/3 cup	150 mL
Semi-sweet dark chocolate squares (1 oz., 28 g, each), cut up	4 1/2	4 1/2
Egg yolk (large)	1	1
Orange-flavoured liqueur (such as Grand Marnier)	1 tbsp.	15 mL
Hard margarine (or butter), cut up	1 tbsp.	15 mL

Whipped cream, for garnish
Fresh raspberries, for garnish
Chocolate curls and shavings, for garnish

Heat whipping cream in medium saucepan on medium-low until bubbles form around edge. Remove from heat. Add chocolate. Stir until chocolate is melted and mixture is smooth.

Add egg yolk and liqueur. Stir well.

Add margarine, 1 tsp. (5 mL) at a time, until well combined. Divide chocolate mixture between 2 small cups or ramekins. Cover. Chill for at least 8 hours or overnight. Makes 1 1/4 cups (300 mL).

Just before serving, garnish with whipped cream, raspberries and chocolate curls. Serves 2.

1 serving: 667 Calories; 54.1 g Total Fat (18.9 g Mono, 2.4 g Poly, 30 g Sat); 205 mg Cholesterol; 46 g Carbohydrate; 4 g Fibre; 6 g Protein; 109 mg Sodium

Pictured above.

Vegetarian Dinner Party

It's not as hard as you think to find tasty vegetarian dishes for guests to enjoy, and this menu is proof of that. This selection of recipes is so varied and satisfying that you won't even miss the meat.

serves 6

Roasted Squash Soup

Hazelnut Rolls

Pasta Torte

Creamy Ratatouille

Steamed Green Beans

Peach And Almond Tart

Roasted Squash Soup

A creamy soup with the delightful combination of sweet pears and spices. When squash is in season, serve this soup in small roasted squash "bowls."

Chopped butternut squash (about 2 3/4 lbs., 1.25 kg)	7 cups	1.75 L
Medium pears, peeled, cored and quartered	2	2
Cooking oil	2 tsp.	10 mL
Salt	1/4 tsp.	1 mL
Cooking oil	1 tbsp.	15 mL
Chopped onion	1 1/2 cups	375 mL
Garlic cloves, minced (or 1/2 tsp., 2 mL, powder)	2	2
Ground ginger	1 1/2 tsp.	7 mL
Ground cumin	3/4 tsp.	4 mL
Chili powder	1/2 tsp.	2 mL
Pepper	1/4 tsp.	1 mL
Prepared vegetable broth	4 cups	1 L
Salt	1/4 – 1/2 tsp.	1 – 2 mL
Whipping cream (or whole milk)	1/2 cup	125 mL
Crumbled feta cheese (about 1/3 cup, 75 mL)	1 1/2 oz.	43 g
Chopped fresh chives, cut into 1/2 inch (12 mm) lengths	1 – 2 tbsp.	15 – 30 mL

Combine first 4 ingredients in large bowl. Arrange in single layer on greased baking sheet with sides. Bake in 400°F (205°C) oven for about 1 hour, stirring twice, until squash is tender and lightly browned.

Heat second amount of cooking oil in large pot or Dutch oven on medium-low. Add onion and garlic. Cook for about 10 minutes, stirring occasionally, until onion is soft.

Add next 4 ingredients. Heat and stir for 1 to 2 minutes until fragrant.

Add squash mixture, broth and second amount of salt. Bring to a boil. Boil for 10 minutes to blend flavours. Cool slightly. Process in blender, in 2 or 3 batches, until smooth. Return to same pot.

Add whipping cream. Heat and stir on medium-high for about 5 minutes until hot.

Sprinkle feta cheese and chives over individual servings. Makes about 8 cups (2 L). Serves 6.

1 serving: 241 Calories; 12.8 g Total Fat (4.7 g Mono, 1.5 g Poly, 5.8 g Sat); 30 mg Cholesterol; 30 g Carbohydrate; 4 g Fibre; 6 g Protein; 846 mg Sodium

Pictured on page 138.

Hazelnut Rolls

Hearty rolls with a chewy crust and a soft, moist centre.

Warm milk	1/2 cup	125 mL
Warm water	1/4 cup	60 mL
Active dry yeast (or 1/4 oz., 8 g, envelope)	1 tbsp.	15 mL
All-purpose flour	1 1/2 cups	375 mL
Salt	1 tsp.	5 mL
Granulated sugar	1/2 tsp.	2 mL
Cooking oil	1 tbsp.	15 mL
Hazelnuts, toasted (see Note) and chopped	3/4 cup	175 mL
All-purpose flour, approximately	1/2 cup	125 mL

Combine warm milk and water in large bowl. Sprinkle yeast over top. Let stand for 10 minutes. Stir until yeast is dissolved.

Add next 5 ingredients. Mix until soft, sticky dough forms. Turn out onto lightly floured surface. Knead, gradually working in enough of second amount of flour, until smooth and elastic. Place dough in greased medium bowl, turning once to grease top. Cover with waxed paper and tea towel. Let stand in oven with light on and door closed for about 1 hour until doubled in bulk.

Top: Roasted Squash Soup, page 137   Bottom: Hazelnut Rolls, above

Punch dough down. Turn out onto lightly floured surface. Divide dough into 6 portions. Shape each portion into 5 inch (12.5 cm) long roll. Place rolls on ungreased lightly floured baking sheet. Cut diagonal slits on top, 1 1/4 inches (3 cm) apart and 1/4 inch (6 mm) deep. Cover with greased waxed paper. Let stand in oven with light on and door closed for about 40 minutes until doubled in size. Bake in 425°F (220°C) oven for 20 to 25 minutes until golden brown and hollow-sounding when tapped. Makes 6 rolls.

1 roll: 299 Calories; 13.3 g Total Fat (9.6 g Mono, 1.9 g Poly, 1.1 g Sat); 1 mg Cholesterol; 38 g Carbohydrate; 2 g Fibre; 8 g Protein; 409 mg Sodium

Pictured on this page.

Note: To toast hazelnuts, place in single layer in ungreased shallow pan. Bake in 350°F (175°C) oven for 5 to 10 minutes, stirring or shaking often, until desired doneness.

Pasta Torte

This creamy, nicely seasoned pasta dish has a unique appearance when cut.

Penne pasta (about 6 oz., 170 g)	2 cups	500 mL
Boiling water	8 cups	2 L
Salt	1 tsp.	5 mL
Large eggs	4	4
Whipping cream (or whole milk)	1 1/2 cups	375 mL
Finely grated fresh Parmesan cheese	2/3 cup	150 mL
Chopped fresh parsley (or 1 1/2 tsp., 7 mL, flakes)	2 tbsp.	30 mL
Chopped fresh sweet basil (or 3/4 tsp., 4 mL, dried), optional	1 tbsp.	15 mL
Salt	1/4 tsp.	1 mL
Pepper	1/4 tsp.	1 mL

Cook pasta in boiling water and first amount of salt in large uncovered pot or Dutch oven for 10 to 12 minutes, stirring occasionally, until almost tender. Drain. Rinse under cold water. Drain.

Combine remaining 7 ingredients in large bowl. Add pasta. Stir. Pour into greased waxed paper-lined 8 inch (20 cm) springform pan. Cover tightly with greased foil. Bake in 350°F (175°C) oven for 60 to 75 minutes until set. Keep covered. Let stand for 10 minutes before cutting. Cuts into 6 wedges.

1 wedge: 432 Calories; 27.7 g Total Fat (8.3 g Mono, 1.4 g Poly, 16 g Sat); 226 mg Cholesterol; 31 g Carbohydrate; 1 g Fibre; 15 g Protein; 386 mg Sodium

Pictured on page 139.

Top and Bottom Left: Steamed Green Beans, page 140   Centre Left and Bottom Right: Pasta Torte, page 138   Centre Right: Creamy Ratatouille, below

Creamy Ratatouille

The many different flavours in this creamy dish blend so well together.

Cooking oil	1 tbsp.	15 mL
Chopped onion	1 cup	250 mL
Garlic cloves, minced (or 1/2 tsp., 2 mL, powder)	2	2
Chopped red pepper	1 cup	250 mL
Chopped yellow pepper	1 cup	250 mL
Small fresh white (or brown) mushrooms, cut in half	4 oz.	113 g
Chopped zucchini (with peel)	1 cup	250 mL
Dry red (or alcohol-free) wine	1/2 cup	125 mL
Can of diced tomatoes (with juice)	14 oz.	398 mL
Granulated sugar	1/2 tsp.	2 mL
Salt	1/2 tsp.	2 mL
Pepper, sprinkle		
Whipping cream (or whole milk)	1/3 cup	75 mL

Heat cooking oil in large frying pan on medium-low. Add onion and garlic. Cook for about 10 minutes, stirring occasionally, until onion is soft.

Add next 4 ingredients. Cook on medium-high for 5 to 10 minutes, stirring occasionally, until vegetables are lightly browned.

Add wine. Heat and stir for 3 to 4 minutes until liquid is almost evaporated.

Add next 4 ingredients. Stir. Bring to a boil. Boil, uncovered, for about 5 minutes until sauce is thickened and vegetables are tender.

Add whipping cream. Heat and stir until very hot, but not boiling. Makes about 3 cups (750 mL). Serves 6.

1 serving: 127 Calories; 7.2 g Total Fat (2.7 g Mono, 1 g Poly, 3 g Sat); 16 mg Cholesterol; 12 g Carbohydrate; 2 g Fibre; 3 g Protein; 317 mg Sodium

Pictured above.

Steamed Green Beans

Trim fresh green beans. Leave whole or cut in half. Place in steamer basket over boiling water. Steam until tender but bright green colour still remains. Immediately add some hard margarine (or butter) and toss until melted. Sprinkle with finely chopped yellow pepper to serve. Pictured on page 139.

Peach And Almond Tart

A tempting blend of peaches and almonds with a nice cinnamon accent.

ALMOND PASTRY

All-purpose flour	1 1/4 cups	300 mL
Icing (confectioner's) sugar	1/3 cup	75 mL
Ground almonds	1/4 cup	60 mL
Cold hard margarine (or butter), cut up	1/3 cup	75 mL
Egg yolks (large)	2	2
Ice water, approximately	2 tbsp.	30 mL

PEACH AND ALMOND FILLING

Ground almonds, toasted (see Note)	1/2 cup	125 mL
Cans of sliced peaches (14 oz., 398 mL, each), drained	2	2
Brown sugar, packed	1/3 cup	75 mL
Ground cinnamon	1/2 tsp.	2 mL
Slivered almonds	1/4 cup	60 mL

Almond Pastry: Process first 4 ingredients in food processor until crumbly.

Add egg yolks and enough ice water, through feed chute and with motor running, just until soft dough forms. Cover with plastic wrap. Chill for 30 minutes. Roll out pastry on lightly floured surface to 12 inch (30 cm) circle. Carefully transfer to lightly greased 11 x 17 inch (28 x 43 cm) baking sheet.

Peach And Almond Filling: Sprinkle ground almonds over pastry to within 2 inches (5 cm) of edge. Arrange peach slices in single layer on top of ground almonds.

Sprinkle brown sugar, cinnamon and slivered almonds over peach slices. Fold 2 inch (5 cm) pastry edge in towards centre to partially cover filling. Bake on bottom rack in 375°F (190°C) oven for about 35 minutes until pastry is lightly browned. Cuts into 6 to 8 wedges.

1 wedge: 409 Calories; 20.2 g Total Fat (12.5 g Mono, 3 g Poly, 3.5 g Sat); 72 mg Cholesterol; 52 g Carbohydrate; 3 g Fibre; 7 g Protein; 139 mg Sodium

Pictured below.

Note: To toast almonds, place in single layer in ungreased shallow pan. Bake in 350°F (175°C) oven for 5 to 10 minutes, stirring or shaking often, until desired doneness.

Peach And Almond Tart, above

Winter Dinner Party

Blowing snow doesn't mean we should all spend winter in hibernation. Turn your back on the chilly weather and celebrate with a house full of friends and this hearty menu.

serves 6

Creamy Carrot Soup

Sausage And Beer Risotto

Apple Cabbage

Pear Tart

Creamy Carrot Soup, below

Creamy Carrot Soup

A sweet, spicy soup with a smooth texture.

Cooking oil	1 tbsp.	15 mL
Chopped onion	1 cup	250 mL
Garlic cloves, minced (or 1/2 tsp., 2 mL, powder)	2	2
Ground ginger	1 tsp.	5 mL
Curry powder	1 tsp.	5 mL
Finely chopped carrot	5 cups	1.25 L
Prepared chicken (or vegetable) broth	5 cups	1.25 L
Salt	1/2 – 3/4 tsp.	2 – 4 mL
Pepper	1/8 – 1/4 tsp.	0.5 – 1 mL
Whipping cream (or whole milk)	1 cup	250 mL

Finely chopped cooked carrot, for garnish
Chopped fresh parsley, for garnish

Heat cooking oil in large pot or Dutch oven on medium-low. Add onion and garlic. Cook for about 10 minutes, stirring occasionally, until onion is soft.

Add ginger and curry powder. Cook for 1 to 2 minutes until fragrant.

Add next 4 ingredients. Stir. Bring to a boil on medium. Reduce heat to medium-low. Simmer, uncovered, for about 30 minutes until carrot is tender. Cool slightly. Process in blender until smooth. Return to same pot.

Add whipping cream. Heat and stir for about 3 minutes until hot.

Sprinkle individual servings with carrot and parsley. Makes 6 cups (1.5 L). Serves 6.

1 serving: 258 Calories; 17.4 g Total Fat (5.8 g Mono, 1.5 g Poly, 9 g Sat); 49 mg Cholesterol; 20 g Carbohydrate; 4 g Fibre; 7 g Protein; 988 mg Sodium

Pictured above.

Sausage And Beer Risotto

This thick, creamy risotto is made with an interesting and very flavourful combination of ingredients. We have suggested using hot sausages but you can use any kind you like.

Olive (or cooking) oil	2 tsp.	10 mL
Hot Italian sausages (or your choice), casings removed (about 6)	1 1/4 lbs.	560 g
Prepared chicken broth	7 1/2 cups	1.9 L
Olive (or cooking) oil	1 tbsp.	15 mL
Finely chopped onion	1 1/2 cups	375 mL
Garlic cloves, minced (or 1 tsp., 5 mL, powder)	4	4
Arborio rice	2 1/2 cups	625 mL
Beer	3/4 cup	175 mL
Chopped fresh parsley (or 3 1/2 tsp., 17 mL, flakes)	1/3 cup	75 mL
Salt, sprinkle (optional)		
Pepper, sprinkle (optional)		
Finely grated fresh Parmesan cheese	2/3 cup	150 mL

Heat first amount of olive oil in large frying pan on medium. Add sausages. Cook for about 15 minutes, turning occasionally, until plump. Remove from pan. Cut into 1/2 inch (12 mm) pieces. Set aside.

Pour broth into large saucepan. Cover. Bring to a boil. Reduce heat to low. Keep warm.

Heat second amount of olive oil in large pot or Dutch oven on medium-low. Add onion and garlic. Cook for about 10 minutes, stirring occasionally, until onion is soft.

Add rice. Stir until rice is coated with olive oil.

Add beer. Heat and stir on medium until beer is absorbed. Add hot broth, 1 cup (250 mL) at a time, stirring until broth is absorbed before adding more. Repeat with remaining broth, stirring constantly, until all broth is absorbed and rice is tender. This should take 25 to 30 minutes.

Add sausage and next 3 ingredients. Stir until sausage is hot. Remove from heat.

Stir in Parmesan cheese. Makes about 8 cups (2 L). Serves 6.

1 serving: 811 Calories; 39 g Total Fat (18.2 g Mono, 4.7 g Poly, 13.9 g Sat); 80 mg Cholesterol; 78 g Carbohydrate; 1 g Fibre; 31 g Protein; 1932 mg Sodium

Pictured on page 143.

Apple Cabbage

This colourful, easy-to-prepare recipe is comfort food on a cold night.

Hard margarine (or butter)	2 tbsp.	30 mL
Tart medium cooking apples (such as Granny Smith), peeled, quartered and thinly sliced	2	2
Shredded red cabbage, packed	2 cups	500 mL
Shredded green cabbage, packed	2 cups	500 mL
Apple juice	1/4 cup	60 mL
Salt	1/4 tsp.	1 mL
Pepper	1/4 tsp.	1 mL

Melt margarine in large frying pan on medium. Add apple. Cook for about 5 minutes, stirring occasionally, until apple starts to soften.

Add remaining 5 ingredients. Heat and stir for about 5 minutes until cabbage is wilted. Do not overcook. Makes about 4 cups (1 L). Serves 6.

1 serving: 77 Calories; 4.1 g Total Fat (2.5 g Mono, 0.5 g Poly, 0.8 g Sat); 0 mg Cholesterol; 11 g Carbohydrate; 2 g Fibre; 1 g Protein; 152 mg Sodium

Pictured on page 143.

Top Right and Bottom Right: Sausage And Beer Risotto, this page
Centre Left: Apple Cabbage, above

Pear Tart

Enjoy the fresh taste of pears and a hint of spice in this delicious tart.

PASTRY

All-purpose flour	1 1/4 cups	300 mL
Granulated sugar	1/4 cup	60 mL
Cold hard margarine (or butter), cut up	1/2 cup	125 mL
Egg yolks (large)	2	2
Ice water	1 tbsp.	15 mL

FILLING

Hard margarine (or butter), softened	3/4 cup	175 mL
Granulated sugar	2/3 cup	150 mL
Large eggs	3	3
Ground almonds	1 1/3 cups	325 mL
All-purpose flour	2 tbsp.	30 mL
Large pears, peeled	2	2
Apricot jam, warmed and strained	2 tbsp.	30 mL

RUM CARAMEL SAUCE

Hard margarine (or butter)	1/2 cup	125 mL
Brown sugar, packed	1/2 cup	125 mL
Whipping cream	1/2 cup	125 mL
Dark rum	2 tbsp.	30 mL
Ground cinnamon	1/2 tsp.	2 mL
Ground ginger	1/4 tsp.	1 mL

Pastry: Combine flour and sugar in large bowl. Cut in margarine until crumbly. Add egg yolks and ice water. Mix until soft dough forms. Cover. Chill for 30 minutes. Roll out pastry on lightly floured surface to about 1/8 inch (3 mm) thickness. Press in bottom and up side of 10 inch (25 cm) tart pan with removable bottom. Trim edge. Cover. Chill for 30 minutes.

Filling: Beat margarine and sugar in medium bowl until just combined.

Add eggs, 1 at a time, beating well after each addition.

Stir in almonds and flour. Turn mixture into tart shell.

Cut pears in half lengthwise. Remove cores. Cut each half into 1/8 inch (3 mm) slices. Arrange in 2 rows across top of filling to form large cross. Bake on bottom rack in 350°F (175°C) oven for about 55 minutes until browned and set.

Brush jam over warm tart. Cool. Cuts into 10 wedges.

Rum Caramel Sauce: Combine all 6 ingredients in medium saucepan. Heat and stir on medium-low until margarine is melted. Boil on medium-high for about 5 minutes until slightly thickened. Makes 1 1/3 cups (325 mL) sauce. Drizzle over individual servings. Serves 10.

1 serving: 639 Calories; 45.3 g Total Fat (27.3 g Mono, 4.9 g Poly, 10.7 g Sat); 122 mg Cholesterol; 53 g Carbohydrate; 1 g Fibre; 7 g Protein; 429 mg Sodium

Pictured below.

Pear Tart, above

An Evening Of Appetizers

An appetizer menu is convenient if you're expecting company throughout the evening, or if the group is too large for a formal sit-down meal. Everyone, including you, is then free to mingle and visit.

serves 10

Shrimp Toasts

Grilled Zucchini Salsa

Shrimp Dumplings

Asparagus Bites

Beef On Lettuce Shells

Pâté Jewel

Toast Rounds

Two-Bite Potatoes

Shrimp Toasts

Crunchy toast topped with a delicious layer of shrimp, garlic and ginger. These will become a favourite!

Raw (or frozen, thawed) medium shrimp (about 20), peeled and deveined	10 oz.	285 g
Egg white (large)	1	1
All-purpose flour	2 tbsp.	30 mL
Granulated sugar	1/2 tsp.	2 mL
Pepper	1/8 tsp.	0.5 mL
Garlic cloves, minced (or 1/2 tsp., 2 mL, powder)	2	2
Green onions, chopped	2	2
Finely grated peeled gingerroot	1/2 tsp.	2 mL
Fish sauce	1 tbsp.	15 mL
Baguette bread loaf, cut into 1/3 – 1/2 inch (8 – 12 mm) slices	1/2	1/2

Cooking oil, for deep-frying

Put shrimp into food processor. Pulse with on/off motion until finely chopped.

Add next 8 ingredients. Process until consistency of thick paste.

Spread 1 tbsp. (15 mL) shrimp mixture on 1 side of each baguette slice.

Heat cooking oil in deep-fryer or large frying pan to about 375°F (190°C). Use tongs to set baguette slices, 3 or 4 at a time, into hot oil. Deep-fry for about 30 seconds until golden. Turn, shrimp-side down, and deep-fry for about 1 1/2 minutes until golden brown. Remove to paper towels, shrimp-side up, to drain. Makes about 20 appetizers. Serves 10.

1 serving: 102 Calories; 5.3 g Total Fat (2.9 g Mono, 1.6 g Poly, 0.5 g Sat); 28 mg Cholesterol; 8 g Carbohydrate; trace Fibre; 5 g Protein; 206 mg Sodium

Pictured on page 147.

Grilled Zucchini Salsa

Colourful, tender-crisp vegetables in a tangy dressing. This fresh salsa tastes even better the next day. Serve on Toast Rounds, page 150, or with tortilla chips.

Garlic cloves, minced (or 1/2 tsp., 2 mL, powder)	2	2
Olive (or cooking) oil	1 tbsp.	15 mL
Pepper, generous sprinkle		
Medium zucchini (with peel), halved lengthwise	3	3
Diced tomato, seeds removed	1/2 cup	125 mL
Finely chopped onion	2 tbsp.	30 mL
Chopped fresh chives (or 1 1/2 tsp., 7 mL, dried)	2 tbsp.	30 mL
Finely chopped fresh parsley (or 3/4 tsp., 4 mL, flakes)	1 tbsp.	15 mL
Balsamic (or red wine) vinegar	1/4 cup	60 mL
Olive (or cooking) oil	2 tbsp.	30 mL
Salt	1/2 tsp.	2 mL

Combine garlic, first amount of olive oil and pepper in small bowl. Brush liberally on cut sides of zucchini. Preheat gas barbecue to medium. Cook zucchini, cut side down, on greased grill for about 3 minutes, dabbing remaining olive oil mixture over outside of zucchini, until dark grill marks appear but zucchini is still firm. Turn. Cook for 2 to 3 minutes until zucchini is tender-crisp. Dice into 1/4 inch (6 mm) pieces. Transfer to medium bowl.

Add next 4 ingredients. Toss.

Combine vinegar, second amount of olive oil and salt in separate small bowl. Add to vegetable mixture. Toss until coated. Cover. Let stand at room temperature for at least 1 hour, stirring several times, to blend flavours. Makes 2 1/2 cups (625 mL).

2 tbsp. (30 mL): 23 Calories; 2 g Total Fat (1.5 g Mono, 0.2 g Poly, 0.3 g Sat); 0 mg Cholesterol; 1 g Carbohydrate; trace Fibre; trace Protein; 58 mg Sodium

Pictured on this page.

1. Grilled Zucchini Salsa, above
2. Shrimp Toasts, page 145
3. Asparagus Bites, page 148
4. Two-Bite Potatoes, page 150
5. Shrimp Dumplings, page 148
6. Toast Rounds, page 150

Shrimp Dumplings

These easy-to-make dumplings are bursting with the taste of shrimp. They are the perfect appetizer for unexpected guests as they can easily be cooked ahead of time, chilled and reheated before serving.

Green onions, cut into 5 pieces each	3	3
Small celery rib, cut into 5 pieces	1	1
Raw (or frozen, thawed) medium shrimp (about 30), peeled and deveined	12 oz.	340 g
Egg white (large)	1	1
Cornstarch	2 tbsp.	30 mL
Soy sauce	2 tbsp.	30 mL
Sesame (or cooking) oil	1 tsp.	5 mL
Hot pepper sauce	1/4 tsp.	1 mL
Chopped fresh cilantro (or fresh parsley), optional	1/4 cup	60 mL
Package of round dumpling wrappers	16 oz.	454 g
Sesame seeds, toasted (see Note)	1 1/2 tsp.	7 mL
Cooking oil	2 tbsp.	30 mL
Hot water	1 1/2 cups	375 mL

Put green onion and celery into food processor. Pulse with on/off motion until finely chopped. Add shrimp. Pulse 3 or 4 times until chopped.

Add next 6 ingredients. Process for 5 or 6 seconds until well mixed and consistency of thick paste.

Moisten edge of 1 dumpling wrapper with water. Place about 1 tbsp. (15 mL) filling in centre. Bring edge of wrapper up towards centre. Pinch into 4 or 5 folds, leaving small opening. Repeat with remaining wrappers and filling. Sprinkle opening with sesame seeds.

Heat 2 tsp. (10 mL) cooking oil in large non-stick frying pan on medium. Add dumplings, 8 to 10 at a time, in single layer. Carefully pour 1/2 cup (125 mL) hot water into pan around dumplings. Cover. Cook for 5 to 8 minutes until dumplings are browned on bottom and liquid is evaporated. Repeat with remaining dumplings. Makes about 30 dumplings. Serves 10.

1 serving: 198 Calories; 4.5 g Total Fat (2 g Mono, 1.5 g Poly, 0.5 g Sat); 37 mg Cholesterol; 29 g Carbohydrate; trace Fibre; 10 g Protein; 513 mg Sodium

Pictured on page 146/147.

Note: To toast sesame seeds, place in single layer in ungreased shallow pan. Bake in 350°F (175°C) oven for 5 to 10 minutes, stirring or shaking often, until desired doneness.

Asparagus Bites

Attractive pinwheel rolls of ham, blue cheese and fresh asparagus. You'll love the delicious cheesy aftertaste.

Block of cream cheese, softened	8 oz.	250 g
Blue cheese, softened	4 oz.	113 g
White bread slices, crusts removed	24	24
Deli cooked ham slices, cut to fit bread	24	24
Cooked fresh (or canned, drained) asparagus spears, cut to fit width of bread slices	24	24
Hard margarine (or butter), melted	1/2 cup	125 mL

Mash cream cheese and blue cheese together well in small bowl.

Roll out bread slices lightly with rolling pin. Spread 1 tbsp. (15 mL) cheese mixture on 1 side of each slice.

Place 1 ham slice over cheese mixture on each bread slice. Lay 1 asparagus spear on each ham slice. Roll up tightly.

Brush each roll with margarine. Arrange rolls, seam-side down, in single layer on ungreased baking sheet. Freeze for about 1 hour until firm. Cut each roll into 4 pieces. Place in resealable freezer bag. Store in freezer. To serve, arrange in single layer on ungreased baking sheet. Bake in 350°F (175°C) oven for 15 to 20 minutes until crisp. Broil for 1 to 2 minutes, watching carefully, until nicely browned. Makes 96 appetizers. Serves 10.

1 serving: 519 Calories; 32.8 g Total Fat (14.7 g Mono, 2.9 g Poly, 13 g Sat); 85 mg Cholesterol; 31 g Carbohydrate; 2 g Fibre; 25 g Protein; 1895 mg Sodium

Pictured on page 147.

Beef On Lettuce Shells

Crisp lettuce leaves filled with a soft, mild-flavoured beef mixture. A nice combination of textures that tastes great served hot or cold.

Lean ground beef	1/2 lb.	225 g
Garlic clove, minced (or 1/4 tsp., 1 mL, powder)	1	1
Finely grated peeled gingerroot	1/2 tsp.	2 mL
Chopped onion	1/2 cup	125 mL
Can of water chestnuts, drained and chopped	8 oz.	227 mL
Pine nuts, toasted (see Note) and coarsely chopped	1/4 cup	60 mL
Green onion, sliced	1	1
Dried crushed chilies	1/4 tsp.	1 mL
Liquid honey	1 tbsp.	15 mL
Water	1/3 cup	75 mL
Soy sauce	1 tbsp.	15 mL
Dry sherry	1 tbsp.	15 mL
Beef bouillon powder	1/2 tsp.	2 mL
Sesame (or cooking) oil (optional)	1/2 tsp.	2 mL
Cornstarch	1 tbsp.	15 mL
Small leaves from romaine lettuce hearts (or Belgian endive or butter lettuce leaves)	20	20

Scramble-fry ground beef, garlic, ginger and onion in medium non-stick frying pan until no pink remains in beef. Drain.

Add next 5 ingredients. Stir.

Combine next 6 ingredients in small bowl until smooth. Add to beef mixture. Heat and stir on medium until boiling and thickened. Transfer to serving bowl. Set bowl in centre of large plate.

Arrange lettuce leaves on plate around serving bowl. Provide several spoons for guests to fill their own shells. Serves 10.

1 serving: 82 Calories; 4.1 g Total Fat (1.6 g Mono, 1 g Poly, 1.1 g Sat); 12 mg Cholesterol; 6 g Carbohydrate; 1 g Fibre; 6 g Protein; 147 mg Sodium

Pictured below.

Note: To toast pine nuts, place in single layer in ungreased shallow pan. Bake in 350°F (175°C) oven for 5 to 10 minutes, stirring or shaking often, until desired doneness.

Beef On Lettuce Shells, above

Pâté Jewel

Liverwurst lovers will enjoy this smooth appetizer. Spreads easily and tastes great on crisp Toast Rounds, this page, or crackers.

Envelope of unflavoured gelatin	1/4 oz.	7 g
White grape juice	1/4 cup	60 mL
Prepared chicken broth	1/2 cup	125 mL
Dry sherry	1 tsp.	5 mL
Hot pepper sauce	1/4 tsp.	1 mL
Fine liverwurst with herbs	8 oz.	225 g
Soft goat (chèvre) cheese (or cream cheese, room temperature)	2 oz.	57 g
Finely chopped fresh parsley (or 1/4 tsp., 1 mL, flakes)	1 1/2 tsp.	7 mL

Gherkins (or dill pickles), for garnish
Pickled onions, for garnish

Sprinkle gelatin over grape juice in small saucepan. Let stand for 1 minute.

Add broth, sherry and hot pepper sauce. Heat and stir until boiling. Remove from heat. Cool in refrigerator, stirring once or twice, until slightly thickened. Pour 1/2 of mixture into lightly greased 3 cup (750 mL) ring mold.

Bottom: Pâté Jewel, above   Top Right: Toast Rounds, this page

Cut liverwurst and goat cheese into chunks. Mash with fork on large plate or pulse with on/off motion in food processor until smooth. Add parsley. Mash or process until combined. Pipe or spoon into mold through centre of gelatin mixture. Carefully spoon remaining gelatin mixture over liverwurst mixture. Tap mold on counter to fill in all spaces. Chill for several hours or overnight until firm. Dip mold in hot water for several seconds to loosen. Invert pâté onto serving plate. Keep chilled until ready to serve.

Place gherkins and onions in centre of pâté to serve. Serves 10.

1 serving: 107 Calories; 8.6 g Total Fat (3.6 g Mono, 0.7 g Poly, 3.7 g Sat); 40 mg Cholesterol; 2 g Carbohydrate; trace Fibre; 5 g Protein; 234 mg Sodium

Pictured on this page.

Toast Rounds

Cut 1 1/2 inch (3.8 cm) rounds from a variety of sliced breads such as dark rye, multi-grain, pumpernickel, herb and whole wheat. Arrange rounds close together on greased baking sheet. Brush with melted hard margarine (or butter) or olive oil. Bake in 350°F (175°C) oven for 10 to 15 minutes until crisp and golden. Pictured on page 146/147 and on this page.

Two-Bite Potatoes

Steam 1 lb. (454 g) red baby potatoes (with peel) for 15 to 20 minutes until tender. Chill. Cut in half. Place, cut side up, on serving tray, removing small slice from ends if needed to stay upright. Make a small indentation by scooping out small spoonful of potato. Filling suggestions:

- Dollop of sour cream with fresh chives or dill sprinkled over top.

- Small rosette of softened cream cheese (plain or flavoured such as herb and garlic or smoked salmon) piped onto potatoes. Garnish with red pepper slice and fresh dill sprig.

- Mix mayonnaise with Dijon mustard (or prepared mustard) to taste. Spoon or pipe onto potatoes. Top with gherkin or dill pickle slice.

- Salsa with sprinkle of grated sharp Cheddar cheese over top.

Pictured on page 147.

Dessert And Coffee

Is your weekend going to be a busy one? Don't put off entertaining, simply invite friends over for dessert and coffee. This menu keeps it simple with a selection that you can serve any time of day.

serves 8

Coffee Treat

Perfect Coffee

Fruit Cocktail Pie

Cherry Strudel Dessert

B'ucca Layers

Coffee Treat

A slightly sweet latte beverage to complement any dessert menu. The foamy top adds a nice touch and can be garnished with cinnamon or chocolate.

Homogenized milk	4 cups	1 L
Granulated sugar	1/4 cup	60 mL
Vanilla	1 tsp.	5 mL
Hot, very strong prepared coffee	4 cups	1 L
Ground cinnamon, for garnish		

Heat milk, sugar and vanilla in medium saucepan on medium until almost boiling. Whisk or beat until foamy.

Pour coffee into mugs. Top with milk mixture. Sprinkle with cinnamon. Makes 8 cups (2 L). Serves 8.

1 serving: 112 Calories; 4.3 g Total Fat (1.2 g Mono, 0.2 g Poly, 2.7 g Sat); 18 mg Cholesterol; 14 g Carbohydrate; 0 g Fibre; 4 g Protein; 71 mg Sodium

Pictured on page 153.

Perfect Coffee

- Always use cold water.

- Use clean (or at least well-rinsed) equipment.

- Use fresh coffee beans. Keep in the refrigerator if you don't use them often or buy just enough for each occasion.

- Grind the beans just before brewing.

- Use the correct size of grind for coffee maker.

- Use about 1 tbsp. (15 mL) ground coffee for each 8 oz. (250 mL) water for a fairly weak coffee. Add more according to taste.

- Pour hot coffee into warmed mugs—what a treat!

- Keep remaining coffee warm in an insulated beverage container rather than on direct heat (whether the stove element or the coffee machine base).

Fruit Cocktail Pie

A smooth, light pie with a mildly sweet, cream-coloured mousse and chunks of fruit dispersed throughout. Garnish with whipped cream and fresh fruit for a special occasion.

Reserved fruit cocktail juice		
Large marshmallows	24	24
Envelope of dessert topping, prepared	1	1
Can of fruit cocktail, drained and juice reserved	14 oz.	398 mL
Baked 9 inch (22 cm) graham cracker crust	1	1
Graham cracker crumbs (optional)	2 tsp.	10 mL

Combine reserved fruit cocktail juice and marshmallows in large saucepan. Heat on low, stirring frequently, until marshmallows are melted. Chill for about 20 minutes, stirring several times, until mixture will mound.

Fold in dessert topping.

Fold in fruit cocktail. Turn out into crust. Sprinkle with graham crumbs. Chill for at least 8 hours or overnight. Serves 8.

1 serving: 274 Calories; 11 g Total Fat (4.4 g Mono, 2.2 g Poly, 3.8 g Sat);
12 mg Cholesterol; 43 g Carbohydrate; 1 g Fibre; 2 g Protein; 204 mg Sodium

Pictured on page 153.

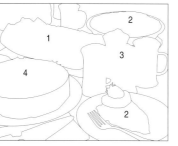

1. Cherry Strudel Dessert,
   page 154
2. Fruit Cocktail Pie, above
3. Coffee Treat, page 151
4. B'ucca Layers, page 154

Cherry Strudel Dessert

Delicious served warm with a scoop of vanilla ice cream or served cold with a dollop of whipped cream.

Package of frozen puff pastry, thawed according to package directions	14 oz.	397 g
Vanilla wafer crumbs	1/4 cup	60 mL
Can of cherry pie filling	19 oz.	540 mL
Grated lemon peel	2 tsp.	10 mL
Vanilla wafer crumbs	2 tbsp.	30 mL
Sliced almonds	1/4 cup	60 mL

Roll out puff pastry on lightly floured surface to 12 × 16 inch (30 × 40 cm) rectangle. Transfer to greased 11 × 17 inch (28 × 43 cm) baking sheet.

Sprinkle first amount of wafer crumbs over pastry to within 1 inch (2.5 cm) of edge.

Combine pie filling and lemon peel in medium bowl. Turn out onto wafer crumbs. Carefully spread to within 2 inches (5 cm) of edge of pastry. Fold sides of pastry up over filling towards centre. Pleat slightly to partially cover filling.

Sprinkle second amount of wafer crumbs and almonds over exposed cherry filling. Bake on bottom rack in 400°F (205°C) oven for about 30 minutes until golden. Let stand for 10 minutes before cutting into pieces for serving. Serves 8.

1 serving: 397 Calories; 21.5 g Total Fat (5.8 g Mono, 11.5 g Poly, 3 g Sat); 2 mg Cholesterol; 48 g Carbohydrate; 1 g Fibre; 5 g Protein; 143 mg Sodium

Pictured on page 152/153.

B'ucca Layers

This easy-to-make, adults-only dessert is rich and chocolatey with a strong liqueur kick. This goes very well with coffee.

Whipping cream	2 cups	500 mL
Instant chocolate (or vanilla) pudding powder	2 tbsp.	30 mL
Hot milk	1/2 cup	125 mL
Licorice-flavoured liqueur (such as Sambuca)	1/4 cup	60 mL
Irish cream-flavoured liqueur (such as Baileys)	1/2 cup	125 mL
Package of chocolate chip cookies (about 27 cookies)	14 oz.	400 g
Milk chocolate melting wafers	1/4 cup	60 mL

Beat whipping cream and pudding powder in medium bowl until stiff peaks form.

Combine hot milk and both liqueurs in small deep bowl.

Line outside bottom and about 1 inch (2.5 cm) up side of 8 inch (20 cm) springform pan with foil to prevent leakage. Briefly submerge each cookie in liqueur mixture. Arrange in single layer in bottom of pan. Cookies should touch each other, but don't be concerned if there are spaces. Spread about 1/3 of whipping cream mixture in even layer over cookies. Repeat with two more alternating layers of cookies and whipping cream mixture. Cover tightly with plastic wrap. Chill overnight. Remove side of pan and foil.

Put chocolate into small resealable freezer bag. Press air out and seal. Place bag in hot water in small bowl to melt chocolate or melt in microwave using short 10 second bursts of high (100%) power, kneading in between, until almost smooth. Do not overheat. Knead chocolate until smooth. Cool to lukewarm. Push melted chocolate to bottom of 1 corner of bag. Cut very tiny piece off corner. Squeeze chocolate over dessert in back and forth motion from 4 to 6 inches (10 to 15 cm) above surface to create lacy design over top. Serves 8.

1 serving: 554 Calories; 32.5 g Total Fat (11.3 g Mono, 1.7 g Poly, 17.6 g Sat); 77 mg Cholesterol; 55 g Carbohydrate; trace Fibre; 6 g Protein; 307 mg Sodium

Pictured on page 152/153.

Feeding Frenzy!

There are going to be days when everyone is hungry and they all turn to you. This menu was created for just such a crowd...a perfect medley to satisfy a lot of appetites!

serves 25

Pleasing Punch

Garlic And Cheese Bread

Easy Marinated Vegetables

Green Bean Salad

Sweet Potato Chili Pie

Sundae Dessert

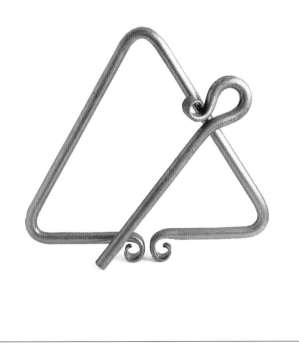

Pleasing Punch

Mix your choice of prepared or concentrated fruit juices with carbonated beverages that complement each other to equal 32 to 40 cups (8 to 10 L). You will need a very large container (such as a Dutch oven or stock pot), or mix up 1/2 at a time. If you're using ice, use more juice concentrate so the flavour won't be watered down as much from the melting ice. Garnish with fresh fruit, such as sliced strawberries and oranges. Pictured on page 156.

Garlic And Cheese Bread

Crispy French bread filled with a rich, creamy spread. Makes a great gooey, cheesy snack that the kids will love!

Hard margarine (or butter), softened	1 cup	250 mL
Garlic cloves, minced (or 1/2 tsp., 2 mL, powder)	2	2
Process cheese spread	1 1/3 cups	325 mL
Green onions, sliced	2	2
Chopped fresh parsley (or 1 1/2 tsp., 7 mL, flakes)	2 tbsp.	30 mL
Dry mustard	1 tsp.	5 mL
Coarsely ground pepper (or 1/4 tsp., 1 mL, pepper)	1/2 tsp.	2 mL
French bread loaves, sliced in half lengthwise	2	2

Beat first 7 ingredients in medium bowl until well combined.

Spread thick layer over cut sides of bread, right to edges. Place cut sides of each loaf together. Wrap loaves in heavy-duty (or double layer of regular) foil. Bake in 400°F (205°C) oven for about 20 minutes until heated through. If desired, loaves may then be opened and broiled to toast cut surfaces. Cut into 1 1/2 inch (3.8 cm) thick slices. Serves 25.

1 serving: 211 Calories; 11.9 g Total Fat (6.4 g Mono, 1.1 g Poly, 3.7 g Sat); 8 mg Cholesterol; 20 g Carbohydrate; 1 g Fibre; 6 g Protein; 543 mg Sodium

Pictured on page 156/157.

Easy Marinated Vegetables

Purchase large quantity of ready-cut mixed bags of broccoli, cauliflower and carrots. Add cherry tomatoes, sliced cucumbers, mushrooms, peppers and onion. Divide among ice cream pails. Pour about 1 cup (250 mL) Italian dressing over contents in each pail. Let stand at room temperature for at least 4 hours, stirring occasionally. Refrigerate if longer than 8 hours and for up to 24 hours. Pictured on page 157.

Green Bean Salad

A tangy, colourful dish with onions and tender-crisp green beans coated in a delicious, sweet sauce. Serve with a slotted spoon.

Fresh (or frozen) whole green beans, cut into 1 inch (2.5 cm) pieces (see Note) Water	12 cups	3 L
Medium onions, sliced Water, to cover	4	4
Cooking oil	1/4 cup	60 mL
White vinegar	4 cups	1 L
Water	1 cup	250 mL
Granulated sugar	4 cups	1 L
Seasoned salt	4 tsp.	20 mL
Pepper	1 tsp.	5 mL

Cook green beans in water in large pot for about 3 minutes until tender-crisp. Drain. Cool.

Cover onion with water in large bowl. Let stand for 1 hour. Drain.

Add green beans and cooking oil. Stir.

Combine remaining 5 ingredients in large saucepan. Heat and stir until sugar is dissolved and mixture is hot. Immediately pour over bean mixture. Cover. Chill for at least 24 hours, stirring twice. Can be kept for up to 3 days. Makes 14 cups (3.5 L). Serves 25.

1 serving: 183 Calories; 2.5 g Total Fat (1.4 g Mono, 0.8 g Poly, 0.2 g Sat); 0 mg Cholesterol; 42 g Carbohydrate; 2 g Fibre; 1 g Protein; 197 mg Sodium

Pictured on page 157.

Note: Use 4 cans (14 oz., 398 mL, each) cut green beans, drained, instead of fresh or frozen.

Top Left: Pleasing Punch, page 155
Top Right: Sweet Potato Chili Pie, page 158
Centre Left: Garlic And Cheese Bread, page 155
Centre Right: Easy Marinated Vegetables, page 155
Bottom: Green Bean Salad, above

Sweet Potato Chili Pie

Delicious and sweet with a distinct chili flavour. Open all cans and use a food processor to chop vegetables while beef is browning, and you'll make short work of this massive recipe! Or assemble the day before to the baking stage, cover and chill overnight. Bake for an additional hour.

Lean ground beef	4 1/2 lbs.	2 kg
Garlic cloves, minced (or 1 1/4 tsp., 6 mL, powder), optional	5	5
All-purpose flour	1/2 cup	125 mL
Seasoned salt	4 tsp.	20 mL
Paprika	1 tbsp.	15 mL
Pepper	2 tsp.	10 mL
Cans of condensed beef broth (10 oz., 284 mL, each)	2	2
Water	3/4 cup	175 mL
Chili sauce	1 cup	250 mL
Cooking oil	1 tbsp.	15 mL
Chopped onion	2 1/2 cups	625 mL
Chopped celery	1 3/4 cups	425 mL
Cooking oil	1 tbsp.	15 mL
Diced red pepper	2 cups	500 mL
Diced green pepper	1 1/2 cups	375 mL
Frozen kernel corn, thawed	2 cups	500 mL
Water	1 cup	250 mL
Cans of Romano (or white kidney) beans (19 oz., 540 mL, each), rinsed and drained	4	4
Chili powder	2 tbsp.	30 mL
Dried whole oregano	1 tbsp.	15 mL
Granulated sugar	1 tbsp.	15 mL
Process Swiss cheese slices	12	12
Sweet potatoes (or yams), peeled and cut into large chunks	4 lbs.	1.8 kg
Water		
Hard margarine (or butter)	1/3 cup	75 mL
Salt	1 tsp.	5 mL
Pepper	1/2 tsp.	2 mL
Large eggs, fork-beaten	2	2
Paprika, for garnish		

Scramble-fry ground beef and garlic in Dutch oven or large frying pan, in 2 or 3 batches, until no pink remains in beef. Drain, reserving about 2 tbsp. (30 mL) fat in pan. Return all beef to pot.

Sprinkle flour, seasoned salt, paprika and first amount of pepper over beef. Heat and stir on medium for about 2 minutes until well combined. Slowly add broth, first amount of water and chili sauce, stirring constantly. Cook, uncovered, for about 10 minutes, stirring occasionally, until mixture is boiling and thickened. Turn into large ungreased roaster with lid or 16 3/4 x 11 1/2 x 2 5/8 inch (41.9 x 28.75 x 6.5 cm) foil pan. (If using foil pan, place on large baking sheet for easier and safer handling.)

Heat first amount of cooking oil in same Dutch oven on medium. Add onion and celery. Cook for about 15 minutes, stirring occasionally, until soft. Add to beef mixture. Stir.

Heat second amount of cooking oil in same Dutch oven on medium. Add peppers and corn. Cook for about 10 minutes, stirring occasionally, until soft.

Add second amount of water. Stir. Add beans, chili powder, oregano and sugar. Stir well. Cover. Simmer on medium for 15 minutes, stirring occasionally, to blend flavours. Add to beef mixture. Stir well. Pack down firmly and evenly.

Cover with cheese slices.

Cook sweet potato in third amount of water in large pot or separate Dutch oven for 15 to 20 minutes until tender. Drain, reserving about 1/2 cup (125 mL) liquid.

Add margarine, salt and second amount of pepper to sweet potato. Mash until margarine is melted. Process, in batches, in food processor, adding reserved liquid a little at a time if necessary to make smooth or continue to mash until fairly smooth. Stir in eggs until well combined. Spoon over cheese. Spread in even layer. (Mixture may also be piped in rosettes or rows for fancier presentation if desired.)

Sprinkle with paprika. Cover. Bake in 325°F (160°C) oven for about 3 hours until heated through. Remove cover for last 1/2 hour to brown top lightly. Let stand for 15 minutes before serving. Serves 25.

1 serving: 415 Calories; 17.5 g Total Fat (7.5 g Mono, 1.4 g Poly, 6.8 g Sat); 72 mg Cholesterol; 39 g Carbohydrate; 5 g Fibre; 26 g Protein; 975 mg Sodium

Pictured on page 157.

Sundae Dessert

A decadent dessert that is handy and inexpensive. This is a delicious ice cream dessert that will garner rave reviews.

Package of maple-flavoured sandwich cookies	12 1/2 oz.	350 g
Carton of butterscotch ripple ice cream	2 quarts	2 L
Chocolate-covered crispy toffee bars (such as Skor), 1 1/2 oz. (39 g) each, coarsely chopped	8	8
Jars of fudge ice cream topping (1 cup, 250 mL, each), heated	2	2
Carton of maple walnut ice cream	2 quarts	2 L
Envelopes of dessert topping, prepared (about 4 cups, 1 L)	2	2
Jar of caramel (or butterscotch) ice cream topping	1 cup	250 mL
Chopped walnuts, toasted (see Note)	1/2 cup	125 mL
Chocolate-covered crispy toffee bar 1 1/2 oz. (such as Skor), finely chopped		39 g

Coarsely crush cookies, in 2 batches, by putting into large resealable freezer bag, squeezing air out and rolling with rolling pin, or by pulsing in food processor with on/off motion several times. Turn into 2 ungreased 9 × 13 inch (22 × 33 cm) pans or large ungreased 16 3/4 × 11 1/2 × 2 5/8 inch (41.9 × 28.75 × 6.5 cm) foil pan. Spread evenly. Lightly pat down in bottom of pan.

Peel carton from butterscotch ripple ice cream. Cut ice cream crosswise into 3/4 inch (2 cm) slices. Arrange in single layer over cookie base. Let stand for about 20 minutes until ice cream is softened. Spread to fill in spaces.

Sprinkle with first amount of chopped toffee bar. Drizzle hot fudge topping as evenly as possible over top. Place dessert in freezer for about 2 hours until firm. (If using foil pan, place on large baking sheet for easier handling.)

Peel carton from maple walnut ice cream. Cut ice cream crosswise into 3/4 inch (2 cm) slices. Arrange in single layer over fudge topping. Let stand for about 20 minutes until ice cream is softened. Spread to fill in spaces.

Spread or pipe dessert topping over ice cream in even layer.

Slowly drizzle caramel topping over dessert topping from about 10 inches (25 cm) above surface in thin stream with side-to-side motion to create fine ribbons. Sprinkle with walnuts and second amount of chopped toffee bar. Cover tightly with foil. Freeze for several hours until firm. To serve, let stand at room temperature for about 20 minutes to make cutting easier. Cuts into 25 pieces.

1 piece: 509 Calories; 24.6 g Total Fat (6 g Mono, 2.7 g Poly, 9.8 g Sat); 44 mg Cholesterol; 71 g Carbohydrate; 1 g Fibre; 7 g Protein; 279 mg Sodium

Pictured below.

Note: To toast walnuts, place in single layer in ungreased shallow pan. Bake in 350°F (175°C) oven for 5 to 10 minutes, stirring or shaking often, until desired doneness.

Sundae Dessert, above

Fondue Fun

Are there any rules to follow when you serve fondue? Only one...relax and enjoy. It's an intimate way to serve dinner and offers a wonderful opportunity to keep the conversation going.

serves 8

Seafood Fondue

Steamed Potato And Veggie Dippers

Sweet Rye Bread Loaves

Soft Banana Cookies

Mocha Chip Fondue

Dessert Dippers

Meringue Kisses

Seafood Fondue

This mild, dip-like fondue is great with Steamed Potato And Veggie Dippers, below. Makes for an intimate dinner setting.

Box of frozen Boston bluefish fillets	14 oz.	395 g
Boiling water, to cover		
Salt	1/4 tsp.	1 mL
Milk	1 cup	250 mL
Block of cream cheese, cut up	8 oz.	250 g
Grated medium Cheddar cheese	1 cup	250 mL
Onion powder	1/2 tsp.	2 mL
Chopped fresh chives (or 1/4 tsp., 1 mL, dried)	1 tsp.	5 mL
Can of crabmeat, drained, cartilage removed and flaked	4 1/4 oz.	120 g

Cook fillets in boiling water and salt in large saucepan until fish flakes easily when tested with fork. Drain. Cool. Flake on plate with fork.

Combine next 5 ingredients in same saucepan. Heat and stir on low until cheese is melted.

Add fish and crab. Stir until heated through. Transfer to fondue pot. Keep warm over low flame. Makes about 3 1/2 cups (875 mL). Serves 8.

1 serving: 254 Calories; 18.4 g Total Fat (5.5 g Mono, 1 g Poly, 10.7 g Sat); 80 mg Cholesterol; 3 g Carbohydrate; trace Fibre; 19 g Protein; 328 mg Sodium

Pictured on page 161.

Steamed Potato And Veggie Dippers

Scrub red or white baby potatoes. Place in steamer basket over boiling water. Cover. Cook for about 15 minutes until tender. Steam other vegetables individually (such as cauliflower florets, broccoli florets, finger-sized carrots, fresh green beans and chunks of peeled yam or sweet potato) in same steamer basket over boiling water until tender-crisp. Cool quickly in ice water to preserve colour and prevent further cooking. Arrange individual vegetables on several small plates or in pretty bowls to pass around the table. Plan about 8 to 10 veggie dippers per person. Pictured on page 161.

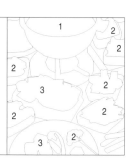

1. Seafood Fondue, above
2. Steamed Potato And Veggie Dippers, above
3. Sweet Rye Bread Loaves, page 162

Sweet Rye Bread Loaves

Golden brown bread that is crusty on the outside but soft and moist on the inside. Use one of the loaves for dunking in the fondue and freeze the other for later.

Warm water	1/4 cup	60 mL
Granulated sugar	1 tsp.	5 mL
Active dry yeast (or 1/4 oz., 8 g, envelope)	2 1/2 tsp.	12 mL
Beer	1 cup	250 mL
Fancy (mild) molasses	2 tbsp.	30 mL
Hard margarine (or butter)	2 tbsp.	30 mL
Salt	1/2 tsp.	2 mL
Rye flour	1 1/2 cups	375 mL
Flaxseed (or caraway seed)	4 tsp.	20 mL
All-purpose flour	2 cups	500 mL
Water, for brushing tops		

Stir warm water and sugar in small bowl until sugar is dissolved. Sprinkle yeast over top. Let stand for 10 minutes. Stir until yeast is dissolved.

Heat and stir next 4 ingredients in small saucepan until margarine is melted. Pour into large bowl. Stir until lukewarm. Add yeast mixture.

Gradually stir in rye flour and flaxseed until smooth.

Add 2/3 cup (150 mL) all-purpose flour. Stir vigorously for 2 minutes. Slowly work in remaining all-purpose flour until dough pulls away from side of bowl and is no longer sticky. Turn out onto lightly floured surface. Knead for about 10 minutes until smooth and elastic. Place dough in greased bowl, turning once to grease top. Cover with greased waxed paper and tea towel. Let stand in oven with light on and door closed for about 1 1/2 hours until doubled in bulk. Punch dough down. Shape into 2 loaves, each about 10 inches (25 cm) long. Arrange, side by side, on large greased baking sheet, leaving space between to allow for rising. Cut 3 or 4 diagonal slashes across top of each loaf. Cover with tea towel. Let stand in oven with light on and door closed for about 1 hour until doubled in size. Brush loaves with water. Bake in 400°F (205°C) oven for 10 minutes. Reduce heat to 350°F (175°C). Bake for 20 to 25 minutes until golden brown and hollow-sounding when tapped. Remove to wire rack to cool. Cut 1 loaf into 3/4 inch (2 cm) thick slices, reserving other loaf for another time. Slices may be cut again into smaller pieces for spearing onto fondue forks. Or serve sliced bread and let your guests tear off their own pieces for spearing and dunking into fondue pot. Makes 2 loaves. 1 loaf serves 8.

1 serving: 129 Calories; 2.1 g Total Fat (1 g Mono, 0.5 g Poly, 0.4 g Sat); 0 mg Cholesterol; 24 g Carbohydrate; 2 g Fibre; 3 g Protein; 94 mg Sodium

Pictured on page 161.

Soft Banana Cookies

The mild, sweet flavour of these soft, cake-like cookies makes them perfect for dunking in Mocha Chip Fondue, page 163. These are also great for dipping into tea or coffee.

Milk	1/4 cup	60 mL
White vinegar	1 tsp.	5 mL
Hard margarine (or butter), softened	1/4 cup	60 mL
Granulated sugar	1/4 cup	60 mL
Brown sugar, packed	1/4 cup	60 mL
Large egg	1	1
Mashed banana (about 1 medium)	1/2 cup	125 mL
Vanilla	1/2 tsp.	2 mL
All-purpose flour	1 1/2 cups	375 mL
Baking soda	1/2 tsp.	2 mL
Baking powder	1/4 tsp.	1 mL
Salt	1/4 tsp.	1 mL
Ground cinnamon	1/8 tsp.	0.5 mL

Combine milk and vinegar in small bowl. Let stand for 10 minutes.

Cream margarine and both sugars in medium bowl. Beat in egg. Add banana and vanilla. Beat well.

Combine remaining 5 ingredients in separate small bowl. Add 1/2 of flour mixture to banana mixture. Stir. Add milk mixture. Stir. Add remaining flour mixture. Mix until just moistened. Drop by rounded tablespoonfuls 1 1/2 inches (3.8 cm) apart onto greased cookie sheets. Bake in 375°F (190°C) oven for 9 to 10 minutes until edges are golden. Let stand on cookie sheets for 5 minutes before removing to wire racks to cool. Makes 40 cookies. Serves 8.

1 serving: 225 Calories; 7.1 g Total Fat (4.3 g Mono, 0.8 g Poly, 1.6 g Sat); 27 mg Cholesterol; 37 g Carbohydrate; 1 g Fibre; 4 g Protein; 253 mg Sodium

Pictured on page 163.

Top Left: Soft Banana Cookies, above
Top Centre: Mocha Chip Fondue, page 163
Top Right and Bottom Right: Dessert Dippers, page 163
Bottom Left: Meringue Kisses, page 163

Mocha Chip Fondue

A rich, shiny, dark, chocolate dip with just a hint of coffee.
Use for dipping cookies or other dessert dippers for a very
decadent treat.

Semi-sweet chocolate chips	1 3/4 cups	425 mL
Skim evaporated milk (or half-and-half cream)	1 cup	250 mL
Instant coffee granules	1 tbsp.	15 mL
Dry sherry	1 tbsp.	15 mL

Combine all 4 ingredients in heavy medium saucepan. Heat on lowest heat, stirring constantly until smooth. Carefully pour into fondue pot. Keep warm over low flame. Makes about 2 cups (500 mL). Serves 8.

1 serving: 234 Calories; 14.3 g Total Fat (4.7 g Mono, 0.5 g Poly, 8.5 g Sat); 10 mg Cholesterol; 28 g Carbohydrate; 2 g Fibre; 4 g Protein; 40 mg Sodium

Pictured below.

Dessert Dippers

Arrange white, yellow or angel food cake cubes, marshmallows and pieces of fruit (such as kiwifruit, cherries, banana, strawberries and star fruit) on a small tray. Ladyfingers are fun too, but to prevent double dipping, provide your guests with small plates for extra dip. Pictured below.

Meringue Kisses

Beat 1 egg white with 1/4 tsp. (1 mL) each of vanilla and cream of tartar until soft peaks form. Gradually beat in 1/4 cup (60 mL) fine granulated sugar (see Note), 1 tbsp. (15 mL) at a time, until stiff peaks form and sugar is dissolved. Spoon or pipe small dollops onto waxed or parchment paper on baking sheet. Bake in 225°F (110°C) oven for 1 1/2 to 2 hours until crisp. Use for dippers. Pictured below.

Note: Processing regular granulated sugar in blender will make fine granulated sugar.

Games 'N' Cards Night

When was the last time you tried your hand at a game of cards? Don't drop this wonderful tradition from your weekend plans. A friendly game at the kitchen table and this menu will keep the conversation lively as the competition heats up....

serves 6

Apple Cider Punch

Crunchy Nut Mix

Spicy Peanuts

Creamy Cheese Dip

Chili Beef

Bacon Biscuits

Apple Cider Punch

In the winter, put this comforting beverage in a slow cooker on Low to keep it warm. Or serve it cold in the summer over ice and garnish with a lemon slice.

Sweet apple cider	6 cups	1.5 L
Medium orange, sliced	1	1
Medium lemon, sliced	1	1
Cinnamon stick (4 inch, 10 cm, length)	1	1
Whole cloves	2	2
Coarsely chopped peeled gingerroot	1 tsp.	5 mL

Combine all 6 ingredients in large pot or Dutch oven. Bring to a boil. Reduce heat to medium-low. Simmer, uncovered, for 5 minutes. Strain. Discard solids. Makes 6 cups (1.5 L). Serve hot or cold. Serves 6.

1 serving: 133 Calories; 0.3 g Total Fat (trace Mono, 0.1 g Poly, 0.1 g Sat); 0 mg Cholesterol; 33 g Carbohydrate; trace Fibre; trace Protein; 8 mg Sodium

Pictured on page 165.

Crunchy Nut Mix

Dark, roasted nuts with a crispy, sweet and spicy coating. Once you start eating this crunchy mix, you won't be able to stop!

Egg white (large), fork-beaten	1	1
Granulated sugar	1/3 cup	75 mL
Worcestershire sauce	1 tbsp.	15 mL
Curry powder	1 tbsp.	15 mL
Chili powder	1 tbsp.	15 mL
Salt	1/2 tsp.	2 mL
Whole almonds	1 1/3 cups	325 mL
Whole cashews	1 1/3 cups	325 mL
Whole pecans	1 1/3 cups	325 mL

Combine first 6 ingredients in large bowl.

Add almonds, cashews and pecans. Mix well until nuts are coated. Arrange in single layer on large greased baking sheet. Bake in 350°F (175°C) oven for about 25 minutes, stirring twice, until crisp and dry. Makes 5 cups (1.25 L).

1/2 cup (125 mL): 364 Calories; 29.9 g Total Fat (18.4 g Mono, 6.2 g Poly, 3.6 g Sat); 0 mg Cholesterol; 21 g Carbohydrate; 3 g Fibre; 9 g Protein; 156 mg Sodium

Pictured on page 165.

Top: Apple Cider Punch, above
Centre Left: Spicy Peanuts, page 166
Centre Right: Crunchy Nut Mix, above
Bottom: Creamy Cheese Dip, page 166

Spicy Peanuts

A salty, spicy and crunchy snack, perfect for a games night. Roasting the peanuts brings out their flavour and makes this an addictive blend.

Hard margarine (or butter), melted	2 tbsp.	30 mL
Cajun seasoning	1 tbsp.	15 mL
Lemon pepper	1 tbsp.	15 mL
Garlic salt	1 tsp.	5 mL
Unsalted peanuts	2 cups	500 mL
Small pretzels	2 cups	500 mL

Combine first 4 ingredients in large bowl.

Add peanuts and pretzels. Stir until coated. Spread out mixture on ungreased baking sheet. Bake in 350°F (175°C) oven for about 20 minutes until crisp and golden. Makes 4 cups (1 L).

1/2 cup (125 mL): 311 Calories; 22.7 g Total Fat (11.6 g Mono, 6.5 g Poly, 3.4 g Sat); 0 mg Cholesterol; 21 g Carbohydrate; 4 g Fibre; 11 g Protein; 734 mg Sodium

Pictured on page 165.

Creamy Cheese Dip

The addition of beer gives this cheesy dip a unique, zippy flavour. Serve with fresh vegetables and assorted crackers.

Block of cream cheese, room temperature	8 oz.	250 g
Grated medium Cheddar cheese	2/3 cup	150 mL
Worcestershire sauce	2 tsp.	10 mL
Chopped green onion	2 tbsp.	30 mL
Beer (or alcohol-free beer)	1/4 cup	60 mL

Thinly sliced green onion, for garnish

Process first 5 ingredients in food processor until smooth. Or place in medium bowl and mash with fork until smooth. Transfer to small bowl. Cover. Chill for 2 to 3 hours to blend flavours. Let stand at room temperature for 30 minutes before serving.

Garnish with green onion. Makes 1 2/3 cups (400 mL).

2 tbsp. (30 mL): 89 Calories; 8.2 g Total Fat (2.3 g Mono, 0.3 g Poly, 5.2 g Sat); 26 mg Cholesterol; 1 g Carbohydrate; trace Fibre; 3 g Protein; 98 mg Sodium

Pictured on page 165.

Chili Beef

A delicious, mildly spiced chili with a thick, chunky texture. Use more or less chili powder as desired.

Cooking oil	1 tbsp.	15 mL
Finely chopped onion	1 cup	250 mL
Garlic cloves, minced (or 1/2 tsp., 2 mL, powder)	2	2
Lean ground beef	1 1/2 lbs.	680 g
Chili powder	1 tbsp.	15 mL
Can of diced tomatoes (with juice)	28 oz.	796 mL
Dry red (or alcohol-free) wine	3/4 cup	175 mL
Tomato paste	3 tbsp.	50 mL
Granulated sugar	1 tsp.	5 mL
Salt	1/2 tsp.	2 mL
Pepper	1/2 tsp.	2 mL
Can of sliced mushrooms, drained	5 1/2 oz.	156 mL
Can of chickpeas (garbanzo beans), rinsed and drained	19 oz.	540 mL
Chopped fresh sweet basil (or 1 tbsp., 15 mL, dried)	1/4 cup	60 mL
Grated medium Cheddar cheese, for garnish		

Heat cooking oil in large pot or Dutch oven on medium-low. Add onion and garlic. Cook for about 10 minutes, stirring occasionally, until onion is soft.

Add ground beef and chili powder. Scramble-fry on medium-high until beef is no longer pink.

Add next 6 ingredients. Stir. Bring to a boil. Reduce heat to medium-low. Cover. Simmer for 1 hour, stirring occasionally. Simmer, uncovered, for 20 to 30 minutes until sauce is thickened.

Add mushrooms and chickpeas. Heat and stir for about 5 minutes until hot. Remove from heat.

Add basil. Stir. Sprinkle individual servings with cheese. Makes 8 cups (2 L). Serves 6.

1 serving: 409 Calories; 21.1 g Total Fat (9.1 g Mono, 2.1 g Poly, 7.2 g Sat); 64 mg Cholesterol; 24 g Carbohydrate; 4 g Fibre; 27 g Protein; 664 mg Sodium

Pictured on page 167.

Bacon Biscuits

Golden brown biscuits with a delicious smoky bacon taste.

All-purpose flour	3 cups	750 mL
Baking powder	2 tbsp.	30 mL
Granulated sugar	1 tbsp.	15 mL
Salt	1/4 tsp.	1 mL
Hard margarine (or butter), cut up	3 tbsp.	50 mL
Bacon slices, cooked crisp and crumbled	6	6
Finely grated fresh Parmesan cheese	1/2 cup	125 mL
Milk	1 1/2 cups	375 mL

Combine first 4 ingredients in large bowl. Cut in margarine until mixture is crumbly.

Add bacon and Parmesan cheese. Stir. Make a well in centre.

Add milk. Stir until mixture just comes together. Do not overmix. Turn out onto lightly floured surface. Press together. Pat or roll out to 3/4 inch (2 cm) thickness. Cut into twelve 3 inch (7.5 cm) rounds with floured cutter. Arrange just touching on lightly greased baking sheet. Bake in 450°F (230°C) oven for 12 to 15 minutes until lightly golden. Let stand on baking sheet for 5 minutes before removing to wire rack to cool. Best served warm. Serves 6.

1 serving: 406 Calories; 12.9 g Total Fat (6.3 g Mono, 1.3 g Poly, 4.5 g Sat); 15 mg Cholesterol; 57 g Carbohydrate; 2 g Fibre; 15 g Protein; 836 mg Sodium

Pictured below.

Chili Beef, page 166

Bacon Biscuits, above

Hot 'N' Spicy Night

Brace yourselves—this hot menu will bring all kinds of energy to the party! This menu selection features a variety of hot and spicy dishes which you can, of course, adjust to fit the mood of your crowd.

serves 4

Iced Lime Drink

Radish And Orange Salad

Veggie Burgers

Yam Chips

Sesame Chicken Strips

Cantaloupe Flan

Iced Lime Drink

A cool, semi-sweet, minty drink that will cool your palate.

Water	4 cups	1 L
Granulated sugar	1 cup	250 mL
Lime juice	1/2 cup	125 mL
Fresh mint leaves, coarsely chopped (or 3 1/2 tsp., 17 mL, dried)	1/3 cup	75 mL
Ice cubes		
Fresh mint sprigs, for garnish		
Thin lime slices, for garnish		

Combine first 4 ingredients in large bowl. Cover. Chill for 4 to 6 hours. Strain into pitcher. Discard solids. Makes 4 1/2 cups (1.1 L).

Add ice cubes. Garnish individual servings with mint sprigs and lime slices. Serves 4.

1 serving: 214 Calories; 0.1 g Total Fat (trace Mono, trace Poly, trace Sat); 0 mg Cholesterol; 56 g Carbohydrate; trace Fibre; trace Protein; 1 mg Sodium

Pictured on page 169.

Radish And Orange Salad

This salad will liven up your table and your taste buds!

Thinly sliced radish	3 cups	750 mL
Can of mandarin orange segments, drained	10 oz.	284 mL
Slivered almonds, toasted (see Note)	1/3 cup	75 mL
Sliced green onion	1/4 cup	60 mL
Dried crushed chilies	3/4 – 1 tsp.	4 – 5 mL
DRESSING		
Olive (or cooking) oil	3 tbsp.	50 mL
White wine vinegar	2 tbsp.	30 mL
Chopped fresh sweet basil (or 3/4 tsp., 4 mL, dried)	1 tbsp.	15 mL
Chili powder	1/4 tsp.	1 mL
Ground coriander	1/8 tsp.	0.5 mL
Salt	1/8 tsp.	0.5 mL
Pepper	1/8 tsp.	0.5 mL

Combine first 5 ingredients in medium bowl.

Dressing: Combine all 7 ingredients in jar with tight-fitting lid. Shake well. Makes 1/3 cup (75 mL) dressing. Drizzle over radish mixture. Toss. Makes about 4 cups (1 L). Serves 4.

1 serving: 199 Calories; 16.9 g Total Fat (11.5 g Mono, 2.2 g Poly, 2 g Sat); 0 mg Cholesterol; 12 g Carbohydrate; 3 g Fibre; 3 g Protein; 109 mg Sodium

Pictured on page 171.

Note: To toast almonds, place in single layer in ungreased shallow pan. Bake in 350°F (175°C) oven for 5 to 10 minutes, stirring or shaking often, until desired doneness.

Veggie Burgers

If you think veggie burgers are only for non-meat eaters, you are missing out! These burgers, with Jalapeño cheese in the patties, are exceptionally good.

Can of chickpeas (garbanzo beans), 19 oz. rinsed and drained		540 mL
Grated Monterey Jack With Jalapeño cheese	1/3 cup	75 mL
Fine dry bread crumbs	1/3 cup	75 mL
Finely chopped red onion	1/4 cup	60 mL
Chopped fresh cilantro (or fresh parsley)	2 – 3 tbsp.	30 – 50 mL
Large egg, fork-beaten	1	1
Ground cumin	1 tsp.	5 mL
Salsa	1/2 cup	125 mL
Hamburger buns, split and toasted (buttered, optional)	4	4

Process chickpeas in food processor until consistency of coarse bread crumbs.

Add next 6 ingredients. Process until well combined. Shape mixture into 4 patties. Preheat gas barbecue to medium. Cook patties on greased grill for about 5 minutes per side until golden brown.

Spread salsa on cut sides of each bun. Place 1 patty on bottom half of each bun. Cover with top halves. Serves 4.

1 serving: 328 Calories; 8.7 g Total Fat (3 g Mono, 1.5 g Poly, 3.1 g Sat); 63 mg Cholesterol; 48 g Carbohydrate; 4 g Fibre; 15 g Protein; 626 mg Sodium

Pictured on page 170/171.

Yam Chips

Cut yam (or sweet potato) into paper-thin slices. Deep-fry, in batches, in hot (375°F, 190°C) cooking oil until lightly browned and crispy. Remove to paper towels to drain. Sprinkle with salt. Pictured on page 170/171.

Iced Lime Drink, page 168

Sesame Chicken Strips

Golden brown chicken strips with a creamy hot sauce.

Boneless, skinless chicken breast halves (about 1 lb., 454 g)	4	4
All-purpose flour	3 tbsp.	50 mL
Salt	1/4 tsp.	1 mL
Large eggs	2	2
Fine dry bread crumbs	1/3 cup	75 mL
Sesame seeds, toasted (see Note)	1/4 cup	60 mL
Cajun seasoning	2 tbsp.	30 mL
Coarsely ground pepper (or 1/2 tsp., 2 mL, pepper)	1 tsp.	5 mL
Curry powder	1 tsp.	5 mL
Cooking oil, for deep-frying		
SPICY DIPPING SAUCE		
Sour cream	1/2 cup	125 mL
Sweet (or regular) chili sauce	2 tbsp.	30 mL
Finely chopped green onion	1 tbsp.	15 mL
Garlic clove, minced (or 1/4 tsp., 1 mL, powder)	1	1

Cut each chicken breast lengthwise into 3 strips.

Combine flour and salt on waxed paper.

Beat eggs with fork in small bowl.

Combine next 5 ingredients in shallow dish. Toss chicken in flour mixture. Dip into egg. Roll in bread crumb mixture until coated.

Deep-fry chicken, in 3 to 4 batches, in hot (375°F, 190°C) cooking oil for 3 to 4 minutes until golden brown and no longer pink inside. Remove to paper towels to drain.

Spicy Dipping Sauce: Combine all 4 ingredients in separate small bowl. Makes 2/3 cup (150 mL) sauce. Serve with chicken. Serves 4.

1 serving: 436 Calories; 21.8 g Total Fat (8.9 g Mono, 5.4 g Poly, 5.4 g Sat); 201 mg Cholesterol; 20 g Carbohydrate; 3 g Fibre; 40 g Protein; 1595 mg Sodium

Pictured on this page and on page 171.

Note: To toast sesame seeds, place in single layer in ungreased shallow pan. Bake in 350°F (175°C) oven for 5 to 10 minutes, stirring or shaking often, until desired doneness.

Top: Yam Chips, page 169
Centre Left: Veggie Burgers, page 169
Centre Right: Radish And Orange Salad, page 168
Bottom: Sesame Chicken Strips, above

Cantaloupe Flan, below

Cantaloupe Flan

A light dessert with a smooth filling, a sweet glaze and a fresh fruit topping. Use honeydew melon and cantaloupe for an eye-catching colour combination.

PASTRY		
All-purpose flour	1 cup	250 mL
Icing (confectioner's) sugar	3 tbsp.	50 mL
Cold hard margarine (or butter), cut up	1/2 cup	125 mL
Egg yolks (large)	2	2
Ice water	1 tbsp.	15 mL
FILLING		
Chopped cantaloupe	1/2 cup	125 mL
Granulated sugar	1/2 cup	125 mL
Finely grated lemon zest	2 tsp.	10 mL
Whipping cream (or whole milk)	1 cup	250 mL
Envelope of unflavoured gelatin	1/4 oz.	7 g
Cold water	2 tbsp.	30 mL
TOPPING		
Large whole cantaloupe (about 1 lb., 454 g)	1	1
Apricot jam, warmed and strained	1/4 cup	60 mL
Orange-flavoured liqueur (such as Grand Marnier)	1 tbsp.	15 mL

Pastry: Combine flour and icing sugar in medium bowl. Cut in margarine until mixture is crumbly. Stir in egg yolks and ice water. Mix until dough forms soft ball. Shape into flattened ball. Cover with plastic wrap. Chill for 30 minutes. Roll out pastry on lightly floured surface to about 1/8 inch (3 mm) thickness. Press in bottom and up side of 8 inch (20 cm) tart pan with removable bottom. Trim edge. Cover. Chill for 30 minutes. Remove plastic wrap and lay parchment paper or foil over pastry shell. Press gently into shell. Fill with dried beans, rice or pastry weights. Bake on bottom rack in 375°F (190°C) oven for 20 minutes. Carefully remove beans and parchment paper. (You can't cook the beans but you can save them for the next time you make pastry.) Bake shell for 15 to 20 minutes until lightly browned. Cool.

Filling: Process first 4 ingredients in blender or food processor until smooth. Turn into medium bowl.

Sprinkle gelatin over cold water in small saucepan. Let stand for 1 minute. Heat and stir on low until gelatin is dissolved. Add to whipping cream mixture. Stir well. Pour into crust. Chill for 2 to 3 hours until set.

Topping: Scoop balls from cantaloupe using small melon baller. Arrange in single layer on top of flan, starting from outside edge.

Combine jam and liqueur in small bowl. Brush over cantaloupe balls. Chill for at least 3 hours or overnight until set. Cuts into 6 wedges.

1 wedge: 520 Calories; 31.7 g Total Fat (15.1 g Mono, 2.3 g Poly, 12.3 g Sat); 121 mg Cholesterol; 54 g Carbohydrate; 1 g Fibre; 6 g Protein; 220 mg Sodium

Pictured above.

Pizza And Video Night

Was your week a hard one? Yes! Don't put off entertaining. Okay! Just call up some friends and invite them over for some homemade pizza and front row seats on the couch as you settle back to watch a movie. Want to come?

serves 6

Spinach And Mushroom Pizza

Pineapple Salami Pizza

Feta Chicken Pizza

Basic Pizza Crust Dough

Triple Chocolate Brownies

Spinach And Mushroom Pizza

An attractive, colourful pizza with generous amounts of toppings. The addition of goat cheese is a nice change from the more traditional mozzarella.

Focaccia bread (12 inch, 30 cm, diameter)	1	1
Pizza sauce	2/3 cup	150 mL
Sliced fresh mushrooms	2 cups	500 mL
Spinach, stems removed	2 cups	500 mL
Soft goat (chèvre) cheese (about 1 cup, 250 mL), broken up	5 oz.	140 g
Finely grated fresh Parmesan cheese	2/3 cup	150 mL

Place focaccia bread on lightly greased pizza pan. Spread pizza sauce on bread.

Top with remaining 4 ingredients. Bake in 500°F (260°C) oven for 15 to 18 minutes until cheese is melted and crust is browned. Cuts into 6 wedges.

1 wedge: 310 Calories; 14.5 g Total Fat (3.5 g Mono, 0.7 g Poly, 7.9 g Sat); 30 mg Cholesterol; 29 g Carbohydrate; 1 g Fibre; 16 g Protein; 746 mg Sodium

Pictured on page 174/175.

Pineapple Salami Pizza

A fresh, juicy pizza with a delicious combination of flavours and textures. Use your favourite salami and try fresh pineapple when it's in season.

Commercial unbaked pizza crust (12 inch, 30 cm, diameter)	1	1
Pizza sauce	2/3 cup	150 mL
Pineapple chunks, drained	2/3 cup	150 mL
Chopped salami	1 cup	250 mL
Sliced ripe olives	1/3 cup	75 mL
Chopped red pepper	2 cups	500 mL
Grated medium Cheddar cheese	1 cup	250 mL
Grated mozzarella cheese	1 cup	250 mL

Place crust on lightly greased pizza pan. Spread pizza sauce on crust.

Top with remaining 6 ingredients. Bake in 500°F (260°C) oven for 15 to 18 minutes until cheese is melted and crust is browned. Cuts into 6 wedges.

1 wedge: 386 Calories; 20 g Total Fat (6.7 g Mono, 1.3 g Poly, 9.6 g Sat); 55 mg Cholesterol; 34 g Carbohydrate; 2 g Fibre; 18 g Protein; 890 mg Sodium

Pictured on page 175.

Feta Chicken Pizza

The scrumptious tastes of sun-dried tomato and smoky bacon add to the unique combination of flavours on this crispy, golden pizza.

Basic Pizza Crust Dough, page 176	1	1
Sun-dried tomato pesto	1/3 cup	75 mL
Whipping cream (or whole milk)	1/4 cup	60 mL
Chopped cooked chicken	1 1/2 cups	375 mL
Bacon slices, cooked crisp and crumbled	4	4
Chopped green pepper	1/2 cup	125 mL
Pine nuts, toasted (see Note)	1/3 cup	75 mL
Chopped fresh sweet basil (or 1 1/2 tsp., 7 mL, dried)	2 tbsp.	30 mL
Crumbled feta cheese (about 4 1/2 oz., 126 g)	2/3 cup	150 mL
Finely grated fresh Parmesan cheese	1/2 cup	125 mL

Prepare pizza dough. Roll out and press in greased 12 inch (30 cm) pizza pan, forming rim around edge.

Combine pesto and whipping cream in small bowl. Spread on crust.

Top with remaining 7 ingredients. Bake in 500°F (260°C) oven for 15 to 18 minutes until cheese is melted and crust is browned. Cuts into 6 wedges.

1 wedge: 381 Calories; 19.9 g Total Fat (6.2 g Mono, 2.8 g Poly, 8.3 g Sat); 71 mg Cholesterol; 26 g Carbohydrate; 2 g Fibre; 26 g Protein; 686 mg Sodium

Pictured on this page and on page 175.

Note: To toast pine nuts, place in single layer in ungreased shallow pan. Bake in 350°F (175°C) oven for 5 to 10 minutes, stirring or shaking often, until desired doneness.

Top Left and Bottom Centre: Spinach And Mushroom Pizza, page 173
Top Right: Pineapple Salami Pizza, page 173
Bottom Left and Bottom Right: Feta Chicken Pizza, above, on Basic Pizza Crust Dough, page 176

Basic Pizza Crust Dough

A crispy, lightly browned crust with a bread-like texture.
Add your choice of toppings and enjoy!

Warm water	3/4 cup	175 mL
Granulated sugar	1/2 tsp.	2 mL
Active dry yeast	2 tsp.	10 mL
All-purpose flour	2 cups	500 mL
Salt	1 1/2 tsp.	7 mL
Olive (or cooking) oil	2 tbsp.	30 mL

Stir warm water and sugar in small bowl until sugar is dissolved. Sprinkle yeast over top. Let stand for 10 minutes. Stir until yeast is dissolved.

Combine flour and salt in large bowl.

Add yeast mixture and olive oil. Mix until dough pulls away from side of bowl and is no longer sticky, adding a little more flour if necessary. Turn dough out onto lightly floured surface. Knead for 5 to 10 minutes until smooth and elastic. Place dough in greased large bowl, turning once to grease top. Cover with greased plastic wrap and tea towel. Let stand in oven with light on and door closed for about 1 hour until doubled in bulk. Turn dough out onto lightly floured surface. Shape into ball. Makes one 12 inch (30 cm) pizza crust.

1/6 of crust: 206 Calories; 5.1 g Total Fat (3.4 g Mono, 0.6 g Poly, 0.7 g Sat); 0 mg Cholesterol; 34 g Carbohydrate; 2 g Fibre; 5 g Protein; 595 mg Sodium

Pictured on page 174 and on page 175.

Triple Chocolate Brownies, this page

Triple Chocolate Brownies

Chocolate is a must for any movie night! These moist, decadent brownies are sure to please anyone with a sweet tooth.

Hard margarine (or butter), cut up	1/2 cup	125 mL
Semi-sweet chocolate baking squares (1 oz., 28 g, each), chopped	6	6
Granulated sugar	2/3 cup	150 mL
Large eggs, fork-beaten	2	2
All-purpose flour	1 1/3 cups	325 mL
White chocolate baking squares (1 oz., 28 g, each), coarsely chopped	5	5
Milk chocolate candy bar (3 1/2 oz., 100 g), coarsely chopped	1	1

Combine margarine, semi-sweet chocolate and sugar in heavy medium saucepan. Heat on lowest heat, stirring constantly, until chocolate is almost melted. Remove from heat. Stir until smooth.

Add eggs and flour. Mix well.

Add white chocolate and milk chocolate. Stir. Spread in greased 8 x 8 inch (20 x 20 cm) pan. Bake in 350°F (175°C) oven for 30 to 35 minutes until just firm. Cool in pan. Cuts into 16 large squares.

1 square: 271 Calories; 14.7 g Total Fat (6.8 g Mono, 1 g Poly, 6.2 g Sat); 30 mg Cholesterol; 34 g Carbohydrate; 1 g Fibre; 3 g Protein; 94 mg Sodium

Pictured below.

Platters Of The World

Would you like to do a little globe-trotting at your next party? Guests will enjoy exploring the cooking styles of Australia, Spain and Thailand with this wide selection of bite-sized morsels.

serves 8

AUSTRALIA

Mini Lamb Patties

Shrimp In Beer Batter

Rosemary Macadamia Nuts

SPAIN

Chorizo In Parsley And Garlic

Crispy Golden Calamari

Sardine Lemon Spread

THAILAND

Chicken Rice Rolls

Pork Satay

Thai Fish Cakes

AUSTRALIA
Mini Lamb Patties

These are often called "rissoles" in Australia. Salsa is very colourful and has a refreshing, sweet taste. Patties can be made up to one hour ahead and kept warm.

Lean ground lamb	1 lb.	454 g
Dry red (or alcohol-free) wine	1/2 cup	125 mL
Minced onion	1/2 cup	125 mL
Garlic cloves, minced (or 1 tsp., 5 mL, powder)	4	4
Large egg, fork-beaten	1	1
Fine dry bread crumbs	1/4 cup	60 mL
Walnuts, finely chopped	1/4 cup	60 mL
Chopped fresh mint leaves (or 1 tbsp., 15 mL, dried)	1/4 cup	60 mL
Finely grated lemon zest	1 1/2 tsp.	7 mL
Salt	3/4 tsp.	4 mL
Pepper	1/8 tsp.	0.5 mL
MANGO SALSA		
Diced mango (or 14 oz., 398 g, can, drained)	1 cup	250 mL
Chopped fresh mint leaves (or 1 1/2 tsp., 7 mL, dried)	2 tbsp.	30 mL
Lemon juice	2 tbsp.	30 mL
Olive (or cooking) oil	2 tsp.	10 mL
Small red chili pepper, seeded and finely chopped (see Note)	1	1
Salt	1/4 tsp.	1 mL

Combine first 4 ingredients in large bowl. Cover. Chill for at least 1 hour or overnight. Transfer to food processor.

Add next 7 ingredients. Process until well combined. Shape into small patties, using 2 tbsp. (30 mL) for each. Preheat gas barbecue to medium. Cook patties on well-greased grill for about 7 minutes per side until no longer pink inside. Makes about 20 patties.

Mango Salsa: Combine all 6 ingredients in small bowl. Makes about 1 cup (250 mL) salsa. Serve with patties.

1 patty with 2 tsp. (10 mL) salsa: 98 Calories; 6.7 g Total Fat (2.7 g Mono, 1.1 g Poly, 2.4 g Sat); 27 mg Cholesterol; 4 g Carbohydrate; trace Fibre; 5 g Protein; 148 mg Sodium

Pictured on page 178.

Note: Wear gloves when chopping chili peppers and avoid touching your eyes.

Shrimp In Beer Batter

Large shrimp are called "prawns" in Australia. Perfectly cooked in a crisp, light batter, these succulent shrimp will make your mouth water.

All-purpose flour	1 cup	250 mL
Salt	1 tsp.	5 mL
Beer	1 cup	250 mL
Cooking oil	2 tbsp.	30 mL
Egg white (large)	1	1
Raw large shrimp (tails intact), peeled and deveined	1 lb.	454 g
Cooking oil, for deep-frying		
HONEY MUSTARD DIPPING SAUCE		
Grainy mustard	1/4 cup	60 mL
Liquid honey	3 tbsp.	50 mL

Combine first 4 ingredients in large bowl. Cover. Let stand for 1 hour.

Beat egg white in small bowl until soft peaks form. Fold into batter.

Holding shrimp by tail, dip into batter. Deep-fry, in 2 to 3 batches, in hot (375°F, 190°C) cooking oil for about 3 minutes until golden. Makes 21 to 25 shrimp.

Honey Mustard Dipping Sauce: Combine mustard and honey in separate small bowl. Makes about 1/3 cup (75 mL) sauce. Serve with shrimp.

1 shrimp with about 3/4 tsp. (4 mL) sauce: 96 Calories; 4.3 g Total Fat (2.2 g Mono, 1.4 g Poly, 0.4 g Sat); 33 mg Cholesterol; 8 g Carbohydrate; trace Fibre; 5 g Protein; 189 mg Sodium

Pictured below.

Rosemary Macadamia Nuts

Macadamia nuts are a popular snack for lots of Aussie kids. Fresh rosemary provides a tasty alternative for grown-ups.

Macadamia nuts	2 cups	500 mL
Hard margarine (or butter), melted	2 tbsp.	30 mL
Coarse sea salt	1 tsp.	5 mL
Fresh rosemary, chopped (or 1 1/2 tsp., 7 mL, dried)	2 tbsp.	30 mL
Coarsely ground pepper (or 1/4 tsp., 1 mL, pepper)	1/2 tsp.	2 mL

Combine all 5 ingredients in ungreased 9 x 13 inch (22 x 33 cm) pan. Bake in 350°F (175°C) oven for 10 to 15 minutes, shaking or stirring occasionally, until lightly browned. Cool. Makes about 2 cups (500 mL).

1 tbsp. (15 mL): 66 Calories; 7 g Total Fat (5.2 g Mono, 0.1 g Poly, 1.4 g Sat); 2 mg Cholesterol; 1 g Carbohydrate; 1 g Fibre; 1 g Protein; 79 mg Sodium

Pictured below.

AUSTRALIA
Bottom Left: Mini Lamb Patties, page 177   Top Centre: Rosemary Macadamia Nuts, above   Bottom Right: Shrimp In Beer Batter, this page

SPAIN
Top Left: Crispy Golden Calamari, page 180   Bottom: Chorizo In Parsley And Garlic, below   Top Right: Sardine Lemon Spread, page 180

SPAIN
Chorizo In Parsley And Garlic

Spicy sausage made even better with the added zip of lemon, garlic and fresh parsley. Great with crusty bread and hearty red wine.

Olive (or cooking) oil	1 tbsp.	15 mL
Uncooked chorizo sausages, cut into 1/8 inch (3 mm) thick slices	4	4
Garlic cloves, minced (or 3/4 tsp., 4 mL, powder)	3	3
Chopped fresh parsley (or 2 1/4 tsp., 11 mL, flakes)	3 tbsp.	50 mL
Lemon juice	2 tbsp.	30 mL
Brown sugar, packed	1 tsp.	5 mL
Pepper	1/8 tsp.	0.5 mL

Heat olive oil in large frying pan on medium. Add sausage. Cook for 5 to 8 minutes, stirring occasionally, until browned. Remove with slotted spoon to paper towels to drain. Reserve 1 tbsp. (15 mL) fat. Discard any remaining fat.

Heat reserved fat in same frying pan on low. Add garlic. Cook for about 5 minutes, stirring occasionally, until very soft and light golden.

Add sausage and remaining 4 ingredients. Heat and stir on medium-low for about 3 minutes until hot. Makes 2 1/2 cups (625 mL).

1/4 cup (60 mL): 322 Calories; 27.1 g Total Fat (13.4 g Mono, 2.4 g Poly, 9.8 g Sat); 59 mg Cholesterol; 2 g Carbohydrate; trace Fibre; 16 g Protein; 831 mg Sodium

Pictured above.

Crispy Golden Calamari

The spice coating is very light which allows the delicate calamari flavour to come through. Serve with lemon wedges.

Cornstarch	1/2 cup	125 mL
Paprika	2 tsp.	10 mL
Garlic powder	2 tsp.	10 mL
Chili powder	2 tsp.	10 mL
Salt	1/2 tsp.	2 mL
Coarsely ground pepper (or 1/4 tsp., 1 mL, pepper)	1/2 tsp.	2 mL
Small calamari (squid) tubes, cleaned and cut into 1/4 inch (6 mm) rings	1 lb.	454 g
Cooking oil, for deep-frying		

Combine first 6 ingredients in medium bowl or resealable freezer bag.

Add calamari, 4 or 5 rings at a time. Toss until well coated.

Deep-fry calamari, in 3 batches, in hot (375°F, 190°C) cooking oil for about 1 minute until golden. Remove to paper towels to drain. Serves 8.

1 serving: 218 Calories; 15.4 g Total Fat (8.6 g Mono, 4.6 g Poly, 1.2 g Sat); 132 mg Cholesterol; 11 g Carbohydrate; trace Fibre; 9 g Protein; 181 mg Sodium

Pictured on page 179.

Sardine Lemon Spread

A quick and easy, fresh-tasting spread to delight your taste buds. Serve with toasted tortilla wedges or crusty bread.

Cans of sardines (7 1/2 oz., 206 g, each), drained	2	2
Chopped fresh parsley (or 2 1/4 tsp., 11 mL, flakes)	3 tbsp.	50 mL
Lemon juice	1 – 2 tbsp.	15 – 30 mL
Chili paste (sambal oelek)	1/2 – 1 tsp.	2 – 5 mL
Salt	1/4 tsp.	1 mL
Coarsely ground pepper (or 1/8 tsp., 0.5 mL, pepper)	1/4 tsp.	1 mL

Break sardines into small pieces in medium bowl with fork.

Add remaining 5 ingredients. Mix well. Makes about 1 cup (250 mL).

1 tbsp. (15 mL): 26 Calories; 1.4 g Total Fat (0.5 g Mono, 0.6 g Poly, 0.2 g Sat); 17 mg Cholesterol; trace Carbohydrate; trace Fibre; 3 g Protein; 97 mg Sodium

Pictured on page 179.

THAILAND
Chicken Rice Rolls

Delicate rice paper rolls filled with a scrumptious chicken filling. Garnish with chopped fresh cilantro or parsley.

Cooking oil	1 tbsp.	15 mL
Ground chicken	1 1/2 lbs.	680 g
Finely chopped red onion	1/2 cup	125 mL
Garlic cloves, minced (or 1 tsp., 5 mL, powder)	4	4
Lime juice	1/4 cup	60 mL
Sweet (or regular) chili sauce	1/4 cup	60 mL
Fish sauce	2 tbsp.	30 mL
Oyster sauce	2 tbsp.	30 mL
Chopped fresh mint leaves (or 1 1/2 – 2 1/4 tsp., 7 – 11 mL, dried)	2 – 3 tbsp.	30 – 50 mL
Chopped fresh cilantro (or fresh parsley)	2 – 3 tbsp.	30 – 50 mL
Warm water		
Rice paper rounds (6 inch, 15 cm, diameter)	16	16

Heat cooking oil in large frying pan on medium-high. Add ground chicken. Scramble-fry for 7 to 10 minutes until chicken is no longer pink and is lightly browned.

Add next 6 ingredients. Heat and stir for about 3 minutes until liquid is evaporated.

Add mint and cilantro. Stir. Cool. Makes 1 2/3 cups (400 mL) filling.

Fill large pie plate 1/2 full of warm water. Soak rice paper rounds, a few at a time, for 2 to 3 minutes until soft. Remove to tea towel to drain. Divide and spoon filling down centre of rice paper rounds, leaving 1 inch (2.5 cm) edge at top and bottom. Fold top and bottom edges to slightly overlap filling. Roll up from side. Makes 16 rice rolls.

1 rice roll: 90 Calories; 2.3 g Total Fat (0.9 g Mono, 0.6 g Poly, 0.4 g Sat); 30 mg Cholesterol; 7 g Carbohydrate; trace Fibre; 10 g Protein; 385 mg Sodium

Pictured on page 181.

THAILAND
Top Left and Bottom Left: Chicken Rice Rolls, above
Centre: Pork Satay, page 182
Top Right and Bottom Centre: Thai Fish Cakes, page 182

Pork Satay

An excellent blend of spices. The pork is tender and sticky with a little crunch. Serve with your favourite satay sauce.

Chopped onion	1 cup	250 mL
Indonesian sweet (or thick) soy sauce	1/2 cup	125 mL
Brown sugar, packed	1/3 cup	75 mL
Cooking oil	3 tbsp.	50 mL
Finely grated lemon zest	1 tbsp.	15 mL
Lemon juice	1/4 cup	60 mL
Garlic clove, minced (or 1/4 tsp., 1 mL, powder)	1	1
Ground coriander	1 tsp.	5 mL
Ground cumin	1 tsp.	5 mL
Ground ginger	1/4 tsp.	1 mL
Cayenne pepper, just a pinch		
Pork tenderloin, partially frozen, halved crosswise and cut lengthwise into 1/8 inch (3 mm) thick slices	1 lb.	454 g
Bamboo skewers (8 inch, 20 cm, length), soaked in water for 10 minutes	16	16

Combine first 11 ingredients in medium bowl.

Put pork into 2 quart (2 L) shallow casserole or large resealable freezer bag. Pour marinade over pork. Stir until coated. Cover or seal. Marinate in refrigerator for at least 6 hours or overnight. Drain and discard marinade. Thread pork, accordion-style, onto skewers. Preheat gas barbecue to medium. Cook skewers on lightly greased grill for about 8 minutes, turning several times, until desired doneness. Makes 16 skewers.

1 skewer: 104 Calories; 5.7 g Total Fat (2.9 g Mono, 1.1 g Poly, 1.3 g Sat); 16 mg Cholesterol; 7 g Carbohydrate; trace Fibre; 6 g Protein; 270 mg Sodium

Pictured on page 181.

Thai Fish Cakes

Spicy, crispy, golden fish cakes with the exotic flavours of lemon grass and cilantro. The dipping sauce tempers the spice and enhances the flavours with a subtle, sweet accent.

Skinless halibut fillet, coarsely chopped	2 lbs.	900 g
Fresh cilantro (or fresh parsley)	1/3 cup	75 mL
Peanut butter	1/4 cup	60 mL
Red curry paste	3 tbsp.	50 mL
Finely chopped lemon grass, bulb only (root and stalk removed)	2 tbsp.	30 mL
Finely grated lime zest	1 tsp.	5 mL
Cooking oil, for deep-frying		
SWEET DIPPING SAUCE		
Granulated sugar	1/4 cup	60 mL
Water	1/4 cup	60 mL
Finely chopped roasted unsalted peanuts	1 tbsp.	15 mL
Sweet (or regular) chili sauce	1 tbsp.	15 mL

Process first 6 ingredients in food processor until smooth and well combined. Using dampened hands, shape into flattened balls about 1/2 inch (12 mm) thick, using 2 tbsp. (30 mL) for each. Cover. Chill for 15 minutes.

Deep-fry fish cakes, in 4 batches, in hot (375°F, 190°C) cooking oil for about 3 minutes until golden. Remove to paper towels to drain. Makes about 20 fish cakes.

Sweet Dipping Sauce: Combine sugar and water in small saucepan. Heat and stir on medium-high for about 1 minute until sugar is dissolved. Bring to a boil. Boil for 2 to 3 minutes until slightly thickened. Cool.

Add peanuts and chili sauce. Makes about 1/2 cup (125 mL) sauce. Serve with fish cakes.

2 fish cakes with 2 1/2 tsp. (12 mL) sauce: 83 Calories; 4 g Total Fat (1.9 g Mono, 1.2 g Poly, 0.5 g Sat); 12 mg Cholesterol; 3 g Carbohydrate; trace Fibre; 8 g Protein; 43 mg Sodium

Pictured on page 181.

Measurement Tables

Throughout this book measurements are given in Conventional and Metric measure. To compensate for differences between the two measurements due to rounding, a full metric measure is not always used. The cup used is the standard 8 fluid ounce. Temperature is given in degrees Fahrenheit and Celsius. Baking pan measurements are in inches and centimetres as well as quarts and litres. An exact metric conversion is given on this page as well as the working equivalent (Metric Standard Measure).

Oven Temperatures

Fahrenheit (°F)	Celsius (°C)	Fahrenheit (°F)	Celsius (°C)
175°	80°	350°	175°
200°	95°	375°	190°
225°	110°	400°	205°
250°	120°	425°	220°
275°	140°	450°	230°
300°	150°	475°	240°
325°	160°	500°	260°

Spoons

Conventional Measure	Metric Exact Conversion Millilitre (mL)	Metric Standard Measure Millilitre (mL)
1/8 teaspoon (tsp.)	0.6 mL	0.5 mL
1/4 teaspoon (tsp.)	1.2 mL	1 mL
1/2 teaspoon (tsp.)	2.4 mL	2 mL
1 teaspoon (tsp.)	4.7 mL	5 mL
2 teaspoons (tsp.)	9.4 mL	10 mL
1 tablespoon (tbsp.)	14.2 mL	15 mL

Cups

1/4 cup (4 tbsp.)	56.8 mL	60 mL
1/3 cup (5 1/3 tbsp.)	75.6 mL	75 mL
1/2 cup (8 tbsp.)	113.7 mL	125 mL
2/3 cup (10 2/3 tbsp.)	151.2 mL	150 mL
3/4 cup (12 tbsp.)	170.5 mL	175 mL
1 cup (16 tbsp.)	227.3 mL	250 mL
4 1/2 cups	1022.9 mL	1000 mL (1 L)

Pans

Conventional - Inches	Metric - Centimetres
8x8 inch	20x20 cm
9x9 inch	22x22 cm
9x13 inch	22x33 cm
10x15 inch	25x38 cm
11x17 inch	28x43 cm
8x2 inch round	20x5 cm
9x2 inch round	22x5 cm
10x4 1/2 inch tube	25x11 cm
8x4x3 inch loaf	20x10x7.5 cm
9x5x3 inch loaf	22x12.5x7.5 cm

Dry Measurements

Conventional Measure Ounces (oz.)	Metric Exact Conversion Grams (g)	Metric Standard Measure Grams (g)
1 oz.	28.3 g	28 g
2 oz.	56.7 g	57 g
3 oz.	85.0 g	85 g
4 oz.	113.4 g	125 g
5 oz.	141.7 g	140 g
6 oz.	170.1 g	170 g
7 oz.	198.4 g	200 g
8 oz.	226.8 g	250 g
16 oz.	453.6 g	500 g
32 oz.	907.2 g	1000 g (1 kg)

Casseroles

Canada & Britain

Standard Size Casserole	Exact Metric Measure
1 qt. (5 cups)	1.13 L
1 1/2 qts. (7 1/2 cups)	1.69 L
2 qts. (10 cups)	2.25 L
2 1/2 qts. (12 1/2 cups)	2.81 L
3 qts. (15 cups)	3.38 L
4 qts. (20 cups)	4.5 L
5 qts. (25 cups)	5.63 L

United States

Standard Size Casserole	Exact Metric Measure
1 qt. (4 cups)	900 mL
1 1/2 qts. (6 cups)	1.35 L
2 qts. (8 cups)	1.8 L
2 1/2 qts. (10 cups)	2.25 L
3 qts. (12 cups)	2.7 L
4 qts. (16 cups)	3.6 L
5 qts. (20 cups)	4.5 L

Index

Index

Index

Index

Index

Index

Quiche, Shrimp 28

Index

Index

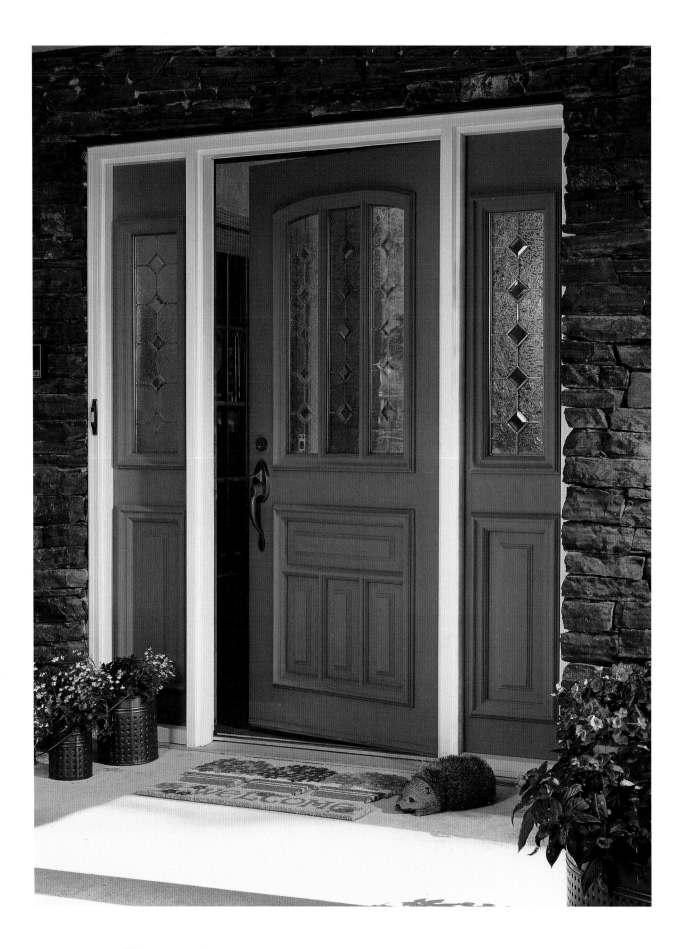